Military Cooperation in Multinational Peace Operations

This edited volume uses theoretical overviews and empirical case studies to explore both how soldiers cope with the new forms of cultural diversity occurring within various multinational military operations, and how their organizations manage them.

Military organizations, like other complex organizations, are now operating in an ever more diverse environment, with the missions themselves being ever more varied, and mostly conducted in a multinational framework. Members of the military have to deal with a host of international actors in the theatre of operations, and do so in a foreign cultural environment, often in countries devastated by war. Such conditions demand a high level of intercultural competence. It is therefore crucial for military organizations to understand how military personnel manage this cultural diversity.

This book will be of much interest to students of peace operations, military studies, international security, as well as sociology and business studies.

Joseph Soeters is Professor of Organization Studies at the Netherlands Defence Academy and Tilburg University. **Philippe Manigart** is Professor of Sociology and Head of the Department of Behavioural Sciences at Brussels Royal Military School.

Cass military studies

Military Advising and Assistance
From mercenaries to privatization,
1815–2007
Donald Stoker

Private Military and Security Companies
Ethics, policies and civil–military relations
Edited by Andrew Alexandra,
Deane-Peter Baker and Marina Caparini

Military Cooperation in Multinational Peace Operations
Managing cultural diversity and crisis response
Edited by Joseph Soeters and
Philippe Manigart

Military Cooperation in Multinational Peace Operations

Managing cultural diversity and crisis response

Edited by Joseph Soeters and
Philippe Manigart

Routledge
Taylor & Francis Group

LONDON AND NEW YORK

First published 2008
by Routledge
2 Park Square, Milton Park, Abingdon, Oxon OX14 4RN

Simultaneously published in the USA and Canada
by Routledge
270 Madison Ave, New York, NY 10016

Routledge is an imprint of the Taylor & Francis Group, an informa business

© 2008 Selection and editorial matter, Joseph Soeters and
Philippe Manigart; individual chapters, the contributors
Typeset in Times by Wearset Ltd, Boldon, Tyne and Wear
Printed and bound in Great Britain by TJI Digital, Padstow,
Cornwall

British Library Cataloguing in Publication Data
A catalogue record for this book is available from the British
Library

Library of Congress Cataloging in Publication Data
A catalog record for this book has been requested

ISBN10: 0-415-44589-2 (hbk)
ISBN10: 0-203-92872-5 (ebk)
ISBN13: 978-0-415-44589-4 (hbk)
ISBN13: 978-0-203-92872-1 (ebk)

Contents

Part III
Afterthoughts

JOSEPH SOETERS AND PHILIPPE MANIGART

Contributors

John Ballard is currently Professor of Strategic Studies at the US National War College in Washington DC. He is the author of a number of articles on military affairs as well as of four books: *Uphold Democracy* (Praeger, 1997), *Continuity during the Storm* (Greenwood, 2000), *Fighting for Fallujah* (Praeger, 2006) and *Triumph of Self-Determination* (Praeger, 2008).

Nejat Basim is currently the director of the Defence Management Programme at the Turkish Military Academy in Ankara. Dr Basim is an expert in the field of cross-cultural studies, organizational behaviour and HRM. He has published a number of books and articles in those areas.

Mehmet Cakar is a research assistant and doctorate candidate in organizational sociology at Baskent University in Ankara.

Andrea van Dijk is a PhD student at the Netherlands Defence Academy and Tilburg University. She holds a BA degree in social studies and a MA degree in theology.

Efrat Elron is a research fellow at the Truman Institute for the Advancement of Peace at the Hebrew University, and teaches organizational behaviour in Tel Hai Academic College and at the Hebrew University in Jerusalem. Her research interests include multinational and military organizations and the role of cultural diversity in them, as well as the study of team and leadership processes. She has authored a number of articles on these issues both in civilian and military academic journals. She is involved in various projects analysing UN peace operations and the enhanced UNIFIL mission, works with IDF in different capacities, and is taking part in the production of TV documentaries on the regional peace operations. She is a member of the editorial boards of the *International Journal of Cross Cultural Management* and *Group and Organizational Management*.

Angela Febbraro obtained a PhD in Applied Social Psychology and is currently a defence scientist R&D in Toronto, Canada. She holds adjunct positions in psychology at York University and Wilfrid Laurier University and sits on the editorial board of the *Canadian Journal of Police and Security Services*. She has published on the subjects of women, leadership and gender integration, and is currently engaged with cultural diversity and inter-group relations in the military and broader context.

Erik Hedlund is a researcher and coordinator of research in educational sciences at the Swedish National Defence Academy in Stockholm. His PhD thesis dealt with the Swedish Officer Training Programme between tradition and change.

Hitoshi Kawano is Professor of Sociology at the National Defence Academy's Department of Public Policy, School of Humanities and Social Sciences, in Yokosuka, Japan. He holds a PhD degree in military sociology from the University of Chicago. His research interests include military history, sociology of combat and peacekeeping, and civil–military relations in post-Cold War Japan. Among his publications are "The positive impact of peacekeeping on the Japan Self-Defense Forces", in L. Parmar (ed.), *Armed Forces and the International Diversities* (India: Pointer Publisher, 2002) and *Gyokusai no Guntai, Seikan no Guntai* [The Army of Death, The Army of Life] (Tokyo: Kodansha, 2001).

Ljubica Jelušič is Professor of (military) sociology, polemology and the anthropology of war at the Faculty of Social Sciences of the University of Ljubljana in Slovenia. She is currently General Secretary of the Research Committee 01 (Armed Forces & Conflict Resolution) of the International Sociological Association.

Anthony King is a reader in sociology at the University of Exeter in the UK. His research focuses on football, social theory and, latterly, the military. He has published extensively on these topics in international journals and he authored a number of books, among which *The European Ritual* (Ashgate, 2003) and *The Structure of Social Theory* (Routledge, 2004). He serves on the editorial board of *Armed Forces and Society*.

Philippe Manigart is Professor of sociology and Head of the Department of Behavioural Sciences at Brussels Royal Military School. He is also associate professor of sociology at the Faculty of Economics of the University of Mons-Hainaut. He has a MA in sociology from the University of Chicago and a PhD from the Free University of Brussels. A member of the Council of the *Inter-University Seminar on Armed Forces and Society*, he has published numerous books and articles on military organizations, European public opinion and security issues in journals like *Armed Forces and Society*.

Rene Moelker is an associate professor in the social sciences at the Netherlands Defence Academy. He has done scholarly work in retrieving the military-relevant texts of sociology icon Norbert Elias, and published articles about this in the *British Journal of Sociology*. In addition, he works on family support during deployment, and is engaged in the longitudinal study on the first German–Netherlands Corps, published in *Armed Forces and Society.*

Jan van der Meulen is an associate professor in the social sciences at the Netherlands Defence Academy and a professor in military social sciences at Leiden University. Together with Joseph Soeters he recently edited a book on cultural diversity in the armed forces, a collection of case studies from 14 countries (Routledge, 2007). In 2005 they edited a special issue of *Armed Forces and Society* on casualty aversion in the armed forces. He is a member of the editorial board of *Armed Forces and Society.*

Bojan Pograjč currently serves as the commander of the 1st SAF Brigade. He holds a MA degree in the social sciences from the University of Ljubljana as well as a MA degree from the National War College in the USA.

Delphine Resteigne is a teaching assistant at the Department of Behavioural Sciences at Brussels Royal Military School. She has a BA (licence) in sociology from the University of Liège and a MA in international relations from the Free University of Brussels. Her areas of research concern mainly organizational and intercultural sociology. She has conducted several quantitative and qualitative studies among cadets and troops in operations.

Anne-Marie Søderberg is Professor at the Department of Intercultural Communication and Management at the Copenhagen Business School. She has been studying for many years national and international mergers and acquisitions with a focus on communication, culture, identity and HR issues originating from M & A integration processes. Apart from publishing articles in international journals she has co-edited a number of volumes, among which are *Cultural Dimensions of International Acquisitions* (Walter de Gruyter, 1998) and *Merging across Borders. People, Cultures and Politics* (Copenhagen Business School Press, 2003).

Joseph Soeters is Professor of organization studies at the Netherlands Defence Academy and Tilburg University. He focuses on international and diversity management. He has been active in intercultural comparative studies in the civilian sector, leading to a co-edited book entitled *Comparing Cultures. Dimensions of Culture in a Comparative Perspective* (Brill, 2004). He has published a textbook on civil wars and terrorism (Routledge, 2005) and with Jan van der Meulen he co-edited *Cultural Diversity in the Armed Forces. Experiences from Fourteen Countries* (Routledge, 2007). He is one of the Vice-Presidents of the Research Committee 01 (Armed Forces & Conflict Resolution) of the International Sociological Association.

Maren Tomforde obtained her PhD in Anthropology from the University of Hamburg; her thesis was based on two years of fieldwork in Thailand on the phenomenon of cultural spatiality. Since 2003, she has been a research associate at the Bundeswehr Institute of Social Sciences, where she works on

German peacekeeping missions, military culture and intercultural communication.

Abdulkadir Varoglu, Colonel, retired, used to be the dean of the Turkish National Defence Academy, and has published a number of academic papers in journals like *Armed Forces and Society, International Journal of Intercultural Relations* and *International Peacekeeping.* Currently, he is the dean of the Faculty of Management Studies at Baskent University in Ankara.

Merete Wedell-Wedellsborg is a clinical psychologist (MA, PhD), who worked in crisis therapy, executive coaching and consulting at the Royal Danish Defence Academy for ten years. Her PhD thesis "The global soldier" (Copenhagen Business School, 2007) was based on three case studies of multinational NATO units in Poland and Italy. She is now working at Right Management in Copenhagen as Senior Consultant and executive coach for leaders in public and private companies.

Louise Weibul is working to obtain her PhD at the University of Karlstad. She works as a researcher for the Swedish National Defence Academy in Stockholm.

Donna Winslow is a former Professor of cultural anthropology at the Free University of Amsterdam. Before that, she occupied a number of positions in (military) teaching and research institutes in Canada. She has published in the field of military studies, based on field work in areas such as Afghanistan and the Golan Heights (in journals including *Armed Forces and Society* and *Canadian Review of Sociology and Anthropology*). Prior to this, she did a number of studies pertaining to social and political relations in French Caledonia. She is currently Director of the Office of the Auditor General of Canada.

Preface

Since the end of the Cold War armed forces have increasingly been engaged with peace operations all over the globe. The scope of these operations is so demanding that most national armed forces are no longer capable of conducting these missions on their own. This pushes them to work together with the forces of other nations. Hence, multinational military cooperation has become a new standard way of operating in peace missions. However, as in the business sector, multinational cooperation between military organizations does not turn out to be easy. There are experiences that seem to be successful and others that are much less so. In this volume we aim to bring together academic reflections and case studies of a number of such experiences.

Over the last couple of years multinational military cooperation has attracted a lot of attention. NATO, for instance, has founded two working groups on this issue. Separate sessions at the World Congress of the International Sociological Association in Durban in 2006 and at the InterUniversity Seminar on Armed Forces and Society in Chicago in 2007 illustrate this new interest even more. In addition, a special seminar on this topic, funded by the Belgian Defence Ministry (research contract ERM HF-04), was organized by the Royal Belgian Military School in Brussels in the fall of 2006. Many authors in this volume attended that seminar, as well as a seminar on cultural challenges in military operations organized by NATO Defense College in Rome in March 2007.

We thank Routledge, in particular Andrew Humphrys and Emily Kindley-sides, for enabling us to publish this volume in their renowned series on military studies, and our copy editor, Sarah M. Hall. We are grateful that our respective employers, the Netherlands Defence Academy and the Belgian Military School, enabled us to do the work that was needed to make the book ready to be printed. We thank all authors – colleagues and friends – for working together with us in this project; it was a nice and rewarding example of multinational cooperation in itself.

Joseph Soeters
Philippe Manigart

Chapter 1

Introduction

Joseph Soeters and Philippe Manigart

The rise of multinational peace operations

In today's globalizing world military organizations are not only becoming more diverse internally, they also operate in an ever more diverse environment. Today's militaries carry out missions all over the world, in culturally, ethnically, and linguistically varying regions. The majority of these operations are conducted by multinational intervention forces, such as UNIFIL in Lebanon, ISAF in Afghanistan and KFOR in Kosovo, or by permanent multinational forces, such as NATO or the Eurocorps. Except perhaps for the US armed forces, national militaries are no longer capable of executing such operations on their own. The current imbalance between demand and resources makes it impossible for most national armed forces to conduct large-scale missions on their own. In addition, the need for legitimacy pushes even the most powerful countries and their armed forces to cooperate with the armed forces of other nations. To be distinguished from *joint* operating (military services of one country working together), this multinational military cooperation is called *combined* operating. In general, in the military one sees the same evolution as in the private sector, i.e. the proliferation of joint ventures, strategic alliances and virtual organizations in an international context.

The mass armed forces of the nineteenth and early twentieth centuries were purely national organizations serving their respective nation-states. To the extent that there was a degree of multinational cooperation, it took the form of coalitions in time of war, as for example the coalition that fought Napoleon's armies or the two alliances that fought during the First and Second World Wars. During peacetime, there was hardly any form of multinational cooperation, such as common exercises, training and doctrines.

The Cold War saw the rise of new forms of multinational military cooperation. On the one hand, permanent conventional military alliances – NATO and the Warsaw Pact – were put in place and, on the other hand, the UN carried out the first peacekeeping operations. Both developments were examples of real multinational military cooperation. NATO and Warsaw Pact armies developed common operational and training procedures, common multinational headquarters and sought a certain degree of standardization (interoperability), mostly in the domain of weapons and support systems. The UN peacekeeping operations of the Cold War, such as the one described by Moskos (1976) in Cyprus, were typically conducted after a ceasefire between the warring parties had been negotiated and there was an agreement to send Blue Helmets as interposition or monitoring forces.

If the Cold War was a time of relative stability for armed forces, now in today's world, the rather straightforward bi-polar conflict has given way to a much messier and fuzzier world. Conflicts may be the result of internal state disintegration or civil war rather than inter-state confrontations of the past. In order to respond to such diverse threats and crises, military organizations are now nearly always operating in the context of a multinational framework. This may be under the aegis of the UN or NATO but also, more recently, of regional supranational organizations, such as the European Union (EU), the African Union (AU), or the Economic Community of West African States (ECOWAS).

These multinational military intervention forces, to the extent that they use modular, or package structures made of various national contingents, resemble matrix organizations. These are temporary structures with a dual reporting and control mechanism: a vertical one, the national contingents, and a horizontal one, i.e. the mission. The advantages of matrix structures are that they are more flexible and adaptive than the functional structures of the national armed forces of the past. They encourage cooperation, conflict resolution and coordination. However, as the command structures are twofold (i.e. the command of the mission versus the national line of command), multinational matrix structures come with problems too. In such environments, it is important that individual team members have considerable tolerance for diversity, confusion and ambiguity since a lot of personnel from different levels within the organization are grouped together in an informal environment where lines of communications are loose and unorganized. It therefore requires highly developed interpersonal skills at all levels. If indeed, in the past, military astuteness and a clear picture of the enemy was sufficient, today, the structural internationalization of the workforce (for instance in multinational headquarters), the multinational character of military contingents during deployments as well as the variety of local populations military task forces have to deal with, have become predominant features of military activities. Members of the military must – in diffuse political constellations – negotiate with belligerents from all sides of a conflict and remain neutral, while at the same time being able to defend themselves against aggression. They also have to deal with a host of international actors in the theatre of operations, including representatives of the United Nations, the media and NGOs (Winslow and Everts 2001). And they must do this in a foreign cultural environment, in a country devastated by war, far removed from family and friends. Such conditions demand a high level of intercultural competence.

As said, even the US armed forces, the most powerful and advanced in the world, need allies from around the globe (NATO, Japan) to perform their duties in large-scale operations, such as in Iraq and Afghanistan. In Europe the fact that national armed forces need to work together has already led to the creation of structural bi-national or multinational arrangements. For example, in Belgium, the two Army brigades are fully integrated into the Eurocorps, together with units from the armed forces of Germany, France, Spain and Luxembourg. The German *Bundeswehr* has been divided into various parts, each of which has merged with other national forces. As a consequence, the first German/Dutch Corps, the Eurocorps, the Multinational Corps North East (containing military from Germany, Denmark and Poland) and others have been formed.

As far as operations are concerned, the picture is equally clear. For instance, Belgian troops are presently deployed, among others, in Afghanistan as part of ISAF and in Kosovo as part of KFOR. But in the last few years, the same troops, or other units, were part of multinational task forces sent to Somalia, Rwanda, Zaire/Congo, Haiti, Cambodia, Turkey. Dutch politicians have made it clear that they only intend to prolong the Dutch military contribution in Southern Afghanistan on the condition other nations are able and willing to work along-side with the Dutch servicemen. Over the years multinational cooperation has become standard procedure for almost all national armed forces, as may be illustrated by the fact that the newly formed EU battle groups – except the UK battle group – are formally obliged to have a multinational personnel composition (see King 2005).

Two forms of multinational military cooperation may be distinguished, i.e. horizontal and vertical multinationality. The former, traditional, type of inter-action within multinational military contingents consists of a simple lining up of individual national units within a battle group. Direct work-related contacts between military personnel from the various national contingents therefore occur only at the level of headquarters (Klein and Kümmel 2000: 316 and Klein 2003: 309). Vertical multinationality, on the other hand, implies a greater degree of cooperation and interaction between the various national components and takes the form of mixed bi- or multinational contingents. Here, work-related interactions between personnel occur at the battalion or even company level. Another dimension of military multinational cooperation is the degree of specialization – simple or advanced – between the various national contingents. In simple integration, there is no task specialization between the various national components constituting the task force and cooperation takes the form of a simple juxtaposition of the national units, while in advanced cooperation, there is a certain degree of specialization.

If one crosses these two dimensions, one obtains four distinct forms of multi-national military cooperation: simple horizontal (for instance, the Eurocorps) advanced horizontal (operation Enduring Freedom in Afghanistan) simple verti-cal (ISAF) and advanced vertical (no example yet; but perhaps one day, some form of an integrated European army).

International management in the business sector

International cooperation is not a phenomenon that is unique to the military. In the world of international business, it has become clear that management in an international context has its own peculiarities. International managers need to take into account that consumers and workforces in different countries are alike in many aspects but unlike in many other. If multinational companies fail to translate these differences into their production and marketing policies, they will undoubtedly face serious difficulties in their global operations. This phenomenon is so pervasive that at today's business schools international management and business are taught in separate courses and programmes.

These programmes are based on empirical knowledge indicating that people differ with respect to values and attitudes along national borders. In repeated studies and overviews (Schwartz 1994; Adler 2002; House *et al.* 2004; Vinken *et al.* 2004; Hofstede and Hofstede 2005; Smith, Peterson and Thomas 2008) systematic national differences have been demonstrated with regard to the way people deal with hierarchies and rules in organizations as well as with gender differences, decision-making, communication styles, and employees' orientation to work. In many studies these differences have been linked to national cultures. Despite globalization and McDonaldization, those national cultures seem to be fairly persistent. But there is more than just values, attitudes and cultures. Even though supranational developments – for instance in the European Union – tend to harmonize national rules and regulations (Drezner 2001), the institutional aspects of multinational cooperation in business remain fairly stubborn and not always easy to deal with. National differences in reward and co-determination systems, for example, can hamper effective decision-making and productive cooperation across borders, even when this occurs within the context of one multinational company (Peterson and Thomas 2007).

Even though business is currently one of the most international phenomena, there have been quite a number of experiences pointing at mutual misunderstanding, conflictual collaboration or even straight failures among business organizations working together. In 1996 estimates were that only half of the business endeavours to cooperate internationally were successful (Cartwright and Cooper 1996). One may argue that since that year learning experiences may have had an ameliorating impact, but still one should not be overly optimistic. In 1998 the German car producer Daimler Benz merged with USA-based Chrysler. From its very inception this bi-national automotive giant experienced difficulties that the partnering organizations never faced when they operated from within their home country only. Almost immediately, experts pointed at differences in national cultures and a lack of balance in the power distribution between the partners. In August 2007 the bi-national automotive giant faced the final curtain: it dissolved into two separate national companies again. This is not to say that multinational cooperation will never be successful; on the contrary, workforce diversity helps to develop more creative solutions to problems, and famous examples of strategic international alliances – for instance in the airline indus-tries – are conquering the world. Yet, cases such as the Daimler/Chrysler venture remind us that multinational organizational arrangements – even though the logic behind them is undisputable – do not always automatically lead to sat-isfying results.

National differences between military organizations and their impact on multinational military cooperation

This is important for the military to keep in mind when starting multinational operations or creating permanent multinational military organizations. A study replicating Hofstede's influential work in the commercial sector (Soeters 1997) has shown that in the military national cultural differences do exist too, and to a large degree these differences are similar to what has been found in business life. However, there was also another remarkable finding: even though signific-ant work-related cultural differences between national armed forces were revealed, there was also something like a supranational military culture. This military culture is – compared to civilian life – more collectivistic (uniforms!), more hierarchy-oriented and less salary-driven than the average civilian working culture. The consequence of this is that military personnel of different origins can often function and get along with each other without too many problems (Elron *et al.* 1999; Ben-Ari and Elron 2001). Famous scholars such as Charles Moskos even claim that military personnel from different countries seem to be better suited to work together than with civilian personnel from nongovernmen-tal organizations (NGOs) or local agencies. Not surprisingly, the military often regards people from NGOs as "strange bedfellows" (Winslow 2002).

However, as said, there are also substantial cultural and institutional differ-ences among the armed forces of different countries (Soeters, Poponete and Page 2006). As in civilian cultural studies (e.g. Ronen and Shenkar 1985), clus-ters of countries closely resembling each other have been identified. In the mili-tary – as in civilian life – an Anglo-Saxon cluster consisting of former British colonies (UK, USA, Canada, Australia, New Zealand) can be discerned as well as a Latin cluster (France, Italy, Spain) and a Germanic cluster. Notwithstanding these results pointing at a certain degree of national heterogeneity, additional empirical research has also demonstrated that the armed forces from NATO countries are culturally more homogeneous than those from so called Partner-ship for Peace countries, i.e. countries from the previous communist alliance (Soeters, Poponete and Page 2006). Hence, the following observation seems to be valid: armed forces (from NATO) are alike in many aspects but they are unlike in many others. But is all this of more than theoretical and academic value? We would argue it is.

Various previous studies have demonstrated and argued that these facts indeed impact on the way operations are conducted. A number of qualitative case studies have made clear that national differences exist with respect to the influence of national politics on the conduct of operations, the way armed forces deal with conflicts including setting more or less ambitious operational goals as well as with respect to operational styles, the use of violence and force protection. Besides, there are clear work-related differences such as in leadership styles, rule orientation, work and living conditions and, more specifically, work load. Finally, there are clear differences in how various national military organizations relate to and communicate with the local population in the area of operation (see, for instance, Duffey 2000; Caniglia 2001; Fitz-Gerald 2003; Olonisakin 2003; Soeters *et al.* 2004b, 2006).

It may even be induced that as a consequence of such differences varying results in effectiveness and (societal) outcomes in the area of operations may be achieved. Of course, the link between differences in operational styles and final results is difficult to ascertain. In peace operations there are simply too many variables in play to make such unidimensional causal inferences. Yet, an observation by Stewart (2007), who acted as a high civil servant in the British area in Iraq right after the invasion in 2003, may be illustrative here. During his work in the area he more than once praised the British forces for their experienced, courageous and pro-active behaviour in the streets. He was much more critical in these aspects of the conduct of the Italian armed forces, who "occupied" another province in the same area of operation. Stewart deemed the Italian units to be too passive. Nonetheless, during his return to the region – one year after he had handed over his position to his successor – he came to an astonishing conclusion:

> I found that Dhi Qar, [...] where I believed the closure of our office and the passivity of the Italian troops would lead to inchoate anarchy [...], had become one of the most secure provinces in Iraq, while Maysan, where the British had fought a prolonged and bloody battle for reform, was highly unstable. The Italian policy of inaction had produced a better result because it had forced Iraqis to take responsibility for their own affairs.
>
> (Stewart 2007: 402)

Of course, this is only one observation, but it is illustrative of the idea that differences in operational styles may lead to differences in outcomes, and sometimes this is happening in surprising ways. What is more, differences in organizational and operational styles may lead to less than optimal cooperation in a multinational military setting. In the civilian business sector this has been observed often, as we saw before. This – the dynamics of multinational military cooperation – is what this volume is about.

Volume's aim and content

Our ambitions in this volume are modest. We will not try to ascertain which national operational styles – under which conditions – lead to the best results. It is much too early to express such bold ambitions. Instead, we want to stick to providing an inventory of the knowledge with respect to military cooperation in multinational peace operations. We will focus on military–military interaction – including its political context – and leave the interaction between the military and NGOs and other local agencies to other publications (e.g. Rietjens and Bollen 2008). But even our modest goals are important given the fact that multi-national cooperation is getting increasingly important in today's peace opera-tions, as it does in international business. In the field of international business numerous publications and journals on cross-cultural management have appeared, and continue to do so. As far as we know this has not been the case so far in the field of multinational military cooperation. With this volume we aim to fill this void.

The volume consists of three parts. The first part contains four thematic overviews, delving into academic and practical knowledge from all sorts of studies and case descriptions concerning one specific facet of organized, military life in a multinational context.

The Canadian scholar Donna Winslow gives us an overview of UN opera-tions, with a focus on African missions. She focuses on how the UN over the last decade has tried to improve the effectiveness of these operations. Given the systematic multinational character of these missions, ensuring interoperability and creating common operational styles (including ethics and legal issues) are crucial to enhance the overall effectiveness of these operations. The UN has for-mulated a number of policy changes in order to deal with these issues.

Israel-based expert Efrat Elron pursues on Winslow's work on the UN and focuses on the organizational level integration mechanisms used by peace opera-tions to overcome the challenges of cultural and national diversity. To support her ideas she looks at a variety of UN missions in the Middle East and beyond through the eyes of their officers and commanders. The unique case of coopera-tion developed between UNIFIL, the Israeli Defence Forces and the Lebanese Armed Forces is presented as an example in which lessons learned serve as the basis for the coordination and liaison between the armed forces on the two sides of the border and the multinational force assigned to keep stability and peace in the region.

Another Canadian scholar, Angela Febbraro, provides us with a chapter dealing with leadership and team diversity in multinational operations. This is a much studied subject in the field of international management, because leader-ship is not conceived in the same way all over the globe. Also in the military, leadership in an international context has attracted considerable attention. Man-agers and commanders play an important role in leading multinational teams and units. They may be more or less sensitive to, and aware of cultural issues, and act accordingly. What goes wrong, and what goes right, and why, are some of the questions that Febbraro aims to answer in the chapter.

Andrea van Dijk, a young Dutch academic, focuses on a much forgotten and neglected factor impeding or enhancing multinational cooperation, in business as much as in peace operations: language skills. Certainly in the Anglo-Saxon world, it is often assumed that speaking English solves all possible language-related problems in multinational cooperation. Yet, not all (military) people speak this language fluently, and as a consequence issues of power and centrality arise.

In the second part of the book we present a number of case studies, which are based on field work in the area of operation or at a multinational HQ. Although armed forces from all over the world are being studied (including those of the USA, Australia, Canada, Japan and Gambia), the main focus is on cooperation between European military organizations. The first reason is that, because of their decreasing resources and increasing tasks they are set to do, European armed forces are urged to work together with forces from other nations. The other reason of course is that research is often conducted in the Western hemisphere, whereas (military) organizations from developing countries have attracted, until now, much less academic attention, regrettably so.

In the first case study (Chapter 6), UK sociologist and anthropologist Anthony King presents a somewhat provocative, yet exciting contribution on the British approach to multinational operations. He wants his readers to grasp the peculiarities of the British defence organization and its service people, in particular its commanders. This will enable the soldiers of other nations to better understand and work together with the British. Among other issues the topic of language will pop up again.

Professor John Ballard from the USA provides a detailed analysis of the multinational operations in East Timor led by the Australian armed forces. In general, these operations were regarded as quite successful, and Ballard deciphers the reasons and the recipe for the success, without closing his eyes for what went less smoothly.

That politics indeed do play a role in multinational military cooperation becomes crystal clear in the chapter co-authored by Turkish academics Abdulkadir Varoglu, Mehmet Cakar and Nejat Basim. They give an account of a quite coincidental sort of military cooperation between two countries that at first glance do not seem to have much in common. A more detailed look, however, reveals that political interests and cultural/religious similarities have brought Turkey and Gambia working together in a project of military cooperation, much to the satisfaction of both partnering countries.

German anthropologist Maren Tomforde conducted an extensive, longitudinal study together with collaborators from Italy on the German–Italian cooperation in Kosovo (KFOR). She points at the concept of transnationalism, which helps her to understand that the Italian and the German service people – although having rather different languages and cultures – seemed to get along with one another pretty well.

Ljubica Jelušič and Bojan Progajč from Slovenia describe the working of a multinational brigade consisting of Italian, Hungarian and Slovenian companies. In general, this has been a very exciting and learning experience, not the least because two former communist countries participated in this multinational brigade. Interestingly enough, at the beginning of their cooperation, issues of language were quite important.

Swedish academics Erik Hedlund and Louise Weibull (together with Joseph Soeters) went to Liberia, on the African West coast. In that country, notorious for its atrocious civil wars that have been going on for years, UNMIL was deployed in 2003. Since then, the situation in the country has much improved. UNMIL mainly consists of African troops, in particular from Nigeria. But there are also contributions from two traditional UN-supporting nations in Europe, Ireland and Sweden. Troops of these countries were put together in one Quick Reaction Force, based on the assumption that this would work out easily. It did not, however, much to the regret of those involved. An interesting learning experience, though.

The Dutch professor Jan van der Meulen and his Japanese colleague Hitoshi Kawano once again bring general politics into the picture of multinational military cooperation. Their case study is about the armed forces of two countries that are far away: the Netherlands and Japan. In Iraq both armed forces became accidental neighbours having to work together in the very South of that violence ridden country. They meticulously show that national politics influence the content of their armed forces' mandate, which in turn dominates the operational activities on the ground. Differences in policies formulated in The Hague and Tokyo led to operational differences in Al Muthanna, Iraq.

Danish experts on intercultural communication Anne-Marie Søderberg and Merete Wedell-Wedellsborg describe and analyse the cooperation in a NATO training centre in Poland, where service personnel from Germany, Poland and Denmark and some ten other NATO member states work closely together. Using the concept of identity the authors carefully compare the different influences that shape the organization's culture and performance; this enables them to reveal interesting insights into the dynamics of that particular training centre.

In the second part's final chapter Joseph Soeters, Delphine Resteigne, Rene Moelker and Philippe Manigart present a carefully conducted, theory-driven comparison of three cases of multinational cooperation in the framework of the ISAF operation in Kabul, Afghanistan. They find support for the impact of a number of determinants that have previously been identified in the field of civilian international management. This research approach produces a much better understanding of factors leading to a rather smooth or – on the contrary – a more strained sort of multinational military cooperation.

In the concluding chapter the editors try to summarize the previous contributions raising a number of dilemma and questions pertaining to factors that have come to be identified as important. Using the well known framework of John Berry (e.g. 2004) regarding cultural integration, they suggest a number of possible organizational arrangements when dealing with multinational military cooperation. Clearly, there are no easy solutions: the issues at stake are simply too complicated. Most important is the idea of continuous improvement based on permanent organizational learning.

We think this book offers a wealth of experiences and insights on the chances of success for multinational military cooperation. Some of the experiences in the chapters have been very promising, some less so, but all experiences are useful to learn about. Multinational military cooperation is here to stay; there can be no doubt about that. The challenge for commanders (and their service people) of so many countries will be to know how to manage the intricacies that are inherently connected to cross-bordering military cooperation. If this volume helps them to acquire this knowledge, it has fulfilled its modest aim.

Part I

Thematic overviews

Chapter 2

The UN

Multinational cooperation in peace operations

Donna Winslow

Introduction

The multinational nature of contemporary peace operations produces a complex web of relations, all of which demand a high level of international cooperation at strategic, operational and tactical levels. Effective cooperation and coordination among states, organizations and individuals is a contributing factor to the success of these missions.

The goal of this chapter is to examine United Nations (UN) efforts to promote multinational cooperation in peace operations. We will see that the UN does this through sharing information, encouraging common training and setting up guidelines and policies. Although the UN itself is an exercise in supra-national norms, its successes and failures underscore the difficulties in maintaining them. It is important to examine UN efforts to improve its peace operations in order to understand how this international body is attempting to improve its performance in some of the most challenging peace operations in the world.

We will focus on the impact of these efforts in current UN operations particularly in Africa where almost half of UN operations and the majority of its peacekeepers are. The largest operations occur in Africa. Take, for example, the breadth of the UN Mission in Liberia where its mandate includes a disarmament, demobilization, reintegration and repatriation programme; support for humanitarian and human rights assistance; support for the reform of security institutions; and, assistance to the transitional government. We will see that the UN cooperates with other agencies in different configurations: integrated operations where the full scope of the operation is managed within a single chain of command; coordinated operations where the UN and other organizations operate side by side under separate command structures but closely coordinate policies and actions; parallel operations where there is no formal cooperation with other organizations; and, sequential operations where the UN precedes or follows a multinational, regional or bilateral force.

There are currently 104,414 personnel serving in 18 operations led by the UN Department of Peacekeeping Operations (DPKO) on four continents in ten time zones, directly impacting the lives of hundreds of millions of people. There are

70,972 troops, 2,541 are military observers and 9,657 are police personnel. In addition, there are 4,852 international civilian personnel, 11,091 local civilian staff and 2,049 UN Volunteers. The challenges they face include a lack of resources, a diversity of languages and training levels and few opportunities to train together before a mission.

The Brahimi Report

After the disasters of the mid-1990s, including the UN's failure to prevent the 1994 genocide in Rwanda or the 1995 massacres in Srebrenica, Bosnia-Herzegovina (both detailed in unusually frank UN reports issued in late 1999), UN member states largely turned away from the organization for major peacekeeping initiatives. This relatively fallow period could have been viewed as breathing space to correct the more obvious problems with UN peacekeeping, but there seemed to be little interest on the part of states to invest more time and money in what was assumed in many quarters to be a failed enterprise (Durch 2001: 1).

In 1999, the UN was suddenly called upon, in rapid succession, to administer Kosovo under the protection of NATO ground forces; to replace the Australian-led mission and launch a new government for East Timor; to replace the Nigerian-led mission in Sierra Leone; and finally, to oversee a shaky ceasefire in the vast Democratic Republic of Congo. The elements of the UN Secretariat responsible for peacekeeping were at this time under-funded, under-staffed, unprepared to run a country (and were politically constrained from preparing to do so even if they had possessed the requisite expertise), and not up to dealing with situations such as ruthless, diamond-smuggling gangs who passed for treaty signatories, such as Sierra Leone's Revolutionary United Front (Durch 2001: 1).

The Panel on UN Peace Operations was announced 7 March 2000 by then UN Secretary-General Kofi Annan. The high-level Panel chaired by Ambassador Lakhdar Brahimi, Under-Secretary-General for special assignments (preventive action and peacemaking) was given a straightforward yet comprehensive mandate: to present a clear set of concrete and practical recommendations to assist the United Nations to improve future peacekeeping activities. The final document generated by the four-month study, *The Report of the Panel on United Nations Peace Operations* is commonly known as the "Brahimi Report." The Brahimi Report represents the first systematic effort to identify and address the technical problems with UN peacekeeping missions and within the United Nations' DPKO. It called for collaboration in planning and standardized training.

The Brahimi Report described the United Nations' inability to bring more men, money and thought to the mission of peacekeeping. The Report revealed the extent to which the UN Secretariat was under-staffed and under-funded. At the time the Report was completed (July 2000) the DPKO had only 32 military officers to plan, recruit, equip, deploy, support, and direct some 27,000 soldiers that comprised the 15 missions underway (Docking 2001: 4). These numbers illustrate a central point of the Report: that the United Nations lacked the resources to effectively fulfil its peacekeeping mission. In fact, the United Nations is a body that is in constant search of material and financial support and coherent political backing from member states.

The Panel recommended the creation of specific Integrated Mission Task Forces that would draw people from those parts of the UN system having specific operational expertise (for elections, for example, or refugee return), as well as from the peacekeeping department's military and police staffs, to sit together and jointly plan and support a field operation. Such collaboration had been sporadic. It recommended that recruitment and training of civilian mission personnel be standardized and make heavy use of information technology for basic familiarization prior to mission deployment. Selected military and police personnel should be pre-trained and on-call in their home countries for rapid setup of headquarters for new missions, and to help train the police and other experts who come to a new mission from dozens of countries (Durch 2001: 17).

In terms of our theme, the Report urged greater international collaboration to create well-trained and appropriately equipped forces for peace operations. One of the persistent challenges is that (as opposed to those carried out during the Organization's first 50 years) a large percentage of the troops in formed military units deployed in United Nations peacekeeping operations, are contributed by developing countries. When developing nations provide personnel for peacekeeping missions, they frequently require outside material and financial support from the UN and bilateral partners, such as transportation, logistics, equipment, and planning and organizational support. Moreover, developing countries lack the resources and opportunities to carry out collective international training. Some even lack the resources to meet international standards in terms of expertise and equipment. The Brahimi Report stated (United Nations 2000: 18):

> Some countries have provided soldiers without rifles, or with rifles but no helmets, or with helmets but no flak jackets, or with no organic transport capability (trucks or troops carriers). Troops may be untrained in peacekeeping operations, and in any case the various contingents in an operation are unlikely to have trained or worked together before. Some units may have no personnel who can speak the mission language. Even if language is not a problem, they may lack common operating procedures and have differing interpretations of key elements of command and control and of the mission's rules of engagement, and may have differing expectations about mission requirements for the use of force.

The Brahimi Report went on to say (United Nations 2000: 19):

> If United Nations military planners assess that a brigade (approximately 5,000 troops) is what is required to effectively deter or deal with violent

challenges to the implementation of an operation's mandate, then the military component of that United Nations operation ought to deploy as a brigade formation, not as a collection of battalions that are unfamiliar with one another's doctrine, leadership and operational practices. That brigade would have to come from a group of countries that have been working together as suggested above to develop common training and equipment standards, common doctrine, and common arrangements for the operational control of the force.

To that end, the United Nations should establish the minimum training, equipment and other standards required for forces to participate in United Nations peacekeeping operations. Member States with the means to do so could form partnerships, within the context of UN Standby Arrangements System (UNSAS), to provide financial, equipment, training and other assistance to troop contributors from less developed countries to enable them to reach and maintain that minimum standard, with the goal that each of the brigades so established should be of comparably high quality and be able to call upon effective levels of operational support. Such a formation has been the objective of the Standing High-Readiness Brigade (SHIRBRIG) group of States, who have also established a command-level planning element that works together routinely.

This led to following key recommendations concerning military personnel:

a   Member States should be encouraged, where appropriate, to enter into partnerships with one another, within the context of UNSAS, to form several coherent brigade-size forces, with necessary enabling forces, ready for effective deployment within 30 days of the adoption of a Security Council resolution establishing a traditional peacekeeping operation and within 90 days for complex peacekeeping operations;
b   The Secretary-General should be given the authority to formally canvass Member States participating in UNSAS regarding their willingness to contribute troops to a potential operation once it appeared likely that a ceasefire accord or agreement envisaging an implementing role for the United Nations might be reached;
c   The Secretariat should, as a standard practice, send a team to confirm the preparedness of each potential troop contributor to meet the provisions of the memoranda of understanding on the requisite training and equipment requirements, prior to deployment; those that do not meet the requirements must not deploy;
d   The Panel recommends that a revolving "on-call list" of about 100 military officers be created in UNSAS to be available on seven days' notice to augment nuclei of DPKO planners with teams trained to create a mission headquarters for a new peacekeeping operation.

(United Nations 2000: 20)

Implementing change

An important number of the Panel's recommendations have been introduced. Improvements include an expanded headquarters staff, primarily in the DPKO[1] which is now more able to plan operations. DPKO's military section is now twice the size of its pre-Brahimi days as is its police division although both are still considered understaffed.[2] The structure and organization of logistics and field support has been improved and the UN Logistics Base in Brindisi, Italy, expanded. There is now an internal process for integrated mission planning and DPKO's Peacekeeping Best Practices Service (PBPS) now generates timely analytical reports for UN Headquarters, operations and mission contributors.

Unfortunately some of the recommendations were subjected to extended discussions and political procrastination. The most important delay concerned the setting up of the Peacebuilding Commission which met for the first time in June 2006. (It had been originally scheduled to start work in December 2005). The rationale behind the Commission is explained by Kofi Annan (2005b: 1):

> All of us have been shocked, over the last fifteen years, by the spectacle of countries apparently emerging from a bitter, destructive conflict, only to slip back again because the international community lost interest too soon and moved on to other crises. One reason for this has been the lack of any international institution specifically devoted to peacebuilding, as opposed to peacemaking or peacekeeping. And therefore I think one of the most encouraging results ... was the decision to fill this institutional void by establishing a Peacebuilding Commission, backed by a small peacebuilding support office within the Secretariat, and a voluntary Peacebuilding Fund.

The Commission requires a high level of international cooperation. It includes an Organizational Committee (made up of 31 member countries) and country-specific committees (this includes country representatives as well as all the relevant contributors such as regional organizations, regional banks and international financial institutions). The Commission's mission statement is described on its website as follows: "The Peacebuilding Commission will marshal resources at the disposal of the international community to advise and propose integrated strategies for post-conflict recovery, focusing attention on reconstruction, institution-building and sustainable development, in countries emerging from conflict" (United Nations Peacebuilding Commission 2006: 1).

The Commission will bring together the UN's broad capacities and experience in conflict prevention, mediation, peacekeeping, respect for human rights, the rule of law, humanitarian assistance, reconstruction and long-term development.

Specifically, the Commission will (paraphrased from United Nations Peacebuilding Commission 2006: 1):

- Propose integrated strategies for post-conflict peacebuilding and recovery;
- Help to ensure predictable financing for early recovery activities and sustained financial investment over the medium to longer term.
- Extend the period of attention by the international community to post-conflict recovery;
- Develop best practices on issues that require extensive collaboration among political, military, humanitarian and development actors.

By improving coordination and reducing duplication of efforts among the many actors who become involved in a country experiencing or coming out of conflict, it is believed that the Peacebuilding Commission will improve overall efficiency and reduce the likelihood of a costly relapse into conflict. The primary aim of the Commission is to strengthen a country's own capacity to recover after conflict and reduce the long-term necessity for recurring peacekeeping operations.

Another important initiative is the Multi-national Standby High Readiness Brigade for UN Operations (SHIRBRIG). The idea for SHIRBRIG began in the 1990s.[3] In the 1995 Statement *Supplement to an Agenda for Peace*, the UN Secretary-General recommended that the UN should consider the idea of a rapid deployment force, consisting of units from a number of member states, trained to the same standard, using the same operating procedures and interoperable equipment, and taking part in combined exercises at regular intervals.

That same year, Denmark established a working group of a number of like-minded member states, all with extensive experience and high standards in the field of peacekeeping, to explore the option of creating a rapid deployment force within the framework of UNSAS. In December 1996, Austria, Canada, Denmark, The Netherlands, Norway, Poland, and Sweden signed a letter of intent of cooperating on the establishment of a framework for SHIRBRIG. A Steering Committee was established to oversee the brigade, and a permanent Planning Element was created (Multi-national Standby High Readiness Brigade for UN Operations 2007).

SHIRBRIG was first declared available to the UN at the end of January 2000 and its headquarters is in Denmark. Following a deployment to the United Nations Mission in Ethiopia and Eritrea, SHIRBRIG assisted in the transition from the Economic Community of West African States (ECOWAS)-led mission in Liberia to the UN-led mission UNMIL. Sixteen nations (Argentina, Austria, Canada, Denmark, Finland, Italy, Ireland, Lithuania, the Netherlands, Norway, Poland, Portugal, Romania, Slovenia, Spain, and Sweden) have signed one or more SHIRBRIG documents, with eight more nations (Chile, Croatia, Czech Republic, Egypt, Hungary, Jordan, Latvia and Senegal) participating as observers (Multi-national Standby High Readiness Brigade for UN Operations 2007).

The SHIRBRIG brigade pool is comprised of a number of similar units exceeding the force requirement. This ensures the deployment of the brigade even if one or more participants decide not to provide troops for a given mission for whatever reason. The nations earmark these forces for participation in a SHIRBRIG operation, but they remain under national command until deployed. The brigade structure is tailored for each specific mission, but could consist of 4,000 to 5,000 troops. The SHIRBRIG concept of operations can be paraphrased as follows (Multi-national Standby High Readiness Brigade for UN Operations 2007):

- Member countries decide on a case-by-case basis whether or not they will participate in any given mission. National decision-making procedures (and thereby national sovereignty) are in no way affected by membership in SHIRBRIG. This is the overarching principle governing members' participation in SHRIBRIG.
- Any deployment involving SHIRBRIG must be mandated by the UN Security Council. Although deployments were initially envisioned under Chapter VI of the Charter, the steering Committee recently agreed to examine more robust operations on a case-by-case basis.
- After a maximum of six months, the mission is either terminated or SHIRBRIG will be replaced by non-SHIRBRIG forces.
- The Brigade's reaction time is 15 to 30 days following the decision of the participating nations to make forces available for deployment upon request by the UN.
- The availability of forces will be based on a brigade pool of resources that will include capabilities to carry out a peace support operation as well as provide for redundancies in such capabilities.
- Units committed to the brigade should be self-sufficient for 60 days.

The elements of SHIRBRIG are the following three entities:

The *Steering Committee* – This executive body is a political-military structure responsible for oversight and supervision, policy-making, and for the SHIRBRIG decision-making and force generation process. The Chair of the Steering Committee rotates annually among the full member participants.

A *Planning Element* – Located at Høvelte Barracks in Denmark, the Planning Element is the permanent multinational military staff composed of officers from the ten member countries that have signed all the SHIRBRIG documents. The Planning Element develops standing operating procedures, carries out operational preparations for deployment, and conducts training of the SHIRBRIG staff and unit commanders. During operations, the Planning Element serves as the nucleus of the brigade headquarters and is augmented by non-permanent staff from the member nations.

A *Brigade Pool* which is comprised of a number of similar units providing a full range of capabilities. These units exceed SHIRBRIG's force requirement in order to ensure the deployment of the brigade. Forces earmarked for the SHIRBRIG brigade remain under national command until deployed. The SHIRBRIG pool of resources also allows flexibility in structuring the force for a specific mission.

The system ultimately depends on arrangements negotiated between the United Nations and individual Member States. The resources agreed upon remain on "standby" in their home country, where necessary preparation, including training, is conducted to fulfil specified tasks or functions in accordance with United Nations guidelines. When necessary, the resources are requested by the Secretary-General, and, if approved by the Member States, are rapidly deployed. The primary responsibility for the training of personnel in the performance of peacekeeping duties remains with Member States. To facilitate standardization, training guidelines for specific United Nations tasks and objectives are published by the Secretariat.

Since its creation SHIRBRIG has participated in a number of UN missions in Africa. From November 2000 to March 2001 it deployed a headquarters of 95 staff officers and support, 200 Danish troops for a headquarter company and one Canadian-Netherlands infantry battalion of 600 troops to the UN mission in Ethiopia and Eritrea. This effort underscored the importance of common standards and training. As Secretary-General Kofi Annan commented, "There, a force that had trained together and developed a high degree of coherence was able to arrive and establish itself quickly in the theatre of operation, thereby sending a message of competence and commitment" (Annan 2002 quoted in Bani 2007: 3).

In March 2003 it provided a planning team to ECOWAS to assist ECOWAS in planning for its mission in Côte d'Ivoire. In September of that same year it deployed 19 members to assist in the formation of the interim headquarters of the UN mission to Liberia. In 2004 it deployed members to Sudan as part of the UN Advanced mission in Sudan; in 2005 it provided the nucleus of the force headquarters in addition to an Italian Headquarters and Security Company (220 troops) for the UN mission in Sudan (Bani 2007: 1–2).

SHIRBRIG was expected to play a role in Darfur. Thus in 2006 SHIRBRIG was asked by the UN to assist DPKO in planning for a possible deployment to establish a Divisional HQ in Darfur, Sudan, as part of the transition of the African Mission in Sudan (AMIS) to UNMIS. The assistance DPKO needed were three officers with the following specialities: medic, air operations, and engineer (water purification). They comprised part of the DARFUR Planning Team, in which they were the only military personnel.

SHRIBRIG has a number of initiatives to assist the African Union and other regional organizations. It has helped establish the African Stand-by Forces (ASF) which is a regional initiative based on the SHIRBRIG model (Bani 2007: 2). To promote cooperation with African forces SHIRBRIG exchanges with regional organizations such as ECOWAS training concepts are discussed (Multinational Standby High Readiness Brigade for UN Operations 2007).

The UN and international cooperation

Jackson's (2006: 2) reflection after evaluating the Burundi mission was that "The UN will seldom be the sole actor in future, so learning how best to engage alongside others is a critical task." As mentioned in the introduction there are four levels of organizational cooperation: integrated operations[4] where the full scope of the operation is managed within a single chain of command; coordinated operations where the UN and other organizations operate side by side under separate command structures but closely coordinate policies and actions; parallel operations where there is no formal cooperation with other organizations; and sequential operations where the UN precedes or follows a multinational, regional or bilateral force.

The United Nations Challenges Project (2006) has mapped a number of operations according to command relations and functions. As they note this is not always clear. For example UN Organization Mission in the Democratic Republic of Congo began as an observer mission protected by peacekeepers but also had short-term security support from the French-led EU operation Artemis, while the UN's own Brigade was being assembled and deployed. Eide *et al.* (2005) point out that there is little agreement on what constitutes an integrated mission at the practical level and that a variety of practices have emerged dependent on the different missions and actors involved.

Sequential operations can lead to "rehatting." "Rehatting" (to blue beret) contingents has become more common place in African deployments. In Côte d'Ivoire the UN operation which was established in 2004 was a successor to ECOWAS and involved rehatting many of the West African troops. ECOWAS also rehatted to the UN in Liberia, Sierra Leone, Côte d'Ivoire and Burundi (see Jackson 2006 for details on Burundi). The United Nations Peacekeeping Best Practices Service (2005: 2) has noted the following problems associated with rehatting: The lack of equivalency between the two forces, the basic lack of logistics requirements, differences in force mandates and capability gaps. The unit's report recommends the establishment of common doctrinal guidelines, key norms to address the critical questions relating to command and control, capabilities required, and the steps necessary to achieve a smooth transition. The absence of these elements is an obstacle to a coordinated approach (see United Nations Peacekeeping Best Practices Service 2005 for details).

Interaction between the UN and regional organizations has become a common feature of contemporary operations and as a result a more coordinated approach has evolved. The UN Secretary General stressed this in his report to the UN Special Committee on Peacekeeping Operations in December 2004. In it he urged member states to "define how the United Nations and other organizations should work together and how peacekeeping demands should be shared" indicating that the aim "must be to develop a system of international capacities that is complementary, flexible and nimble" (Annan 2004: paras 8, 71). This thought was repeated in his *In Larger Freedom* report (Annan 2005a): "The time is ripe for a decisive move forward: the establishment of an interlocking system of peacekeeping capacities that will enable the United Nations to work with relevant regional organizations in predictable and reliable partnership." Of course these partnerships will have to be adjusted according to the operation and the characteristics of the organization.

Only a few multinational organizations can use force for more than self-defence: the EU, the African Union (AU), the UN, NATO, and ECOWAS. Other organizations can intervene diplomatically or politically. The Organization for Security Cooperation in Europe (OSCE) can provide observers for a peace operation. Some organizations such as the Arab League, the Association of Southeast Asian Nations (ASEAN), AU, OAS, and OSCE wish to confine their activities to their membership states while other organizations such as NATO roam far afield.

The development of regional dimensions of African peacekeeping has been the most substantial and could be seen as a response to the UN's inability to meet all the peace and security needs of the continent. The African Union, created in 2001 as the successor to the Organization for African Unity, believes that it has an important continental perspective necessary to efforts to prevent and resolve conflicts in Africa. In 2004 the AU launched a Peace and Security Council to serve as a collective security and early warning arrangement that would facilitate timely and efficient regional responses to conflict and crisis (see www.africa-union.org for details). The AU has been active in peace missions in Burundi, Ethiopia and Eritrea, and Sudan. The AU is also developing an African Standby Force comprising of civilians, police, and military and hopes to establish a strategic headquarters and brigades of about 4,500 troops each in each of the five African regions by 2010. AU peacekeepers are trained and able to work under UN command as well as in AU-led missions.

The most visible and draining of AU activities has been the Darfur mission. There is certainly a need for cooperation and collaboration in this case and the Security Council requested that the UN Mission in Sudan closely and continuously liaise and coordinate at all levels with the African Union Mission in Sudan with a view towards expeditiously reinforcing the efforts to foster peace in Darfur, especially with regards to the Abuja peace process and the African Union Mission in Sudan. All AU resources went into the mission which still remains chronically under-staffed and ill-equipped.

Nevertheless, the mission has also been a catalyst in the development of the AU's peacekeeping capacity. Thus, in March 2005, the AU and the Regions agreed on a "Roadmap" for the operationalization of the African Standby Force. The Roadmap takes stock of the developments in each Region and at AU level, and spells out the requirements for progress. Just like the decision to intervene in Darfur, the Roadmap is an ambitious plan. Work is taken forward in each key area via a series of decentralized workshops involving the participation of the Regions as well as international donors. An example of a Regional organization is the Southern Africa Development Community which sponsored several peace

operations field exercises in the 1990s but, with the exception of the brief operation in Lesotho (1998–1999), its members have been contributing forces to
peacekeeping through the United Nations or the African Union. These include
the UN mission in the Democratic Republic of Congo and the African Mission
in Burundi, which merged into the UN Operation in Burundi, ONUB, later
BINUB, in June 2004.

Subregional groupings have also developed their own peace and security
mechanisms, each with its own structure, priorities and capabilities. In West
Africa a peacekeeping capacity was formalized through the ECOWAS mechanism for conflict prevention, management, resolution, peacekeeping, humanitarian relief and security. Made up of 15 West African states ECOWAS has
mounted operations in Liberia, Sierra Leone, Guinea Bissau, and Côte d'Ivoire.
It has also approved a Military Vision and Strategy, a Force Structure, a Logistics Depot Concept, and a Concept of Development, and its Member States have
pledged units and personnel for a Task Force, a HQ Staff, and a Main Brigade of
6,500 men. ECOWAS cooperates with the UN and the AU on several of the
above peace initiatives (United Nations Challenges Project 2006: 62).

In terms of the theme of this chapter, the Roadmap lays great stress on "collaboration and cooperation" with bilateral and international partners, specifying
that assistance will be necessary for the establishment of the planning elements,
the AU logistical depots and the provision of other logistic support, the African
Standby Force training and exercise program and, last but not least, the financing of operations (United Nations Challenges Project 2006: 61). The European
Union has earmarked some $300 million to support future AU peacekeeping
operations. In April 2004, America launched a five-year $660-million plan
called the Global Peace Operations Initiative. The plan was implemented to train
and equip foreign troops – most of them African – for peacekeeping missions in
their own regions (Holt 2005: 6).

In addition to collaboration with regional organizations UN operations cooperate with each other regionally. For example, the proximity of UNMIL
(Liberia) to UNAMSIL, later UNIOSIL (Sierra Leone) and ONUCI (Côte
d'Ivoire) creates an opportunity for cooperation and information sharing concerning smuggling and militias. Unfortunately this useful form of regional cooperation is not formalized and remains at the discretion of mission heads.

In order to build capacity in the regional organizations, common doctrine and
training need to be developed. In the next section we will look at shared training
which promotes interoperability and cooperation.

Training

The UN Challenges project underlines the need for multinational training:

> There is a critical need for participants in peace operations to train together:
> Participants in peace operations shouldn't meet for the first time in the

maelstrom of a peace operation. The earlier in one's education and training that one is exposed to the often different views of other disciplines, the more readily one can adapt to the needs of cooperative work in the field. Preparing together in advance of deployment may take three forms: formal training on cooperation and coordination; joint participation in multi-disciplinary seminars and courses; and, training together in exercises specifically focused on cooperation and coordination.

(United Nations Challenges Project 2006: 124)

Seminars, courses and exercises aimed at enhancing interoperability between and among military, police, and civilian expert participants in peace operations are growing in number, complexity, and sophistication. The UN has encouraged new partnerships to reinforce Africa's capacity for conflict prevention, peace-keeping, and peace-building. Bilateral efforts have provided field training and classroom instruction in peacekeeping, and have helped develop regional training centres. For example France first launched RECAMP (Renforcement des Capacités Africaines de Maintien de la Paix/Reinforcement of African Capacity to Maintain Peace) in 1997, and Senegalese troops participated in phase one while their counterparts in Gabon received training in phase two. Military personnel from all Southern Africa Development Community (SADC) countries plus non-SADC contribute soldiers to the military training exercises. Under the aegis of the UN and in agreement with the OAU, the RECAMP Programme aims at helping African states to acquire military capabilities to enable them to conduct peacekeeping operations on the continent.

The US sponsors African Contingency Operations and Training Assistance and the African Crisis Response Initiative that seeks to help African nations to respond to humanitarian crises and peacekeeping missions in their region. The African Crisis Response Initiative's objective is to enhance the capacity of African nations to better perform peacekeeping and relief tasks through the promotion of common doctrine, interoperability and standard communications technology among African forces. The US-sponsored programme Operation Focus Relief trained seven African battalions for deployment to the UN mission in Sierra Leone. In 2007 the creation of US Africa Command (AFRICOM) was announced. The main focus of AFRICOM will not be military operations; rather it will emphasize training programmes, civil affairs and the professionalization of African armed forces.

The British fund a Military Advisory and Training Team and Peace Support Teams programmes, and programmes from Norway, Canada, and Denmark provide additional training and equipment assistance, while other countries have helped to enhance skills, further doctrinal standardization, and improve logistical capacity. EU Member States train an average of 100 African military officers in Europe every year and 1,000 in Africa itself (United Nations Challenges Project 2006: 133).

Within the UN system itself there have been a number of positive developments in peace operations education and training, including advances in, and general acceptance of, the UN's structure, policies and resources, standards and guidelines for peace operations education and training, and new and enhanced institutions for the development and delivery of education and training. Particular progress within the UN system includes the rejuvenation of the UN DPKO Peacekeeping Best Practices Service (PBPS) and its work to develop a coherent body of peace operations policies and guidelines for the UN system; the development of PBPS's comprehensive and interactive website; and the publication of the 2004 *Handbook on UN Multidimensional Peacekeeping Operations*. The PBPS not only provides a repository for lessons-learned but also facilitates their incorporation in education and training.

ITS is the DPKO training and evaluation service. It provides standardized training, mission training for specific deployments, produces documents, visits missions, and has web links, web training guides, correspondence courses in peacekeeping operations in addition to the courses offered by the United Nations University. ITS has developed Standardized Training Modules (STMs). These have been developed in cooperation with a large number of national education and training institutions and governments. Some 75 Member States contributed to the development of the level-one modules, 50 engaged in level-two development, and more than 50 states were involved in the 2004 deliberations and 2005 trials on level three.

The three STM levels have different objectives. Level one is basic or "universal" training (basic knowledge of peacekeeping, the UN system, codes of conduct, command and control, safety and security – 16 modules in all). Level-two modules are more specific, designed to provide training for specialists, including military observers, military staff officers, and civilian police who will function as monitors, trainers, or mentors. STM level three is intended to create a standardized management training package for senior military leaders/managers that could also form an element of a standardized management training programme for senior civilian and civilian police staff in UN peace operations. The course has now been named the UN Senior Mission Leaders Course (STM3) and there are now 28 modules to draw on, with other under development. The UN's concept for STM level three is to partner with several Member States across all regions to develop and conduct the senior management training (United Nations Challenges Project 2006: 116–118).

The UN tells us that the importance of preparing individuals and groups for peace operations is receiving growing acceptance from Member States. The number of training centres, including regional centres, is also on the increase. The UN is working with a number of Member States and regional organizations to create region-wide approaches and cooperation in providing education and training for peace operations, which will contribute to interoperability. The concept should expand to ensure that training centres are multidisciplinary and deal with non-military education and training as well as military. Examples of developing regional cooperation in this area include ECOWAS efforts in West Africa and the European Union Group on Training. Centres such as the Kofi

Annan International Peacekeeping Training Centre in Ghana not only train local military, police, and civilians, but also undertake a regional role. Within the NATO Partnership for Peace framework a number of countries have developed Partnership for Peace Centres of Excellence, specializing in a number of areas of peace operations (United Nations Challenges Project 2006: 118).

Conclusions

Chapter 14 in this book points out that cooperation becomes easier the more heterogeneous the unit. Certainly current UN operations are very heterogeneous. This said, we can assume that language might pose a significant problem for nations working alongside each other. For example Bangladeshi officers working in Côte d'Ivoire are busy trying to learn French in order to better communicate with the locals and with their French counterparts. Moreover we have seen that UN training plus the other regionally focused training initiatives aim at establishing common understandings of such things as the way the UN works and Rules of Engagement. It is important to note that the UN cannot affect the peacekeeping doctrine that Blue Helmets use since this doctrine is produced for each national contingent by the troop contributing nation.

Another important point is that soldiers, police, and civilian personnel serve together in complex peace operations, but rarely train together beforehand, and often have very little direct knowledge of the others' professional culture. The need to embed a culture of cooperation in individuals as a principal operational requirement was a lesson identified during operations in the Balkans, East Timor, Burundi, Sierra Leone, Liberia, the Democratic Republic of Congo, and Afghanistan (United Nations Challenges Project 2006: 124). Moreover, it is unlikely that the UN will be a sole actor in future operations. This means increased cooperation with regional organizations and member states. There is little opportunity to prepare for this eventual collaboration.

Most peace operation exercises, simulated and live, are conceived, organized and implemented by military organizations, national and international. The military has for some time recognized the need for non-military contributions to the scenarios and actual play of exercises, in the interests not only of realism, but also with a view to achieving a greater training value for the military itself. As missions become more integrated and complex civilian actors must train alongside peacekeepers in the same manner as they will be required to work with them.

The Report on Integrated Missions by Eide *et al.* (2005) examined training opportunities within eight current missions and concluded that "only two had integrated training cells and those that existed were insufficiently resourced." There is certainly a need for more training once in mission due to the new issues that require attention and understanding and that were not covered in national preparations. Moreover, such training is of particular benefit if it is done in multidisciplinary (civilian–military) groups. The Report observes that common training is a valuable tool for enabling better interoperability between conflicting organizational cultures. The UN has urged Member States to work with and support the DPKO development of an Integrated Training Services, in-mission integrated induction and specialized training, and to offer specialized training resources from national peace operations training centres for attachment to specific integrated mission training units. In this way, the UN hopes to promote multinational as well as multiorganizational cooperation.

Notes

1 The DPKO is in charge of evaluating the requirements of a potential peace operation, providing recommendations to the Security Council through the Secretary-General, and responsible for mission planning. DPKO recruits troops and police from contributing countries, matches requirements to budgets, determines equipment and logistical needs, sets up pre-deployment training and oversees deployment of the forces. Among many other jobs, they also work within the UN to integrate mission planning with offices responsible for humanitarian, political and relief efforts, such as the Office of the Coordination of Humanitarian Affairs, the Department of Political Affairs, and the UN High Commission on Refugees, among others (Holt 2005: 3).
2 Holt (2005: 3) tells us that in New York, roughly two dozen people, for example, are in charge of recruiting and managing the UN's civilian police, which total about 6,000 in the field. The job is especially difficult, since most police are recruited as individuals or in small units, unlike peacekeepers.
3 The SHIRBRIG is not to be confused with the idea of a UN "Army"/emergency-response unit. The idea of a UN emergency force first surfaced after the Second World War, when hopes for an activist world body were at their highest. But it was not until 1994, in the aftermath of the Rwanda genocide, that it was considered seriously. At that time, the United States worried that it would become an out-of-control "UN army," and developing countries felt threatened by what they saw as an interventionist force directed by the West. A combination of lack of enthusiasm from the rich and opposition from poor countries resulted in the shelving of the project (see Diehl 2005; Ward 2006 for details).
4 For an ICRC critique of Integrated missions see www.icrc.org/Web/eng/siteeng0.nsf/html/6DCGRN. For The UN Report on Integrated missions see Eide et al. 2005.

Chapter 3

The interplay between the transnational and multinational

Intercultural integrating mechanisms in UN peace operations

Efrat Elron

Introduction

The significant quantitative increase of UN peacekeeping missions in the last decade is intertwined with the transformation of their qualitative profile, which can be seen in their expanded mission spectrum. Although there are continuous widespread debates regarding the nature and responsibility of peace mission operating under the UN (for a review see Bellamy *et al.* 2004 and Hebeger 2007), on the ground contemporary peace operations extend far beyond the monitoring and verification tasks of their predecessors, and their mandates are expanding on multiple horizons (e.g. Findlay 2002; Paris 2004; Ramsbotham 2000). Peacekeepers are increasingly charged with nation-building tasks like economic rehabilitation, democratization, building civil institutions and working police forces, humanitarian aid, and repatriation of refugees. At the same time, missions are being deployed in settings considered less and less ripe for conflict resolution, adding to their mandates authorization higher levels of intervention capabilities, including the use of force to differing degrees. In many cases multinational forces are needed to intervene quickly and on an ad-hoc basis in crisis situations which are ambiguous, dangerous, and complex.

Partnerships in and around a multinational force need to be based on multiple formal and informal integration and coordination mechanisms that contribute to the different dimensions of mission effectiveness, as all actors are interconnected in numerous ways (Elron 2007; Tetsuro 2005). The added complexity of the peace missions in terms of mandate, tasks, and structures highlight the necessity and importance of effective and smooth cooperation between the militaries taking part in the multinational forces constituting the backbone of the peace operations. A unified effort and unified goals within the force, over and above the national interests and cultures and in fit with the mandate and mission are essential. No less important are the identification, creation and enhancement of common interests with the parties whose peace the force is mandated to keep, going beyond national and cultural differences and different legal systems governing discipline and the use of violence.

At the same time, national and culturally-based military uniqueness and differences need to be taken into account and even capitalized on. Numerous studies in the fields of social psychology, conflict resolution, and international management demonstrate that the most effective strategy to reach a state of coherent and integrated multicultural organizations and societies are the ones that advocate group or organizational unity and cohesion while allowing uniqueness to exist in ways that both preserve cultural identity and capitalize on its advantages (e.g. Bartlett and Ghoshal 1989; Doz *et al.* 1981; Elron 1997; Berry 2005; Halevy and Sagiv 2007). Initial explorations of this notion when looking at military cooperation aspects in the multinational forces (e.g. Elron 2007; Moelker *et al.* 2007) indicate that this balance can be the best overall strategy to enhance overall peace operations' effectiveness in several ways.

Based on a multi-phase study conducted mainly in peace operations located in the Middle East and in peacekeeping training centres in Canada and Ireland, this chapter will focus on how formal and informal organizational integrating arrangements mechanisms enable the forces to function as integrated units[1] with Bartlett and Ghoshal's theory of transnational organizations serving as a guiding framework.

The study

A qualitative interview-based study was conducted with military officers and UN officials in several different sites and in four stages. The first stage of the study took place with peacekeepers who served in UN peace operations situated in the Middle East, deployed at the borders between Israel and the neighbouring Arab countries. These forces all had the mandate of observing and monitoring, and included UNDOF (United Nations Disengagement Observer Force), deployed on the Israeli–Syrian border, UNIFIL (United Nations Interim Force in Lebanon) in its pre-SC 1701 phase, and UNTSO (United Nations Truce Supervision Organization), the first UN peace mission whose military observers staff observation posts on the Golan and in southern Lebanon, serving under UNDOF and UNIFIL. Additionally, interviews were conducted with officers from IDF liaison unit responsible for the coordination activities with the peacekeeping forces.

The second stage consisted of interviews with experienced veterans of peace missions who served as instructors in UN-related training centres: the Canadian forces Peace Support Training Centre in Kingston, the United Nations School in the Irish military, and the Pearson Peacekeeping Centre in Canada. The Italian military headquarters in Rome was the fourth site. The aims of the second stage were mainly getting data on a relatively large number of peace missions from interviewees who had vast experience in peacekeeping and could relate to several missions, getting information on a variety of locations, missions types, force compositions, and operational circumstances. Secondly, we wanted to get a post-mission perspective on the study's main questions with officers who are back in their country, their discourse less influenced by a specific mission's norms or the UN values.

At the third stage of the study UNTSO's Jerusalem headquarters and Tiberias station and UNDOF's alpha site in the Golan were revisited, and the findings from the first two stages presented to an audience of military officers and civilian officials. Following the presentations we asked for their comments on our findings, and later interviewed each of the officers individually.

Our interviewees in the first three stages included: (1) 74 military officers ranking from Captains to Generals (the majority ranging from Majors to Lt. Colonels), including UNTSO and UNDO force commanders; (2) eight UN senior officials within missions who held position such as chief administrative officers and political advisors to the mission; (3) three IDF officers from the liaison unit, including the commander of the unit.

The fourth stage was conducted with military attaches in Israel, UNIFIL officers serving in the enhanced UNIFIL, with officers from the Italian Lagunari regiment before they deployed to Lebanon (the latter as part of the preparations and filming of a TV documentary about UNIFIL). All interviewees belonged or served in culturally diverse environments such as the mission headquarters or particular positions of leadership that require such contact (UNTSO being an observer mission with individuals coming from 23 countries and being constantly in international contact an exception).

Theoretical background

Most contemporary UN peace operations and their multinational forces are modular matrix structures with the resulting potential advantages and dilemmas typical of temporary organizations with a dual reporting and control mechanism, as contingents report both to the mission's Force Commander and to their nations. The organizational structure of each mission is different, although with experience across a number of multidimensional missions, some standard core structures are emerging. In most integrated missions the Head of the Mission is a civilian SRSG (Special Representative of the Secretary General) who is responsible for the implementation of the mandate and has authority over all components of the UN mission, with the military Force Commander and one or two civilian Deputy SRSGs in charge of the civilian components (in the Middle East missions the military Force Commander has the highest authority over the missions). The military Force Commander coordinates the national contingents through a Force Headquarters, usually collocated with the mission headquarters. Each national unit or contingent is directly commanded by its own national commander, and countries contributing military contingents normally deploy a national command element to the mission area. The national contingents' headquarters report back to the national authorities on national and mission issues. Recently, there has been stronger collaboration between the UN and regional organizations – mainly the African Union and European Union – and a reliance on their significant troop participation in peace operations. The cooperation between the UN and regional organizations, making the double reporting a triple one at times, will remain out of the scope of this chapter.

Using the framework presented by Soeters and Manigart in the introduction to this book, the UN missions are complex organizations in terms of military multinational cooperation, with both horizontal and vertical multinationality. The main national contingents are usually aligned in a simple horizontal geographical lining up, with each contingent independently or as part of a sector responsible for a separate and defined geographical area and performing the basic tasks of the mission. At the same time smaller national units performing specialized tasks such as engineers, medical personnel, or de-miners are under the category of complex verticality. They are often located within the area of operations of the main contingent, having direct interactions with their personnel. In most cases the specialized units are also dependent on part if not all of the larger contingents' logistics. In some of the cases they are also under the command of the national contingent commander, in other times they are directly under the force commander authority, depending on the unit's specific role and the mission's structure (e.g. a hospital allocated to each contingent and/or one central hospital for the whole mission).

Underneath the structural complexities of UN peace operations reside four interrelated phenomena: first, the UN is the world body whose purpose is to maintain international peace and security by helping resolve armed conflicts between or within states through diplomatic means and/or military means that take place in the form of the peace operations. For peace operations to succeed, the UN forces must be seen as having both international legitimacy and impartiality. Consequently, a key principle of peacekeeping is that UN forces come from a multitude of member states. In other words, the aim of the UN and its peacekeeping forces is to achieve transnationalism through multinationalism. Second, for military personnel serving in peace operations, there is an inherent tension between membership in the multinational forces and the membership in their national military establishments (see for instance Ben-Ari and Elron 2001). A related difficulty is the national units having to surrender some control and have less autonomy, not an easy challenge since most national armed forces have an inherent strong identity and pride, crucial to its functioning (Moelker *et al.* 2007). Moreover, military personnel in particular do not like to be dependent on other nations, especially when there is potential for life-threatening and dangerous situations and there is a gap in perceived levels of military professionalism of the contingents involved (Elron *et al.* 2003). Issues of control and integration are therefore especially salient, and therefore troops staffing multinational forces belong concurrently to two military hierarchies: that of the UN mission and that of their 'home' military establishment. Legault (1967: 40) terms this a condition of 'double allegiance', and it is the interplay between the two allegiances that explains many of the tensions that mark such forces. A salient example is nations' different motivations and interests to join the multinational forces as manifested in the interpretation of the Rules of Engagement (ROE) of an operation, the level of willingness to engage in active combat, and the extent to which national restrictions and caveats are imposed on troops (Elron 2007). On the ground, this tension is especially felt by the senior officers at the missions' headquarters and contingent commanders, who are in direct touch with their home countries. These tensions are described by one of the force commanders in an interview:

> It is mostly felt when casualties begin. Then, there is a choice, like in Somalia, where you have 35 things going on and someone has got to make a choice whether the Australian battalion goes here or the Italian battalion. One is more dangerous than the other and a lot of things are happening in this area and not in that area and some of the policies that the UN is holding may be victimizing the troops, and then national countries do get involved. And this is very difficult for countries when they make this commitment to the UN, when they may have casualties and they do not have control.

Moreover, these national interests are often translated into competition between national contingents over positions and influence within the mission (Born *et al.* 2000).

Third, in the larger context of the UN organization is the egalitarian idea of the world as an aggregate of nation states that are formally equal but different, and whose relations are regulated legally (e.g. Ghosh 1994; Gupta 1992; Robertson 1992). In the reality reflected in the Security Council membership, whose resolutions are responsible for the creation of peace operations, there is an unequal distribution of power, with the more powerful actors dominating the council, the UN and the world's political system. The dividing line of power and wealth is reflected in the missions. The categories of 'Developed/Developing' and 'First/Third World' are used even if not formally, and they are often used to arrange militaries as entities that are placed along a continuums of superior and inferior. The UN's ideal of autonomous national cultures that are somehow equal conceals a topography of power. The inclusion of 'Third World' countries in UN forces seems to lessen and keep (or strengthen) this topography simultaneously. 'Third World' militaries come with significantly lesser equipment and training and are perceived as less professional by their Western partners. The following candid statements were typical of many of our study's participants: 'It might be so that we would like to invite more European battalions to participate in missions, but we have to invite all the countries' (Irish officer, UNIFIL) and 'there were some discreet talks about how sometimes it's difficult for a Westerner to receive orders from a force commander who is not' (Norwegian officer, UNIFIL).

A recent study by Resteigne and Soeters (2007) on Belgian troops in UNIFIL concludes that being under the UN flag may be more difficult for European troops than serving on a NATO mission, and cultural and organizational differences are more pronounced and varied.

With the increased significance of NATO operations and the war in Iraq, the stronger nations gradually withdrew from most UN missions, finding the participation in them less significant combined with perceptions of the effectiveness of some UN operations too limited and the UN leadership as ineffective and bureaucratic. The largest contributors to the missions have become the militaries of developing countries, namely Bangladesh, Pakistan, and India. A compelling signal of the underlying interests behind this trend is the renewed involvement of Europe in UNIFIL II after the recent Lebanon War, the Middle East being a potentially closer and more immediate threat to Europe, and Lebanon a state attracting the political involvement of some European actors (Biscop 2007; Elron 2007). The renewed UNIFIL became the largest contribution of Europe and the EU to any current UN force. In fact, UNIFIL's is Europe's first large-scale contribution to the UN since Bosnia, enhancing the attractiveness of the mission with many nations insisting on a contribution (a significant turnaround from UNIFIL's previously perceived ineffectiveness). An Indian officer serving in the renewed UNIFIL II described the force as 'NATO-heavy' and the Indian battalion at times having to prove and re-prove its professionalism and value to the mission.

On the more micro level, a related implication is the advantage of those countries whose language is English, the formal language in most missions, and those individuals that speak it fluently. In the words of a Canadian instructor from the Pearson Peacekeeping Centre describing his experiences in Iraq:

> Anybody who's an English speaker, coming from America, Britain or Canada, and your English is very good, they want to get you up into jobs that are like operations, training officers [...] and as bad as it sounds, it's better for the headquarters and the job itself.

These sentiments are echoed by a Swedish officer in UNTSO describing the formal meetings held in the Tiberias post:

> The tendency is that you listen, that the native English speakers take less time to speak because for them it's not a problem and they don't have to plan what to say so they get more dominant and people tend to listen to them because they are more well spoken and sound good, so it's perceived as a good idea. It's not necessarily a good idea but they express it in a good way [...] they tend to get more involved into certain tasks and indirectly they have more impact.

Lastly, peace operations are multinational meeting places where cultural differences between the militaries come into play, including approaches to peacekeeping itself (Resteigne and Soeters 2007). A comment representing one of many differences described to us by our interviewees was:

> We are more mission oriented, so we have our mission statement, and we say "this is what we are here to do," and we do it to the absolute best of our

ability [...] that's up to us as professionals. There are some countries that would rather sit down and drink coffee, eat cakes and not do that, just drive around and go shopping.

(Australian officer, UNTSO)

The view from the other side was described by a Dutch officer in the same mission: 'My Australian commander takes some of the most important decisions without consulting with me and the rest of his team. This is not the way its done in my country.' He continues describing the consequences of this specific difference:

> It affects my loyalty – it's not that I would ever do anything explicit against him, but I wouldn't go out of my way to prevent the consequences of his more problematic decisions. You could say that there are times I don't mind seeing him fall.

Controlled integration and interoperability are crucial to overcome the some-times complex implications related to the processes described above and to achieve overall operational success in the multinational and multidimensional environment characterizing the UN multinational forces areas of operation. Effectiveness of a mission depends on coordinated, synchronized, and accurate military actions and integrated responses under a unified command structure, fluent and functioning decision-making processes, and a broader and deeper understanding of the operational area (e.g. Elron 2007; Fitz-Gerald 2003; Szvircsev Tresch 2007). One of UNTSO's force commanders, speaking of his overall experience in multinational forces, indicates that:

> The internal integration of a peacekeeping mission is the first priority for the Head of Mission. He must strive for a unity of effort amongst the various component of the mission, with an aim to synchronize the planning and activities to meet the mandated tasks.

Emphasizing this need and the inherent risk related to missions taking place where conflicts are at times unresolved, an Italian battalion commander, a veteran of five different missions, including Kosovo, Somalia, Lebanon and Albania states:

> We are always at risk. If you move through a foreign and unfamiliar country to accomplish your mission, meeting people, needing to make agreements, establishing relations, finding camps for troops, when you travel and you are a stranger in a country without a strong control of the situation [...] the risk is different in each mission.

Cultural diversity in organizations and teams can be an asset rather than merely a liability. Culturally diverse teams tend to have a broad range of task-relevant capabilities, skills, knowledge, and viewpoints at their disposal, as long as they are able to overcome their potential cross-cultural difficulties and process losses to allow these different perspectives within the team to be heard and capitalized on (DiStefano and Maznevski 2000; Earley and Mosakowski 2000; Elron 1997; Stahl *et al.* 2006; Halevy and Sagiv 2007; Van Knippenberg and Schippers 2007). Recent studies suggest that differences in some cultural dimensions can be aligned by raising the salience of similarities of other dimension (Cunningham and Sagas 2004; Maloney and Zellmer-Bruhn 2006; Miura and Hida 2004). In the case of multinational forces, the strength of military culture and values, shared by members of armed forces from around the world (e.g. Bellamy 1996; Soeters and Recht 1998; Moskos 1976), serves to decrease the potential negative effects of the cultural differences (Elron *et al.* 2003), and helps create a basic sympathy and quick cohesion between the troops (Ben-Shalom *et al.* 2005; Moelker *et al.* 2007).

What then are the organizational processes used in the UN multinational forces to reach intercultural interoperability and a common mission identity? Integrating mechanisms and processes can be operating at the UN secretariat level, mainly the Department of Peacekeeping Operations (DPKO), within peace operations, and within the TCCs. Some processes are aimed at two or all three of the levels simultaneously. An additional lens to understand the UN and its multinational forces is through models and theories in the field of international management. Multinational Corporations (MNCs) who operate in multiple countries are exposed to cultural, institutional, and economic heterogeneity. Bartlett and Ghoshal (1989) offer an influential model, suggesting for MNCs to have a competitive advantage by capitalizing on diversity, by seeking global integration for coordination, standardization, and efficiency and simultaneously attending to local responsiveness that takes into account differences between national units. No less important is the process of worldwide learning, which allows utilization of lessons learned, different experiences and innovations developed in the different units around the globe. The model relates to the mechanisms we identified – while one type mechanism increases control through centralization of decision making and policies, a second type emphasizes national and cultural differentiation, uniqueness and identity, and is represented in its pure form mostly by the geographical and functional separation of the contingents or units. A third type of process, relying on the interplay between the first two – practices that are based on inclusive processes while emphasizing national identities – is the most prevalent in the peace operations we looked at. The fourth type, which is becoming more prominent as the missions become more complex, uses formal and informal learning mechanisms that integrate knowledge from different constituents, including knowledge based on different national experiences and the resulting operational and strategic solutions. Next we discuss some of the integrating mechanisms our investigations into the inside of peace missions revealed.

Integrating mechanisms

Super-ordinate goals

Despite some of its weaknesses, the UN continues to embody principles and ideals that are shared by the global international community, and which form the basis for its peace operations. The higher values such as 'peace' or 'international justice' are highly esteemed in all cultures. Take for example Italy's national interests as presented by an Italian senior officer in an official military gathering in Israel: 'Maintain capable, effective, and flexible armed forces in response to present and future challenges and in order to guarantee the defence of national interests, to contribute to extending security worldwide, and to the management of international crises.'

These interests, and the wish to help the world's community and the Middle East achieve peace, were strongly echoed in the interviews with the officers of the Lagunari regiment. Hence multinational military activities based on these values offer uniquely integrative missions (Elron et al. 1999). It is a long established finding in social psychology that the institution of super-ordinate goals is one of the most effective techniques for resolving inter-group conflicts and increasing inter-group cooperation (Sherif et al. 1961). Accordingly, our interviews indicate that officers tend to invest more in pro-social behaviours, including tolerance toward cross-cultural misunderstandings and making efforts to collaborate across cultural barriers.

Our interviewees gave us numerous examples of the effectiveness of this integrating mechanism. A senior New Zealand officer serving in UNTSO explained:

> I think that inside the different governments, and also inside each military unit, there is the strong will to help the people. The final target is something that gathers everybody around the same table to work together. You can overcome frictions and problems if you understand, if you trust that the final objective, the long-range goal, is to enable peace to happen.

A more sentimental description comes from an Italian commander recollecting his missions when he was interviewed in the Italian military headquarters:

> The common sense of guilt of our nations that did not intervene before and after a war that made [...] because you can't avoid seeing kids without one leg or women without one arm and when you see this kind of thing you understand that the war is not anymore a big game in the desert [...]. Now war is something that involves 90% civil population [...]. So I think that if a soldier has this consciousness and these feelings cannot avoid to feel pity toward this population. If you are a man, if you are a real warrior, a characteristic of a real warrior for me is to feel pity [...] this is part of the human being.

An Irish instructor, describing the motivations and sentiments typical of his troops, said:

> I think this altruistic streak is still very valid in people. I think a lot of people still care about the job they are doing in an altruistic fashion. Now, is it valid for everybody all the time? – No, it's not. But, it's there and it's a factor, even though it's not the only factor.

Speaking of the way he trains, explaining how these values are disseminated and strengthened, he added:

> If you are lecturing, for instance, if you bring soldiers with you anywhere, you must explain why you are doing it and why you are going on that mission. For example, if you are going on a humanitarian mission, for instance – to Rwanda, to Honduras, obviously the "why" is very important there. And why the Irish government is sending them somewhere. I mean this is the least they can expect.

The use of symbols

The most visible mechanism that combines uniformity with differentiation is the missions' participants' uniform. The blue helmets and berets with the UN's blue symbol worn on the soldiers' shoulders are widely associated with UN peace-keeping troops and are worn in all UN missions. This image signals membership in an entity transcending any single national establishment and the soldiers' role as peacekeepers. Yet a closer look reveals that soldiers are also wearing the uniforms of their national armed forces, with their national insignia worn on their other shoulder. One relatively modern communication means, the email, repeats the double symbolism – many contingents have the symbol of the UN on one side of the sender's name, their national flag on the other side.

At the interface between the operational and the symbolic, military peacekeepers engage more frequently in humanitarian endeavours. Various contingents operating currently as part of UNIFIL, take part in the 'Quick Impact Projects' programme that launched a series of developmental projects in South Lebanon to fortify links with the local population. The Indian contingent, for example, constructed a children's park named the 'Indo-Lebanese Friendship Park'. Other programmes, undertaken with the contingent resources included providing veterinary assistance, conducting yoga classes, and teaching English to kids. The Italian contingent helped inaugurate a volleyball and basketball court and has offered 6,000 fruit saplings. These contributions are a compelling example of a mission level initiative that allows contingents to launch unique projects, at least partly related to specific national and cultural expertise they bring with them. Moreover, some of the projects taken by the Indian battalion were the brainchild of the Indian deputy commander of the force, and were adapted by the Commanding officer of the

Indian battalion – a unique mission Headquarter-field cooperation based on national affiliation within the force and capitalizing on the best of both worlds to enhance the overall mission capabilities.

Accountability

Accountability is 'the condition of being answerable for conducting oneself in a manner that is consistent with relevant prescriptions for how things should be' (Schlenker and Weingold 1989: 24). When such conditions exist, images of standards and expectations of an audience are made salient for one's behaviour, and in anticipation of being judged, individuals will attempt to match their behaviour to those standards (Gelfand and Realo 1999; Schlenker and Weingold 1989). Soldiers in peace operations have to respond to two main audiences, that of their national commanders and soldiers and commanders, and that of the peace operation's various participants and recipients – troops from other countries, civilian counterparts, the local population whose peace the operation is mandated to keep. Peace operations are particularly high accountability situations because of their intense internal and external symbolic processes, and peacekeepers become official and non-official representatives of their country and the peace mission, having to respond to both images, intertwined to different extents. This is well reflected in the following:

> The fact that you have your blue beret on you and that you are wearing your national flag here, you now know that even though you may be a small element you are an ambassador of your country. That in itself is enough to make you do a good job.
>
> (Irish officer, training centre)

All nations who contribute troops use conscious formal and informal processes to enhance their troops' identity as representatives of their country, and to match their behaviours with military and peacekeeping standards. Some countries enhance accountability by using pre-deployment selection criteria to choose those who will be sent to the missions, at the unit and the individual level. An Indian officer from the current UNIFIL told us:

> My battalion is 300 years old, and very highly decorated. We have vast experience with the war against terror (the battalion's main deployment is in Kashmir) in the past 20 years. We have trained and equipped for a whole year before arriving here, and we all came with new uniform. We know well that whatever we do we are perceived as Indians. This is also why officers sent to the headquarters positions will only be the best ones.

The notion of accountability was strongly conveyed in the formal pre-deployment training in both Canada and Ireland. Similar processes were reported by many other participants. It is then transmitted continuously in the mission. Next is a typical example of a commander conveying to his troops the importance of their 'ambassador-ness':

> One of the things I've put great emphasis on when talking to my soldiers was that we were ambassadors and our country will be judged both militarily and socially, which is also important. I tell them that anybody who is selected to go overseas has to bear the national flag, that even subconsciously you don't want to project anything negative.
>
> (Irish officer, training centre)

An additional process, in some countries with stronger implications than others, is the use of the evaluation reports from the mission, reported by a senior New Zealand officer from UNTSO:

> If a New Zealand officer goes off as Lieutenant Colonel and works in an organization with twenty countries, he's going to get a report written on him or her. And at the end you can say 'great ambassador', but sometimes the truth must be told, and the reporting officer writes 'arrogant' [...]. If they don't get a good report, in New Zealand's case, we will certainly look at it.

The values of the UN are repeatedly communicated in the different parts of the Standardized Generic Training Modules created by the DPKO's Integrated Services Unit. The modules are the backbone of national pre-deployment training. Smaller booklets describing the UN, its vision and structure, and briefing about issues such as the basic duties of peacekeepers, security, liaison and negotiation, are given to every solider in the mission. This is the UN's way to ensure its basic values reach the troops. The significance of the specific mission is also part of the pre-deployment training, later continually stressed in the mission itself by commanders.

Formal standardization of command and control

The DPKO uses several formal means to resolve legal as well as technical command and control issues not only in the missions, but also prior to the national contingents' deployment. These include unifying command and control terms, concepts and definitions and standardized contracts. At the same time they all explicitly take into account national differences by putting formal and agreed upon limits to the contact between the UN and the TCCs.

The basic concept of 'United Nations Operational Authority' refers to the authority transferred by the Member States to the United Nations to use the operational capabilities of their national military contingents, units and/or military personnel to undertake mandated missions and tasks. The Authority is vested in the Secretary-General and the Security Council. It involves the full authority to issue operational directives within the limits of a specific mandate, an agreed period of time, and a specific geographic area which is the mission area as a whole. Generally, this process takes place when national military personnel and units arrive in the mission area. However, it intentionally does not include responsibility for a variety of administrative control and personnel matters, such as pay and promotions. These functions remain a national responsibility. For example, while the UN pays a uniform monthly rate, intended to cover mission expenses for the individual, the salaries remain a national responsibility (and a cause for a major difference between first- and third-world countries). In regard to disciplinary matters, while the UN is responsible for the good conduct of all military personnel, the discipline indoctrination and sanctions remains the responsibility of the nations. Similarly, the 'United Nations Operational Control' is the authority granted to the military commander to direct forces assigned to accomplish specific tasks or missions, to deploy units or personnel, and to retain or assign tactical control as required by the operational necessities. However, each of these directions has to be in consultation with the national contingent commanders and approved by the UN Headquarters.

Levels and details of contingents' self-sustainment and functions like logistics support, major equipment (e.g. internal operational communication and personal operational equipment to laundry and cleaning), provisions supply maintenance and transportation are agreed on separately, vary for nations and missions, and are considered a joint responsibility of the UN and the TCC, mutually coordinated through standardized contracts called Memoranda of Understanding (MOUs). The MOU establishes the responsibilities of the UN Headquarters, the peacekeeping mission itself, and the TCC. Practically speaking, it allows a TCC to send additional National Support Elements of different types – operational, logistic, and administration. At the same time, these initiatives need to comply with UN standards, and prior to deployment the DPKO personnel will undertake a pre-deployment inspection and will conduct periodic verification inspections in the mission area to confirm the readiness, serviceability, and usage of the agreed on equipment.

At the individual mission level, Standard Operating Procedures (SOPs) are created by force headquarters in alliance with DPKO policies. These consist of basic operational procedures, and are used as a reference for standard activities, relying on experience in both traditional and recent multidimensional missions with specific mission conditions. In the spirit of integration combined with differentiation, while the peacekeeping doctrine used by member states preparing for peace operations needs to be consistent with the doctrine produced and used by UN peacekeeping missions in general, the conduct of some specialized military tasks, reconnaissance patrols for example, is a national responsibility.

Knowledge sharing and mutual learning

The international management literature frames knowledge management as a crucial means for learning and for overall effectiveness related to the two broad organizational goals that organizations must meet to be effective, the managing of interdependence and uncertainty (e.g. Bartlett and Ghoshal 1989; Zellmer-Bruhn and Gibson 2006). This section will emphasize intra-mission knowledge sharing and learning integrating mechanisms. Knowledge usually flows better within an organization's boundaries than across them (Miller *et al.* 2007), and provides unique opportunities for mutual learning and facilitating inter-unit cooperation. In peace operations, each of the participants carries a unique nationally based knowledge, usually combined with experience from past peace missions, joint operations and other cooperative frameworks (e.g. NATO headquarters). Unique knowledge can stimulate the creation of new knowledge and at the same time contribute to organizational units' ability to innovate. The DPKO's recommendation is that a central key to mission effectiveness is the sharing and passage of information among the leadership throughout the various components of headquarters and down to the working levels in each component. This can be achieved by frequent meetings with component commanders and key advisors, repeatedly clarifying the current situation in the mission area, and prioritizing actions and planning. The sharing of advice from the strategic levels through available communication means is also crucial. Subsequently, key staff should share this information with their colleagues and subordinates so that common messages and guidance permeate throughout the mission. The Spanish East sector commander in the current UNIFIL for example, conducts commanders' meetings regularly, specifically requesting the representatives of each of the contingents to describe how their own military approaches operational and strategic level challenges.

Positive knowledge management norms also signal to teams the desirability of developing better practices (Anand *et al.* 2003; Zellmer-Bruhn and Gibson 2007), and allow better implementation of solutions, increases attention to learning activities, and stimulates inquiries about alternative practices. Additionally, the exchange and sharing of professional knowledge has overall positive impacts on individual members' satisfaction with their tasks and their organization and increases team cohesion (Edmondson 1999). Moreover, Gibson and Vermeulen (2003) found that the availability of a knowledge management system interacted with the presence of demographic subgroups in teams to influence reflective communication. A typical discussion of the different advantages of this kind of intra-mission knowledge exchange at the headquarters is expressed by an Irish peacekeeping training officer:

> You get different opinions on a subject. I'm not saying you can find the truth, the truth is very elusive, but you can have a better understanding of it if you are getting different opinions. It's not just from an Irish perspective or an American perspective or a Canadian perspective or wherever, so I think that in that respect it is very important. The rotations with people coming in and out all the time increases all of that [...] and increases training and builds up relationships.

At the national military level, Banerjee (1995: 14), for instance, in talking about the Indian military, suggests that participation in multinational frameworks provides exposure to other militaries and has allowed the comparison of strengths and weaknesses. It also gives the opportunity to get familiarized with advanced equipment and weapons, to train in complex and sophisticated communications systems, to receive surplus equipment and to change attitudes of officers and NCOs. The importance of learning from others, formally and informally, was repeatedly stressed in the interviews as an important and rewarding part of the participation to multinational environments. This consequence was discussed by an Italian officer:

> I was very happy when they sent me, they told me for the first time to go to Lebanon. And then 'you have to go to north Iraq' and then in Somalia. We are happy because it is a chance to know people and to test yourself and to check the preparation of your troops comparing with the preparation of the other troops, it is a good chance to improve your capability, to increase your efficiency. I think that these are the reasons to which we are happy to have these opportunities.

Next is the discussion of three additional important integrating mechanisms, namely the creation and use of Joint Mission Analysis Cells, joint training before the mission and in it, and the informal knowledge sharing conducted extensively by the mission's officers.

Joint mission analysis cells

One of the most recent knowledge integrating mechanisms is the Joint Mission Analyses Centres (JMAC), serving as advisory units to the Head of Mission (SRSG or Force Commander, depending on the structure of the mission) in the larger missions and created by the DPKO much as a result of the shock waves felt throughout the UN after the Baghdad bombing (Benner *et al.* 2007). The JMACs' main objectives are to provide the mission's senior management with advice on mission specific strategic issues and their implementation at the operational levels. In practice, JMACs are responsible for information and intelligence management, combining experts from different areas (e.g. military, political, economic, police, civil affairs, human rights, safety and security, and press and information). Part of JMAC's information comes from military contingent commanders, its personnel composition intentionally representing a variety of nationalities, with the intention of taking national experiences as a source of learning. JMAC products include long-, medium- and short-term strategic assessments, risk and threat assessments, early warning and critical information reports, as well as thematic reports. The JMACs have been fully implemented in two integrated missions in the past year (MONUC in Congo and MINUSTAH in Haiti), and are in different stages of implementation in other missions. UNIFIL

II is an example where the unit will be responsible not only for analysing political processes taking place in Lebanon but also in the wider Middle East.

Joint training

The crucial importance of joint training, in large part a result of the increasing threat of global terror, has been recognized by many national militaries and by international and regional organizations like NATO and the African Union. This recognition was followed by a dramatic increase in the frequency of joint military training on a bi- and multilateral basis. NATO Training Group has been under the Supreme Allied Command Transformation Headquarters since 2004, an indication of its importance. It is one of the most important means of the expression of the Joint Education and Training (JET) Policy. These trainings and NATO's missions in Kosovo and Afghanistan play an important role in NATO militaries becoming more similar, partly a result of NATO standardization processes, and partly a result of the militaries becoming more familiar with each other. These mechanisms, even if outside the UN, help enhance the smoothness of internal cooperation within UN peace missions. The current UNIFIL, which is based mostly on the participation of NATO and EU nation members, serves as a prominent example, as this composition was requested by Lebanon, Israel, and the European TCCs as the negotiations on SC resolution were taking place during the Lebanon War. The impact of these trainings is described by a European military attaché posted in Israel who served in several missions, including UNIFIL Headquarters:

> You come to a mission like UNIFIL, and there is the basic standardization which is becoming stronger, and there is a certain common language that is there and you pick it up quickly in the mission to get going together.

Recently, however, joint exercises, operations and information sharing include more NATO partners who are not NATO and EU members, with the aim of enhanced interoperability and information sharing. India is a good example for increased cooperation, and a five-nation war game taking place in 2007 involved the Indian, Singaporean, Japanese, Australian, and US navies. What used to be a bilateral US–Indian exercise has become a multilateral one, and India for the first time has adopted some of the related NATO procedures. While First- and Third-World distinctions indeed continue to exist, this cooperation is beginning to make the separation lines less defined.

On the ground, the contingents familiarize themselves with other units through joint patrols in the areas of operations, joint training in specific military activities like reconnaissance and rifle shooting, and mutual professional visits at the officer level at other contingents' headquarters:

> We have a very good relationship with the Spanish battalion [...] we had joint exercises. We go out to their battalion, they come to ours. We familiarize

ourselves with their ways of working and with their territory [...]. It makes the cooperation better, also in the case of a crisis. We also share our expertise in terms of understanding the mission better.

(Indian officer, current UNIFIL)

Joint activities and training on the ground can therefore serve as an inclusive integrating mechanism not only at the mission level but also at the national level.

Informal exchanges of knowledge

Peacekeepers are extensively engaged in informal mutual exchange of military and cultural knowledge. Peace operations provide ample opportunities – tasks that have significant stretches of inactivity, security procedures that force troops to remain on base, limited options to meet non-soldiers, eating messes, and the mission's varied leisure facilities – in which most of our interviewees referred to this kind of learning as a key part of their lives as peacekeepers. The one-time or continuous exchanges involved a combination of sharing information, comparing, and debating. When military topics emerged they ranged from tactical operational features (e.g. command and control of their units, the ROEs, ways of patrolling, force protection, weapons) to national strategic level thinking and concepts. Comparisons were also made between missions the officers participated in. An interesting description of a typical exchange is offered by a Canadian trainer in Kingston:

When you are doing patrols in Iraq and it's 55–56 degrees Celsius, and you are not used to the heat, you know – temperate Canada does not have that heat – so, how do you deal with it? You ask people who come from such areas – Senegal, Uganda, in Indonesia when they are doing jungle fighting [...]. You ask questions and you learn [...]. You offer information and you share information.

He then discusses the consequences of this specific of conversation: 'Bringing it with me back I can't use it here, but the knowledge of how others work has allowed me to be better prepared the next time I go overseas.'

A different interaction is described by an Italian officer who served in Kosovo, emphasizing the relational consequences of an informal professional exchange:

Since the first day we succeeded in establishing immediately a warm touch with them, we spent the night explaining them documents – to the Egyptians – documents in NATO language that is not understandable for an officer from a different army [...]. The Egyptians were very proud, very brave but they were not in NATO. So we spent nights talking about our militaries from every aspect. After one month we established an extremely close contact by means of this sacrifice and we succeeded in gaining their trust.

Risky events and situations can also bring out a condensed form of professional exchanges, somewhat similar to the ones described in detail by Ben Shalom *et al.* (2005) in their study on cooperation and creation of trust between combat units in the Al-Aqsa intifidah. All current UNIFIL officers from different contingents reported that the two 2007 terror attacks, one resulting in the death of six Spanish battalion soldiers, created a bout of intense discussions that included national past experiences with terror and options for preventing future attacks, many of these discussions taking place between officers from different nations.

Cohesion building activities

A prevalent and salient organizational mechanism that has become part of the social fabric in the missions is the deliberate cohesion-building activities in the form of a range of educational, cultural and sport events designed to introduce national cultures to each other. These activities help create a common *esprit de corps* and a unique identity for the specific mission. Furthermore, the allocation of time and space for such activities enhances the potential for spontaneous interpersonal interactions that allow better and deeper acquaintanceship between members of different cultures, and signal that the meeting of cultures in social settings is desirable (see Moelker *et al.* 2007). There are numerous examples of such activities, some of which have become famous traditions – the celebration of national days, happy hours, sports competitions.

Interestingly, these same activities are also a way to enhance cultural sensitivity via the emphasis of cultural differences. The celebration of national days, in which culture-specific food is served, culture-specific music is played, and culture-specific activities take place serves to differentiate one country from the others and highlight its uniqueness. In terms of the typology of the integrating mechanisms model, these social activities allow for both the creation of shared bases and the seeking of cultural knowledge, and serve therefore as a powerful example of the third type of mechanism. In some missions they have the additional benefit of breaking the routine by travelling to the location the event takes place at. Take for example a day-long sports competition involving all the regional peace operations that took place in 2005 in an army base in the centre of Israel near Tel Aviv. Both UNIFIL and UNDOF also have national clubs at their headquarters' base, serving national food and drinks. While these serve as gathering places for those who want to feel closer to home also in terms of company, they also present an opportunity to invite one's friends and colleagues who come from different cultures and present one's nation in an informal atmosphere.

Other activities are the creation and initiative of unit commanders, embedded in a context encouraging these activities. These are mostly used for the creation of social cohesion without the emphasis on the uniqueness of cultures. The Austrian military police commander in UNDOF describes such an activity with his own group of colleagues and soldiers:

> One of the things we have, especially during summer time, every Friday evening, is more or less a small party here in the office, where we are all together. That is the chance to sit together with all your guys and to speak to each other, and that's the moment when people come closer.

Many times, however, these meetings evolve into or include the comparison between nations and cultures. Observing social events at UNTSO, much of the talk involved the comparing of national food, eating and drinking habits and customs – at times promoting one's own, at others complimenting others', with some comments aimed at making fun or being cynical about either. All in all, this kind of bantering helped create a pleasant atmosphere while allowing the participants of the events to gain more intimate knowledge about their colleagues.

Many informal social activities and interactions happen at the individual level, and going out when possible is a favourite activity of peacekeepers. Drinking, eating, and partying are central to the creation of sentiments of cooperation and affiliation. These gatherings seemed to have been at times more important than the more formal briefings and meetings or conclaves. Eating and drinking together both signal commonality, afford relaxed circumstances for interaction and are part of the minute exchanges through which trust is created. A Senior Norwegian officer in UNTSO described these important advantages:

> I think that's an advantage for the formal meetings as we know more of each other, actually, and then it's more relaxed when it comes to formal meetings. You have a better understanding of each other, and we build up a sort of confidence, and we can discuss issues more freely.

In our interviews, numerous instances were mentioned in which informal social activities with members of other national forces was a means to enhance familiarity and create social bonds that also eased the mutual functioning and coordination on the job. An interesting example was described by an Italian officer serving at the headquarters in Albania which was mainly managed by British officers. Difficulties in getting information related to his job were solved after inviting some of the British officers to a dinner at the Italian mess where closer informal relationships were created.

These contexts, however, at times served to reveal the tendency to interact with others who are perceived to be more similar. In these instances, while cultural unity is created within the group, it also serves to keep other cultures at a distance, thus keeping the distinction between the First and Third Worlds, as a Canadian observer in UNTSO reports: 'Most of my interactions were with the

Swedish and Irish officers. We always met, went for a walk, for a beer, and then talked about this and that.'

In other instances, it could be the distinction between the First-World US with the CANZ countries (Canada, Australia. and New Zealand) and those whose native language is not English and/or Third World. An Italian officer described the outings with his colleagues to a headquarters club:

> If I am with native English speakers, I find myself not being able to follow the nuances of a conversation, not understanding the jokes and having to pretend in a three second delay that I do, so I feel more comfortable with those who speak as slow as I do […]. Italians connect very well with the Spanish, Portuguese and South Americans, so on some nights it's their company or that of other Italians that I will seek.

Another Italian officer indicated: 'When there are five Italians and one American we will all speak in English. Q: and if there are five Italians and three Americans? A: then after a few minutes we will naturally split into two groups.'

Interestingly, drinking habits seem to be another source of potential dividing line, and intense beer-drinking shared by North Americans and North Europeans can keep away those who prefer wine-drinking or no drinking at all. Overall, however, language and nationality are just two factors, and as with relationship in all places chemistry and common interests are indeed a significant part of one's choices with whom to socially interact, and can overcome national barriers.

Conclusion

The UN has been going under major transformation and reform processes in the past decade to increase its operational capabilities in peace operations. Intercultural interoperability is becoming a major issue as part of this effort. The DPKO, Member States, and command and control practices within the missions play a major part in this extensive effort. In this study we examined the sources of the ability of the multinational forces within UN peace operations to achieve a working level of cooperation despite their high national and cultural diversity and multiple cultural fault lines. Our main findings are that the nature of the UN peace operations and their tasks have led to the prevalent use of integrating mechanisms that emphasize the interplay between the transnational and multinational – the use of inclusive practices while simultaneously allowing and even emphasizing national identities and customs. These include the practical and symbolic use of superordinate goals, the formal standardization of military capabilities, operational methods and procedures created at the UN headquarters and at the mission level, the notion of accountability, different forms of knowledge sharing and mutual learning, and formal and informal cohesion-building activities. An understanding of these mechanisms and how they are implemented can result in greater success in the carrying out of peacekeeping missions, more so as intercultural tensions are always bound to affect mission effectiveness, even if its influences may be hard to capture as these tensions many times exist beneath the surface – the overall similarity because of the strong military cultures. Moreover, it may have important implications for the operation of all organizations that face cultural diversity.

For future studies and practice, more attention needs to be paid to the unique aspects of leadership and command in multinational missions. It is a crucial factor hardly investigated yet. The effects of intercultural training on officers, with an emphasis on developing their intercultural skills and abilities, global mindset and cultural intelligence (e.g. Black and Mendenhall 1990; Fowler 2006; Levy *et al.* 2007; Thomas and Fitzsimmons 2007) needed for this type of command need to be examined, as do the effects of previous international experience and career demands and opportunities at the national militaries. The changed cultural composition of many peace operations, especially those operating in Africa, is an issue in current research. Taking a closer took at the different implications of integrating mechanism in different kinds of missions, their overall relation to more aspects of mission effectiveness and the conscious and practical use by commanders in the field will take the understanding of cultural challenges in military operations one necessary step further.

Note

1 The guiding theoretical framework for the study was presented in an article published in 1999 by Elron, Shamir, and Ben-Ari in *Armed Forces and Society*.

Chapter 4

Leadership and management teams in multinational military cooperation

Angela R. Febbraro

Introduction

As history demonstrates, the challenge of leading a multinational military team is not altogether new, as nations, since the earliest times, have associated with each other in order to achieve a common purpose (Elron *et al.* 1999). Military forces must depend on each other to achieve their mission often because of a lack of resources, logistics, or personnel to conduct independent operations, and sometimes because building an international coalition can lend legitimacy to an operation (Soeters and Bos-Bakx 2003). Increasingly, and particularly since the end of the Cold War, the employment of military forces in multinational contexts demands a broader range of leadership competencies and a greater collaborative effort than previously required (MacIsaac 2000). Contemporary military operations often consist of new partners who typically have not trained together and who have very different military traditions and cultures (Marshall *et al.* 1997). Further, since the end of the Cold War, multinationality has occurred lower down in the chain of command, making it an issue for a broader range of personnel, whether at the strategic, operational or tactical level (Stewart, Macklin *et al.* 2004). Multinational forces face a number of issues that stem from inter-group relations and dynamics, which themselves emanate from differences in culture, language, religion, class and gender customs, work ethics, military values, and political systems (Lescoutre 2003; Plante 1998). In short, the units of multinational military teams vary in their agendas, leadership and command structures, and cultures (Klein *et al.* 2000). Furthermore, although differences in language, terminology, military doctrine, and command organization may have all been present in previous military operations, these differences are often exacerbated by the degree of cultural diversity, the level of interaction among units, and the limited preparation time available in most military operations today (Marshall *et al.* 1997).

McCann and Pigeau (2000) emphasize that building an effective multinational military force in today's operations requires that a leader be able to weld together military personnel from different cultures and who have varying abilities and expectations. This ability to integrate diverse forces, or "intercultural competence," will become increasingly important, as military operations depend more and more upon effective teamwork among members of diverse cultural backgrounds (Klein *et al.* 2000; Plante 1998; Winslow, Heinecken and Soeters 2003). Indeed, Winslow and Everts (2001) argue that "cultural interoperability" – the shared way by which multinational military coalitions or alliances "do business" – is key to mission success.

This chapter begins with an examination of the leadership competencies that are important in the context of leading multinational military teams. It then examines differences in leadership styles among national militaries that are related to national cultural differences. In addition, the chapter explores research in the business and management literature in order to illuminate military team performance and cooperation in a multinational context. As will be discussed, cultural heterogeneity within teams may be advantageous in certain contexts, but disadvantageous in others. Finally, the chapter discusses recommendations for leadership and team training in the multinational military context, which may lead to, or enhance, cultural interoperability or integration, and thus, multinational military cooperation.

Leadership of multinational military teams

Although many definitions of leadership have been proposed in the military and scientific literatures, analysts generally agree that, rather than reflecting universal qualities of effectiveness, different leadership styles will emerge as effective, depending on the organizational or cultural context. For example, Gurstein (1999) argues that the requirements of a military leader in the multinational (e.g. peacekeeping) context is similar in many ways to those required of a leader in any other military context: the capacity to motivate; to direct while including; to articulate and instil a sense of common direction and purpose; and to distil, reflect, and project unifying symbols and cultural values. However, each of these requirements is rendered more complex, and potentially more problematic, in a multinational, multicultural, multilingual context, such as the highly political environment that is typical of a United Nations (UN) peacekeeping mission. Furthermore, abilities in mediation, conflict resolution, negotiation, diplomacy, cultural sensitivity, and behavioural flexibility are all considered central to the task of leading a multinational peacekeeping force, but are typically not included as criteria in leadership selection and training (Gurstein 1999). Other analysts have also suggested that the requirements for leading a multinational coalition are more demanding and difficult than the requirements for leading a national force. Bowman (1997) points out, for example, that coalition leaders must clearly understand that coalition politics may override coalition military logic, and that coalition leaders must be persuasive, not coercive, and sensitive to national needs. Similarly, Barabé (1999) argues that the multinational force commander faces unique integration and unity of effort issues. Against a diversity of political and other impediments, the commander must blend the skills of component forces so that the whole is, somehow, greater than the sum of its parts.

Moelker *et al.* (2007), who studied German–Dutch cooperation in Kabul, Afghanistan, suggest that the role of leadership is critical in maintaining a multinational unit's morale, in keeping good relations with other units in the mission, and in creating cohesion within the unit. However, Elron *et al.* (1999) suggest that the creation of cohesion and trust in multicultural military settings may be more difficult to achieve than in unicultural military settings, and that commanders must play an integral role in establishing such trust within a multiculturally diverse force. In short, increased cultural diversity within military teams will ramp up the degree of complexity in the military commander's task at all levels, multiply the challenges facing military leaders, and require new skills in negotiation, liaison, persuasion, and teamwork (Shamir and Ben-Ari 2000; Stewart *et al.* 2004).

C.J.R. Davis (2000) argues that because of the political nature of multinational coalitions, the fact that commanders typically have restricted authority to direct and control personnel and material, and the fact that doctrinal unity of command is rarely achieved in multinational coalitions, operational commanders must focus on achieving *unity of effort* towards common multinational objectives, as opposed to *unity of command*. Such unity of effort or purpose may be gained through cooperation and mutual confidence between coalition partners and the force commander; through rapport and patience; through respect for different cultures, religions, and values; through an understanding and knowledge of each member's national goals, objectives, capabilities, and limitations; through the identification of the appropriate mission for participating nations; and through the assignment of equitable tasks in terms of burden and risk sharing (C.J.R. Davis 2000). Unity of effort requires cooperation to achieve the same ends within the commander's intent, which must be disseminated and understood throughout the multinational force; however, understanding intent will be a more complex issue when compounded by linguistic and cultural differences (Potts 2004). Recognizing the overriding impact of politics, C.J.R. Davis (2000) proposes three strategies to maximize unity of effort within a coalition: innovative command structures that satisfy national constraints; thorough coordination and consensus-building leading to the appropriate employment of forces; and the development of mutual confidence and cooperation within the coalition's senior commanders and staff (e.g. through leader development and education). In addition, direct personal contact, whenever possible, will be critical to ensuring unity of effort and a common understanding of commander intent (Potts 2004).

Whatever the similarities and differences between various national forces, multinational military commanders must recognize the difficulty of integrating national forces into a successful cooperative effort. Thus, the multinational leader must build consensus regarding common goals and objectives, for it is this consensus that will provide the glue to bind the multinational force together (C.J.R. Davis 2000). As Bisho (2004) suggests, successful multinational leaders will be those who best handle operational realities by applying the proper blend of vision, determination, patience, tolerance, and flexibility. Further, as R.G. Davis (2000) points out, a multinational military leader must be sensitive to the fact that the participating forces in a multinational operation are not always equally capable, and thus must assign individual forces the missions that they are able to accomplish. This calls for political awareness, patience, tact, respect, and mutual understanding on the part of the multinational leader, based on knowledge of other nations' languages, history, and, importantly, culture (United Kingdom Doctrine for Joint and Multinational Operations 1999; Barabé 1999). Similarly, mutual respect for the professional ability, culture, history, religion, customs, and values of national participants will serve to strengthen relationships. The military leader must respect the individual terms of service of the national forces (e.g. leave and promotion rules, decorations policies, restrictions on types of acceptable assignments), which may vary dramatically across contingents. Finding a means to reconcile these differences with the accomplishment of the mission is a significant responsibility for the commander of a multinational peacekeeping force (Gurstein 1999). The commander must integrate all the national contingents together into a strong and coordinated team, and by personal example, must motivate the team. Further, there must be mutual understanding between the operational level commander and component commanders to ensure unity of effort. In multinational operations, elements from other nations may be embedded within each component, but they may be more responsive to their national chain of command than to a multinational military commander (Soeters and Bos-Bakx 2003). The effective multinational military leader will overcome any friction caused by these tensions through innovative conflict resolution techniques and by applying a variety of leadership approaches to deal with diverse national aims or cultural differences (MacIsaac 2000).

Shamir and Ben-Ari (2000) suggest that, in addition to finding innovative ways to reward and manage troops (aspects of *transactional* leadership), multinational military leadership will require several aspects of *transformational* leadership (Bass 1998; Yukl 1998), including individual consideration (e.g. sensitivity to members' needs, respecting differences, and providing opportunities for development) and intellectual stimulation (e.g. challenging others' assumptions and stereotypes, encouraging a viewing of the world from different perspectives, and fostering critical and independent thinking). Thus, a multinational commander must be willing to adopt and apply the principles of transformational leadership in addition to the more typical transactional leadership approach, and moreover, must be capable of transitioning from one approach to the other (MacIsaac 2000; Shamir and Ben-Ari 2000). In addition, Champagne (1999) argues that an operational commander in a multinational context must be able to deal with social complexity, or the multiplicity, diversity, and intricacy that is found in social dynamics and interconnections. Leaders will need both conceptual and social competencies (i.e. "social intelligence") in order to achieve success in high-tempo, diverse multinational operations (Stewart *et al.* 2004; Zaccaro 1999, 2002). For example, leaders will require the ability to conduct cross-cultural dialogue and adapt their communication style to the situation, to engage in active listening, and to be perceptive and sensitive to other cultures (Teo 2005). Indeed, transculturally skilled multinational military commanders will be required to transcend and accommodate cultural differences, in order to integrate people of different cultural backgrounds together in a unity of purpose (Graen and Hui 1999). Thus, the challenge for multinational military commanders is to select and train "transculturals" – those individuals who transcend cultural differences and who can bring people of different cultures together (Graen and Hui 1999). Such notions speak to the importance of developing "cultural intelligence," which has been defined as "a person's capability for successful adaptation to new cultural settings" and includes being aware that behaviours may have different meanings for different cultures, using context-appropriate cultural knowledge when interacting with individuals from other cultures, and being able to switch readily between different cultural frames for sense-making (Cooper *et al.* 2007: 315).

In a similar vein, Elron *et al.* (2003) discuss interculturally effective leadership behaviours such as (a) *integrating differences* (e.g. bringing different cultural perspectives and preferences together, resolving differences among them, and generating integrative solutions and compromises); (b) *bridging differences* (i.e. communicating across differences, making efforts to understand them, and building shared bases and commonalities, such as a shared military professionalism, lessons learned, mission-specific experiences, and supraordinate goals); and (c) *tolerating differences* (i.e. passive actions or inactions that allow others the space to act freely according to their own cultural values, beliefs and norms; suspending quick judgement; and avoiding treading on others' cultural "comfort zone," such as not ridiculing others' religious customs or practices) (see also Mannix and Neale 2005). Along a similar theme, Vora and Kostova (2007) suggest that those capable of integrating "multiple organizational identifications" will be more successful in handling complex organizational goals than others, and that a sense of "oneness with multiple entities" (e.g. national interests as well as broader, multinational goals) can allow individuals to leverage their understanding of those entities and work towards fulfilling multiple goals. In the multinational military context, multinational commanders, in possessing multiple organizational identities and in acting as "bicultural interpreters," may explain and interpret broader multinational mission goals as well as understand the national interests of team or unit members, thus enhancing inter-unit and multinational cooperation.

Reflecting these themes, Cremin *et al.* (2005) have also discussed the behavioural characteristics of effective multinational military leaders. These behaviours include: adopting a flexible and adaptive command and leadership style in accordance with the foreign contingents under their command (e.g. by adopting, in certain contexts, a more consensus-based, persuasive command style, being willing to compromise and negotiate, and avoiding more dictatorial styles of command); building personal and professional relationships with foreign contingents by paying them visits and, where possible, socializing with them (i.e. "eating and drinking at the operational level"; see King this volume); establishing a shared "frame of reference" for the operation (e.g. by instilling a common sense of purpose and adopting common operating procedures); and engendering understanding and trust between the different nations by negotiating and building relationships (see also Stewart *et al.* 2004). Further, the knowledge, skills, and attributes (or KSAs) of effective multinational commanders include leadership and coaching skills (e.g. advising and guiding subtly, without causing offence); cognizance of other nations from a variety of perspectives (military, political, cultural, and historical) and of how they relate to one's own nation; empathy towards other nations (being able to appreciate the perspectives, constraints, and drivers of another national commander or component/contingent); and self-awareness and self-control (i.e. being able to step back and consider how one's behaviour comes across to a foreign national) (Cremin *et al.* 2005).

Importantly, the themes regarding multinational military leadership discussed by researchers have also been reflected in the writings and experiences of military commanders, themselves. For example, Major General Roger Lane (2006), former Deputy Commander of the Italian-led NATO Rapid Deployable Corps deployed to Afghanistan, and responsible for the day-to-day operational management of 10,000 individuals from 36 nations in the HQ NATO/International Security Assistance Force (ISAF), writes that the multinational commander requires a number of key attributes, including excellent interpersonal and team-building skills, the ability to cope with change and uncertainty, excellent negotiation and decision-making skills, political acuity, professional and technical expertise, creativity, pragmatism, patience, empathy, emotional intelligence, and emotional resilience. Lane (2006) further points out that by bringing commanders together from different backgrounds and experiences, the multinational commander employs cultural diversity, creates new insights and opportunities, and generates "buy-in." Resonating with themes presented earlier, Major General Lane points out that it is critical that the multinational commander is able to provide consistency so that all share the same vision and perspective, or in other words, a common operating intent (McCann and Pigeau 2000), and is able to instill unity of effort, if not unity of command. Likewise, Canadian General Roméo Dallaire (2000) discusses some of the lessons he gleaned from his experiences as Commander of the United Nations Mission for Rwanda (UNAMIR) in 1993–94. He argues that operations in the current global context require a much broader range and depth of knowledge than those acquired in conventional warfighting training programmes, and that militaries must ensure that their personnel develop the linguistic, cultural, and analytic skills needed for such operations. According to Dallaire, the situation in Rwanda, in which close to one million people were murdered or displaced, illustrates the military's general failure to understand the cultural dimensions of conflicts in theatre. For example, the military's lack of understanding of the importance of the simple radio in disseminating information and hate propaganda in Rwanda played a role in extremists' murder of the acting prime minister of Rwanda and ten of the Belgian soldiers assigned by UNAMIR to protect her. Dallaire (2000) argues that such situations demonstrate that many factors besides raw military power – including cultural perceptions and social sensitivities – can influence success in operations.

In short, the broad array of skills required for effective leadership in multinational military contexts is more complex and demanding than the leadership competencies required in national and culturally homogenous military forces, and will present unique challenges in the contemporary global context (for a more detailed discussion, see Gurstein 1999).

Cultural differences in national leadership styles

As noted in the previous section, the effectiveness of different military leadership approaches will vary depending on the context (e.g. multinational vs national). Moreover, the ability to transition from one leadership style to another, depending on the cultural or situational context, will be critical to multinational leadership, as different nations within a multinational military contingent will value and respond positively to different styles of leadership. This is evident from the literature on organizational behaviour. For instance, as part of the Global Leadership and Organizational Behavior Effectiveness (GLOBE) studies of 62 nations involving 17,000 middle managers (House *et al.* 2004), Den Hartog *et al.* (1999) found that while some leadership traits (e.g. decisive, positive, just, and intelligent) were seen as universally positive, and other leadership traits (e.g. ruthless and egocentric) were seen as universally negative, a number of leadership traits (e.g. sincerity, evasiveness, cunningness, sensitivity, and enthusiasm) were indicative of effective leadership in some cultures but not others. Similarly, because of the diverse values and core beliefs of different societies, concepts of leadership are culture-bound; for example, authority might be based on achievement, wealth, education, charisma, or birthright, depending on the nation or culture (Lewis 2000). In some societies, leadership is individual, or even despotic, and authority and decision-making structures are hierarchical; in other societies, leadership is collective, and authority and decision-making structures are more collaborative (Lewis 2000). Further, in individualistic cultures, perception of charisma is based on how well an individual fits the characteristics of a good leader, whereas in collectivistic cultures, charisma is based on group performance outcomes (Gelfand *et al.* 2007). Similarly, there is evidence for the culture-specific enactment of transformational leadership; in India, for instance, the *svadharma* orientation (following one's own dharma or duty) is an important component of transformational leadership. As an additional example, paternalistic leadership (a hierarchical form of leadership in which a leader guides subordinates in a manner resembling a parent, and in return expects loyalty and deference) has a positive impact on employee attitudes in collectivistic and hierarchical cultures (e.g. Turkey), but not in individualistic or egalitarian cultures

(Gelfand *et al.* 2007; for military examples, see Soeters *et al.* 2004b). The most effective leaders, therefore, will be those who can adapt their leadership style to suit the particular cultural context.

Beginning in the 1970s, Dutch social and organizational psychologist Geert Hofstede made a comprehensive attempt to capture national value and cultural differences through a cross-cultural classification scheme of work-related values in organizations (Handley and Levis 2001). On the basis of data from over 100,000 respondents in over 50 national subsidiaries of the United States-based multinational company IBM (he later added data from an additional ten countries), Hofstede defined four independent cultural dimensions: *power distance, uncertainty avoidance, individualism–collectivism, and masculinity–femininity* (Hofstede 1980, 1983; Hofstede and Hofstede 2005). *Power distance* relates to the amount of respect and deference between those in superior and subordinate positions, or the extent to which the less powerful in a system accept and expect an unequal distribution of power (see also Klein *et al.* 2000). *Uncertainty avoidance* relates to planning and the creation of stability as a means of dealing with uncertainty. *Individualism–collectivism* relates to whether one's identity is defined by personal goals and achievements or by the character of the collective group to which one belongs. *Masculinity–femininity* refers to the relative emphasis on achievement versus interpersonal harmony and concern for others.[1] Hofstede has subsequently assessed the four original value dimensions among thousands of IBM employees in 72 national cultures and in 20 languages (Hofstede and Hofstede 2005; see also Gerstner and Day 1994; and House *et al.* 2004). Although the generalizability and validity of Hofstede's cultural dimensions have been questioned (Klein *et al.* 2000), and although other researchers have attempted to classify culture according to various other dimensions,[2] Hofstede's model is the most prominent and the most elaborated, and thus his work is generally seen as a major advance in understanding and measuring differences in national culture and values (Handley and Levis 2001). In particular, the dimensions of power distance and uncertainty avoidance have been viewed as useful conceptualizations of national cultural differences relevant to leadership (Klein *et al.* 2000). Power distance appears to describe a leadership style, while uncertainty avoidance relates to the concept of risk assessment in leaders' decision-making (Klein *et al.* 2000).[3]

Since Hofstede's work was first introduced, many military researchers and analysts have incorporated his dimensions, and other related factors, into their analysis of cultural barriers to teamwork in a multinational military context. For example, Bowman and Pierce (2003) have described four cognitive cultural barriers to teamwork that they argue influence communication, coordination, and decision-making in multinational military contexts. Expanding on Hofstede's conceptualizations, these four dimensions include power distance, tolerance for uncertainty, the individualism/collectivism dichotomy, and cultural differences in reasoning. In Bowman and Pierce's (2003) terms, *power distance* describes the extent to which less powerful individuals in a system accept inequality. In low power distance relationships, working patterns are more egalitarian and team processes are more collaborative and interactive. In contrast, in high power distance teams, leaders tend to be directive, thereby constraining team creativity and collaboration. *Tolerance for uncertainty* reflects the amount of discomfort experienced by an individual or team in the presence of unknown factors. A low tolerance for uncertainty is marked by a search for details through rules and structure, whereas individuals (i.e. leaders or teams) who act or make decisions in the face of incomplete knowledge are exhibiting a high tolerance for uncertainty. This difference can cause problems within a team, or among teams, if individuals or teams with high and low tolerances must work together. One individual or team will start slowly, collecting as much information as possible, while the other individual or team will move quickly toward an end product or solution. The *individualism/collectivism* dichotomy reflects a preference for working alone or in a group. This dimension includes a preference for building relationships among team members as contrasted with a focus on individual task achievement. Individualists often view the mission as primary and relationships among team members as secondary, whereas collectivists view team relationships as critical to producing a viable team product. Finally, cultural differences in *reasoning* can also emerge in the context of multinational military teams. Such differences may be related to concrete versus hypothetical thought patterns: hypothetical thinkers are capable of envisioning several solutions to a problem, whereas concrete thinkers prefer to have detailed plans of action and often use previously used solutions to solve new tasks. These differences can cause problems in a team setting when a course of action is unclear or when conditions require changes to a plan. The hypothetical thinker is capable of generating several possible solutions, while a concrete thinker may view this as avoiding the problem at hand (Bowman and Pierce 2003).[4] In short, cognitive cultural differences may negatively affect such military teamwork and command and control (C2) tasks as planning, problem detection, situation awareness, uncertainty management, and decision-making. Indeed, if commanders (and team members) assume that others interpret and react as they do, manage uncertainty as they do, and think about real and hypothetical issues as they do, then there can be considerable problems (Klein 2005; Klein *et al.* 2000).

As mentioned above, the cultural dimensions of *power distance* and *uncertainty avoidance* appear to be especially pertinent to leadership and command. Differences in power distance, for instance, are reflected in leadership style, as well as the interpersonal power and influence between the superior and the subordinate. In cultures with low power distance, we would find more collaborative, egalitarian working patterns and team interchanges, less centralized or top-down decision-making, and flatter organizational structures (Handley and Levis 2001). It is interesting to note that even among NATO nations, there are variations in power distance. For example, some studies have shown Norway and Denmark to be low on this dimension while Turkey, France, and Belgium have been found to be high on power distance, which is associated with a more top-down, hierarchical, authoritarian leadership style (Hofstede 1980; Soeters *et al.* 2004; cf. Elron *et al.* 1999). Similarly, Soeters (1997) found strong cultural differences in power distance in the military academies of 13 nations, with the United Kingdom (UK) military academy showing the highest level of power distance among all the academies studied (see also Soeters and Bos-Bakx 2003; and Soeters and Recht 2001). Interestingly, it has been observed that the militaries of nations with high power distance, such as France and Italy, resent and ultimately have refused to be placed under the operational command of other nations (Soeters *et al.* 2006).

Significantly, there are also implications of power distance for mission command, or the command doctrine underlying manoeuvre warfare. Mission command is designed to achieve unity of effort, a faster tempo, and initiative at all levels; it requires decentralization of authority and decision-making (R.G. Davis 2000). The emphasis is on the development of skills and the transmission of a commander's intent so that personnel at all levels can function effectively when unexpected events occur with no time for additional input from above (Handley and Levis 2001). Comfort with this approach will vary with differences in power distance (Klein *et al.* 2000; United Kingdom Doctrine for Joint and Multinational Operations 1999; Soeters *et al.* 2004). Specifically, those cultures that are low in power distance will be comfortable with the mission command approach to C2, whereas those cultures that are high in power distance will be less comfortable with this approach (Stewart *et al.* 2004). As Potts (2004) suggests, some nations have inscribed the concept of mission command into their military cultures, allowing subordinates considerable freedom of action and discretion to take the initiative within the commander's intent as circumstances change (see, for instance, Chapter 6, this volume). Others expect to command, and be commanded, by detailed orders, with a need for frequent reporting back to superiors and further direction as circumstances change. Potts (2004) argues that nations must work towards a common understanding of mission command in order to maximize effectiveness in multinational operations, while recognizing and accommodating different approaches. Similarly, Soeters (1997) has argued that commanding officers of international military units should be aware that their leadership or management styles are not necessarily understood in the same manner by different nations, and that they should show mutual understanding and promote multinational teamwork on an equal-status basis, with shared interests and common goals for all nations involved. Once again, one way to achieve this is for leaders to adapt their leadership styles to suit the situation and cultures of their component forces.

Differences in uncertainty avoidance, or the extent to which members of a culture experience uncertainty as stressful and the extent to which they take actions to avoid uncertainty, are also relevant to leadership, and in particular, to decision making (Hofstede 1980; Hofstede and Hofstede 2005). For example, leaders who are high on uncertainty avoidance experience change and ambiguity as highly stressful; thus, they may seek out rules that will provide structure and order for change, and are uncomfortable with making decisions in the face of uncertainty (Klein *et al.* 2000). Members of a culture or military organization that score high on uncertainty avoidance will have standardized and formal decision-making procedures (Handley and Levis 2001). In contrast, those who are low on uncertainty avoidance are more comfortable making decisions in the face of uncertainty (Hofstede 1980; Hofstede and Hofstede 2005). In organizations with low uncertainty avoidance, decision-making procedures will be less formal and plans will continually be reassessed for needed modifications (Handley and Levis 2001). Uncertainty avoidance also influences a national group's readiness to adapt in the face of an unexpected development. High stakes, time pressure decision-making is coordinated when multinational collaborators are similar on uncertainty avoidance and risk assessment. However, it is difficult for people who value spontaneity and last-minute decisions to coordinate actions with those who need firm, committed plans. When operations include people with different levels of tolerance for uncertainty, there can be tension and fear. A leader or decision-maker with high uncertainty avoidance is likely to follow the procedure regardless of circumstances, whereas a leader or decision-maker with low uncertainty avoidance may be more innovative (Handley and Levis 2001). Further, members of a culture or military organization that are high on uncertainty avoidance are also less likely to be comfortable with mission command (Stewart *et al.* 2004). Among NATO nations alone, Portugal and Greece are rated high on uncertainty avoidance while Denmark is rated as low (Hofstede 1980). Thus, the challenge for a leader or commander is to recognize cultural differences in these areas and use them to balance perspectives rather than to create disharmony (Klein *et al.* 2000).

Other researchers have also investigated cultural differences in the context of multinational military operations, in particular as they relate to leadership. For example, a study of the cadet officers of 13, and later 18, military academies in mostly Western nations, referred to earlier, found substantial international cultural differences (see Soeters 1997; Soeters and Bos-Bakx 2003; and Soeters *et al.* 2006). Thus, the cadet officers of Italy were found to score high on power distance and uncertainty avoidance; the US (West Point) cadets also scored high on uncertainty avoidance, but the British (Sandhurst) cadets had by far the highest scores on power distance among all 18 academies, including those of Brazil and Argentina. Further, a similar pattern of cultural heterogeneity within the military was found not only among the young cadet officers in the academy study, but also in a study at the NATO Defense College in Rome.[5] However, despite the cultural differences, the study of military academies also showed that there exists a type of supranational military culture: in comparison to business organizations, the military cultures in the countries studied turned out to be relatively bureaucratic, hierarchical and institutional. Compared to their counterparts in the civilian world, the cadet officers in general had higher scores on power distance and lower scores on individualism and masculinity; this pattern confirms common notions about differences between civilian and military organizations (e.g. that military organizations are more hierarchical and value collectivism more than civilian organizations; and that earning high salaries and striving for individual achievement are not as highly valued in military organizations as they are in civilian business organizations). The result of this supranational military culture is that the military personnel of different nations can often function together without too much difficulty, particularly when they come from culturally similar nations, such as NATO countries (Soeters and Bos-Bakx 2003; Soeters *et al.* 2006). Nevertheless, cultural heterogeneity will impact international military cooperation in many ways, even within NATO alliances. Furthermore, certain conditions may make the development of an international frame of reference or "international military outlook" among military personnel difficult: military units must maintain a national line of responsibility; time frames are often tight; the sense of urgency is generally high; and personnel are constantly rotated (Soeters and Bos-Bakx 2003; Soeters *et al.* 2006).

To illustrate some of the challenges that may arise in international military operations, Soeters and Bos-Bakx (2003) described two intercultural encounters that took place during recent peacekeeping missions: the Anglo–Dutch cooperation in Cyprus and the US–Danish cooperation in Bosnia. In the Anglo–Dutch case, problems arose mostly because the Dutch military had difficulties with the hierarchical, high power distance customs within the British Army. For example, the Dutch soldiers in Cyprus criticized the rank-based separate mess halls and canteens and the prohibition against platoon commanders drinking a beer with the soldiers with whom they had worked all day. The authoritarian way in which orders were issued by the British Army leaders was also foreign to the Dutch, who were more accustomed to the jovial tone generally used by Dutch commanders when explaining their plans and orders. The friction became so intense that the Dutch military staff in the Hague found it necessary to intervene: a special commission investigated the situation and prepared a report with several recommendations, including the importance of getting to know one's own culture and the culture of the other, and of not ridiculing other cultures. These recommendations have been presented to commanders and used during training before other Dutch soldiers deployed to Cyprus. The importance of these recommendations is that they are not ethnocentric (i.e. the "Dutch way of doing things" was not considered superior to the "British way of doing things"). Similar tensions as in the Anglo–Dutch case also arose in the US–Danish cooperation in Bosnia. Unlike the Danish Army, the US Army is high on power distance and uncertainty avoidance. These differences were reflected in Danish military culture, in which phrases like "obey orders," "work by the book," and "comply with military law," favoured by Americans, are relatively less important. In contrast, Danish officers used civilian criteria to describe the nature of their job (e.g. they possess a "results orientation") and favoured a decentralized military structure. Thus, there were important similarities between the Anglo–Dutch experience in Cyprus and the US–Danish experience in Bosnia in terms of the issues that emerged in international military cooperation. In both case studies, the authoritarian approach of one partner (US or UK) was inconsistent with that of the other military (Dutch or Danish), leading to friction and challenges to multinational military cooperation.

Cultural diversity within teams: advantage or disadvantage for multinational military cooperation?

The research studies discussed above suggest that multinational military teams may face a number of challenges related to cultural factors. Still, research in the management and other scientific domains has shown that there can be positive, as well as negative, aspects of team cultural diversity. Consistent with cognitive resource diversity theory (or information-processing and problem-solving approaches), value in diversity comes from increased creativity, innovation, flexibility and problem solving ability (Mannix and Neale 2005). A variety of perspectives and experiences in culturally diverse teams can bring more information and ideas into the team, stimulate thinking, and bring different networks of contacts and resources into the team. If these diverse perspectives, experiences and resources are relevant to the team's task, then high-quality outcomes may be expected. However, if the variety in perspectives, experiences, and resources within the team is not relevant to the team's task, then there is no basis for expecting diversity to enhance the team's activity. Thus, the effect of team diversity will depend, to some extent, on the nature of the task (Mannix and Neale 2005; Staples and Zhao 2006).

Accordingly, it has been suggested that task complexity or difficulty may affect the relationship between team diversity and performance (Sartori et al. 2006). For complex tasks that require team members to pool their resources, having diverse perspectives and resources should aid the team's collaborative effort, and therefore, performance. In contrast, diversity can be counterproductive when dealing with simple, routine tasks; this is because diverse perspectives may complicate simple tasks and impede performance by creating delays or introducing conflict. Similarly, it has been suggested that task interdependence moderates the relationship between team diversity and performance (Sartori et al. 2006). High task interdependence requires that team members depend on each other for expertise, resources, and knowledge in order to achieve their task, whereas low task interdependence allows members to work as individuals with little need for coordination. In the case of high task interdependence, once again, cultural diversity may be a source of innovative knowledge, perspectives, or experience, if relevant to the task. Otherwise, conflict may result. In the case of low task interdependence, cultural diversity may be irrelevant, assuming that team members are in fact able to work independently. Thus, to the extent that multinational military teams are engaged in complex tasks, cultural diversity may be an advantage. However, conflict may occur if multinational military teams are engaged in simple, routine tasks or if the diverse perspectives they bring are irrelevant to the task.

In addition to the nature of the team's task, the effect of cultural diversity on team outcomes is significantly affected by time (Staples and Zhao 2006). When groups initially form, they know little about each other, and conflicts may occur. But, as team members interact over time, the potentially positive effects of diversity (e.g. diverse perspectives and ideas, innovation) may emerge. Watson *et al.* (1993) demonstrated this pattern in a longitudinal laboratory study of the interaction process and performance of culturally homogenous and culturally diverse groups. These groups consisted of 173 upper-level under-graduate American management students who were studied for 17 weeks; the culturally diverse or heterogenous groups included at least two nationalities and three ethnic backgrounds in a four- or five-person team. Initially, the homo-genous groups scored higher than the heterogenous groups on both perform-ance and process effectiveness (e.g. heterogenous team members perceived their team-mates as "too controlling" and disagreed about what was important). But over time, both types of groups showed improvement on process and performance, and differences converged. By the end of the study, there were no differences in process or overall performance between the two types of groups, but the heterogenous groups scored higher than the homogenous groups on two task measures: range of perspectives identified and alternatives generated. Thus, although a high degree of cultural diversity did appear to constrain process and performance in newly formed groups, these negative effects disap-peared over time.

Perhaps one key to explaining such findings, besides the importance of time and the positive impact of diverse perspectives in heterogenous groups, is the fact that both types of groups received feedback about their process and performance over the course of the study. Watson *et al.* (1993) concluded that providing performance and process information at regular intervals may be a feedback feature that organizations, such as multinational military teams, should utilize in order to counter the possible negative effects of cultural diversity. More recently, Gelfand *et al.* (2007) have suggested that culturally heterogenous teams perform at least as effectively as homogenous teams over time *and* when leaders help to prevent communication breakdowns and broker hidden know-ledge between culturally diverse members. Still other researchers have sug-gested the importance of time in understanding the impact of cultural diversity on work team performance. Toh and Denisi (2007) suggest that longer inter-action can reduce the importance of *surface-level attributes*, such as ethnicity or nationality, and increase the importance of *deep-level attributes*, such as shared personal values. Similarly, Elron's (1997) study of top management teams within multinational corporations found that, contrary to expectations, cultural heterogeneity within such teams did not result in lower social cohesion, possibly because any negative effects of value dissimilarity in long-term groups like top management teams may become insignificant over time.

On the other hand, the effect of time on the performance or process of culturally diverse teams is not a simple or straightforward matter, and may also play out differently in real-life military settings compared to laboratory experiments with management students. The results of a longitudinal six-year study of the 1st German/Dutch Army Corps (from 1995 to 2001), for example, found that after an initial period of euphoria, culture shock between the two cultures developed over time (Soeters and Bos-Bakx 2003). Fortunately, this situation was reversed after a positive experience of collaboration during the Kosovo crisis and a challenging experience of working together in the binational headquarters. In keeping with the contact hypothesis in social psychology, both time and *quality of the experience* played important roles in learning to value the other group. Thus, although knowledge from the business sector may be useful in illuminating the multinational military context, the performance of multinational military teams depends on a number of factors, including the nature of the task (creative problem-solving), the cultural composition of the team, the maturity of the team (e.g. the time factor), and, significantly, the qualitative experience of the team.

Furthermore, some studies have suggested a U-shaped or curvilinear relationship between national composition and performance, such that highly heterogenous multinational military teams, with many nationalities of equal size, and highly homogenous military teams, with few nationalities and one nationality clearly outnumbering the others, may outperform teams and organizations that are moderately heterogenous (see Chapter 14, this volume; Peterson and Thomas 2007). In other words, all else being equal, high and low diversity teams show the least amount of conflict, the most effective communication patterns, and the highest level of satisfaction, planning, and cooperation. The highly heterogenous teams emphasize rules and practices that are inclusive rather than exclusive, and therefore are more open to their members' ideas and input; these teams develop the highest levels of team identity. Moderately heterogenous teams (i.e. teams composed of two or three more-or-less equally sized nationalities) tend to display dysfunctional interactions (e.g. members accuse each other of not fully understanding, or of being the source of problems), communication difficulties, and low team identity. Further, Gelfand *et al.* (2007) suggest that highly heterogenous teams outperform moderately heterogenous teams because they avert subgroup fractionalization and faultlines. To illustrate, Søderberg and Wedell-Wedellsborg (2005) compared a multinational corps consisting of personnel from three countries (Germany, Denmark, Poland) with a multinational military training centre consisting of personnel from 15 countries. In the latter, high-diversity organization, national identities played a minor role, whereas in the former (moderate diversity) organization, national identity seemed to be an organizing principle – the basis for coalitions, a source of conflict, and the standard explanation for problems (see also Chapter 14, this volume).

Other research, of a an experimental nature, has also shed light on the conditions under which cultural diversity may be associated with positive (or at least neutral) effects. Staples and Zhao (2006) found that culturally heterogenous teams (i.e. teams that consisted of diverse members, based on language spoken, country of birth, nationality, and individualism/collectivism score on Hofstede's 1994 Values Survey Module) were less satisfied and cohesive, and experienced more conflict, than homogenous teams, although there were no significant differences in team performance. However, an examination of just the heterogenous teams found that the performance of the virtual heterogenous teams (i.e. those teams that were geographically distributed and that communicated via an electronic synchronous chat system or audioconference phone system) was superior to the performance of the face-to-face heterogenous teams (i.e. those teams that were physically co-located). Staples and Zhao (2006) suggested that the reductive capabilities of collaborative technologies (e.g. electronic communication) are beneficial for newly formed diverse teams, in that they may reduce the negative effects of diversity early in the life of a diverse team (in this case, the teams interacted for only one hour).

Although studies such as those described above are encouraging about the potential positive impact of cultural diversity, other studies have demonstrated more negative results. For instance, in a study of 111 work teams in four American organizations in the manufacturing and insurance industries, Kirkman *et al.* (2004) found that team race heterogeneity was negatively related to team empowerment and multiple indicators of team effectiveness. In addition, demographic dissimilarity between team leaders and their teams based on race was negatively related to empowerment and team leader ratings of team effectiveness. Kirkman *et al.* (2004) suggested that the negative effect of racial diversity in these industries reflects a broader trend of the persistence of racial tension in the United States.

To further explain the negative effects associated with cultural diversity, some of the major theories proposed by analysts include social identity theory, social categorization theory, and the similarity/attraction paradigm. According to these theories, the negative effects associated with cultural diversity are due to the creation of in-groups and out-groups. People implicitly categorize themselves into groups according to salient cues, such as demographics, and identify more closely with people they perceive as being similar to themselves. They do this in order to achieve and maintain positive self-identity and in order to reduce uncertainty. As in- and out-group characteristics become more salient, individuals become more biased towards their in-group; they engage in the expression of ethnocentric attitudes, stereotyping, distancing, and the disparagement of people in other categories (Billig and Tajfel 1973; Tajfel 1982). Further, emotional attachments to the in-groups become potential sources of interpersonal conflict with members of out-groups, which in turn reduces satisfaction and team performance in diverse groups (Staples and Zhao 2006). Similarly, social categorization undermines team members' trust in each other's abilities and acceptance of differences. Consistent with social categorization theory, empirical research has shown that racial heterogeneity is associated with reduced commitment (Riordan and Shore 1997), cooperation (Garza and Santos 1991), communication (Hoffman 1985), consideration (Cady and Valentine 1999), and team effectiveness (Hackman 1987). However, social identity theory also identifies a number of strategies for reducing problems in inter-group relations, by creating alternative categorizations among individuals (Tajfel and Turner 1986). These strategies can be used to enhance identification with the diverse team, for example, through the creation of supra-ordinate goals and re-categorization, through rituals aimed at identification of the diverse group as an entity, and by focusing on the celebration of a common goal (see also Elron *et al.* 1999).

In a slightly different vein, however, Berry (2004) suggests that encounters between diverse cultural groups can be solved in a number of ways, depending on (a) whether one wants to maintain one's own culture and identity and (b) the relationship sought among other groups. If one does not value one's own cultural identity and if one does not seek relationships with other groups, then the result will be marginalization; such a situation should be avoided during multinational military operations. If, however, one does not value one's own cultural identity, but one values the cultures of other groups, then it would make sense to assimilate to (or adopt) the cultural practices of other groups. In general, the assimilation strategy tends to develop if one party clearly dominates the other; and it can work well if the smaller (non-dominant) party agrees to assimilate. For instance, this strategy can be seen in air forces that use the same (mostly US-dominated) technology. On the other hand, if one values one's own cultural practices and if one rejects the other group's practices, then separation may be the best strategy. Indeed, in many military operations, this is the actual practice (e.g. in the Balkans, all national contingents of a certain size were assigned their own geographic area of responsibility). Under this separation strategy, each national group could work and live on its own without continuously being confronted by other cultural practices. Further, this separation strategy can be strengthened by giving each national contingent its own role in a system of international division of labour. For instance, in Iraq, the Dutch worked together with a Japanese contingent, but there was a strict division of roles: the Japanese were mainly responsible for civic activities (e.g. building power facilities) while the Dutch were responsible for military tasks such as patrolling, security, and guarding (see Chapter 12, this volume). Although separation may be an effective strategy, many analysts believe that in the end mutual accommodation is the best strategy, because this leads to true integration in which the best of many worlds are merged into something perhaps better than all previous contributing cultures. This integration strategy involves the acceptance by dominant and non-dominant groups of new ways of working based on the input of all. In order to achieve this integrative ideal, however, power relations must be balanced so as to prevent the domination of some over others. At the same time, people must be adept at working in intercultural contexts, which, as discussed below, requires intercultural training.

Recommendations for leadership and team training in the multinational military context

The importance of training in the multinational military context cannot be over-stated. Undoubtedly, an important means for developing cultural diversity as a productive asset rather than a source of conflict and prejudice in multinational military teams is through intercultural training (Christian *et al.* 2006). Below are discussed several general recommendations for leadership and team training in the multinational, intercultural context.

Gillespie (2003), for instance, offers suggestions for preparing leaders in the skills needed to deal with national and cultural frictions and for achieving unity of effort in modern multinational military contexts. These suggestions include foreign language and foreign cultural training, as well as training in generic intercultural issues in multinational military operations that is supplemented by nation-specific information just prior to operations or exercises (see also Stewart *et al.* 2004). However, Gillespie (2003) points out that all personnel who are likely to be involved in multinational operations must be made aware of cultural issues that may affect interoperability, and thus, argues that cross-cultural train-ing and instruction should be given to all personnel prior to deployment. As Bowman (1997) argues, the more personnel available who are experienced in the cultures of various national partners, the smoother the operations will be. Further, multinational military planning exercises could significantly improve initial operational responses to emerging crises. Such training exercises will help to overcome any initial confusion and cultural problems by identifying them in a training situation before an actual crisis occurs (Gillespie 2003).

Similar in intent to the above recommendations, Graen and Hui (1999) have proposed a comprehensive global training model to prepare leaders for global leadership. This global training model, which may be applied to leaders of multinational military operations, involves: (a) transcultural skill development; (b) third-culture making skills; (c) cross-cultural creative problem-solving skills; and (d) ethical skills. *Transculturals*, as alluded to previously, are those who grow beyond their own cultural socialization so that they can understand differ-ent cultures with minimal biases, make valid cross-cultural judgements, and develop cross-cultural partnerships (see also Elron *et al.* 2003). Those with *third-culture skills* are those who can use cross-cultural partners to understand, reconcile, and transcend systematic cultural differences and build a third culture (such as a global military culture?) in which both (or multiple) cultures can cooperate. Third cultures involve the bridging and transcending of two or more cultures. In bridging cultural differences, third cultures involve ways to bring compromises between the different cultural practices, and cross-cultural partners develop organizational practices and management techniques and programmes that are acceptable to members of each culture. Those with *multinational cre-ative problem-solving skills* are those who can mediate and negotiate multina-tional interests in a creative problem-solving context. Those with *ethical skills* are those who can understand multinational ethical conflicts and have the means to deal with them. Graen and Hui (1999) propose that training involving these four skills should continue throughout the career for both individual leaders and teams. As Bowman (1997) suggests, the intercultural education of officers and others will help change perceptions and stereotypes concerning the roles and abilities of other nations, and thus will play a critical role in the leadership of change.

Indeed, in addition to intercultural training and development for individual leaders, commanders should also develop intercultural awareness among members of their teams (Winslow *et al.* 2003). Towards this end, commanders must establish a training and development programme to close any critical gaps that have been identified, and must develop multilingual standard operating procedures (SOPs), cultural awareness training, staff training at the headquarters level, and education in a basic code of ethics (Plante 1998). For UN peacekeepers, for instance, such training may include an understanding of the broader global political context of peacekeeping, a recognition of the diversity of national interests which must be accommodated within a multilateral peacekeeping mandate, and a set of materials and standards that articulate broad ethical standards and codes of conduct (Gurstein 1999). Commanders must also create awareness of the *benefits* of diversity through both words and actions (Winslow *et al.* 2003). As mentioned earlier, multinational commanders should stress the joint character of the mission as the *superordinate goal* for everyone involved in order to achieve a unity of effort. Commanders should emphasize the *equal status* of all groups involved in the operation, and if necessary, boost the status of any low-status groups (Soeters and Bos-Bakx 2003; Soeters and Recht 2001). Commanders should make decisions so that members of every group can maintain their dignity without loss of face. Such principles of inter-group relations can be complemented by policies that enhance intercultural encounters, such as concrete collaboration with diverse groups and preparation before deployment, and should be integrated into the whole training period before, and preferably during, deployment (see Soeters *et al.* 2004). For these tasks, commanders must carry the primary responsibility.

Some analysts have suggested other strategies for overcoming cultural differences and instilling intercultural competence. For example, Klein *et al.* (2000) have proposed a *cultural lens* concept that captures cultural differences in reasoning, judgement, and authority structure (see also Klein 2005). A cultural lens is a metaphor to allow those involved in C2 operations to see their world as if through the eyes of other participants, and to understand how options are conceptualized and evaluated by others. According to Klein *et al.* (2000), the ability to *decentre* that is brought about through the cultural lens can support the anticipation of actions, facilitate accurate judgements, and lead to the effective negotiation of differences. Further, seeing the world through the cultural lens of others may increase common vision in the face of divergent views (Klein 2005). In short, a cultural lens is a tool that multinational leaders (and teams) can use to strengthen common ground and the coordination of action, and to enhance understanding and cooperation in the context of multinational military operations (see also Lewis 2000).

Finally, in a spirit similar to the cultural lens concept, Ely and Thomas (2001) have proposed a perspective on diversity, called the *integration and learning perspective*, which seeks to build more deeply and comprehensively on the varied skills, experiences and ways of thinking of a diverse workforce. According to this perspective, cultural differences can be a source of growth, learning and insight, rather than conflict, but only if these differences are acknowledged and actively explored. Foldy (2004) suggests that the integration and learning perspective is different from much of the cultural sensitivity literature in that it does not presume to know, given a person's cultural identity, what that person's cultural experiences might be. Moreover, Foldy argues that both the integration and learning perspective and more generic learning frames and skills must be present in order to enhance heterogenous work group effectiveness and performance. According to Foldy, holding "learning beliefs" and adopting "learning behaviors" allows groups to undertake the difficult work of expressing and working with culturally based beliefs. Foldy suggests that *learning from and across cultural difference* could be one path towards enhanced performance in heterogenous organizations.

Conclusion

Multinational military operations will become more prevalent in the future as nations seek alternate methods of resolving conflict and new collaborative partners (C.J.R. Davis 2000). With the increasing complexity of contemporary military operations, future multinational military commanders will face a myriad of challenges, including, significantly, the integration of culturally diverse teams (C.J.R. Davis 2000). This integration, which will involve bonding and bridging, will demand a broad range of leadership skills and competencies, including the ability to overcome cultural barriers to international cooperation (such as cultural differences in power distance and decision-making), and an ability to harness cultural diversity as a positive asset, rather than a source of conflict. There is a substantial body of research that demonstrates the positive impact that an effective leader can have on multicultural team performance (Salas *et al.* 2004). Through the development of intercultural competence among multinational leaders and their teams, cultural diversity in such contexts can be used effectively as a positive resource for promoting multinational military cooperation.

Notes

1   Since Hofstede's original work, a fifth dimension, *long-term orientation*, has been added. The fifth dimension was not constructed on the basis of IBM data, but was

derived from an additional study that focused on typical Asian cultural aspects, which exist in varying degrees throughout the world. Long-term orientation refers to the level of perseverance and acceptance of gradual change in a society or community (Soeters *et al.* 2006).

2 For example, Trompenaars and Hampden-Turner have focused on a mix of value and behavioural patterns, and Schwartz has classified culture according to ten value types (Waldherr *et al.* 2006).

3 Hofstede's other dimensions also have implications for leadership, however. For example, masculinity/femininity may affect whether the leader (and team members) are more focused on the task/achievement or on harmonious interpersonal relationships. Individualism/collectivism may affect whether the leader (and team members) are focused more on their own personal goals or the goals of the collective. Long-term/short-term orientation may affect whether the leader (and team members) are open to change or seek to uphold traditions.

4 For a discussion of how dialectical reasoning and counterfactual thinking may also be related to cultural differences in decision-making and reasoning among leaders and teams, see Klein (2005) and Klein *et al.* (2000).

5 There was one exception, however: Page in his study found that German career officers displayed far higher levels of power distance and masculinity than the German student officers in the academy study (Soeters *et al.* 2006).

Chapter 5

Tough talk

Clear and cluttered communication during peace operations

Andrea van Dijk

Introduction

With the change of traditional warfare into peace operations, language has become an essential tool in the coordination and management of operational tasks in multinational military cooperation. The importance of English as the military lingua franca in this regard has increased proportionately to the expansion of the number of nationalities that participate in military missions (Crossey 2005). In order to prevent a linguistic confusion in the theatre of operations, the English-language policy has often been installed to 'command and control' the internal communication structures of the military organization. Depending on the degree of linguistic proficiency, language, however, has proved to be an ambivalent tool for it can both empower as well as disempower the voice and job performance of the military personnel.

The importance and implications of language (in)competence moreover does not restrict itself to the perimeters of the military organization, they are also applicable to the environments in which peace operations take place. The experience of military officers and academics has taught that the military lingua franca will not suffice as an accepted and efficient means of communication in non-western environments. In order to optimize the interaction and exchange of information between peacekeepers and the local population, the military organization should enact the channels of cross-cultural communication in the expeditionary environment by implementing a (basic) knowledge of the local vernaculars and interpreter interventions into its corporate language policy.

Although both subjects are equally important, this chapter will only elaborate on the influence of language on the communication structures of multinational military cooperation. Through a theoretical account of the origin and development of language management within multinational companies, and participatory observation during an international military exercise in Germany, this chapter seeks to investigate and analyse the implications of language (in)competence on military communication in a multinational context.

Language management in multinational companies

Although scholars in international management have largely contributed to an understanding of cross-communication processes by analysing the various cultures and nationalities within multinational corporations, they for a long time 'managed' to overlook the one aspect of communication that holds the fabric of international organizations together. Communication cannot exist without language, and yet it was this very aspect of human interaction that was structurally forgotten and neglected in cross-communication research (Feely and Harzing 2003). Over the last five years however, organizational scholars, have come to acknowledge that language is the carrier of international communication and professional understanding (Adler 2002: 73–102; Marschan-Piekkari et al. 1999: 422). Studies on communication dynamics in multinational corporations have gained an insight into the often strained relationship between parent and host national companies (Marschan-Piekkari et al. 1999: 425; Feely and Harzing 2003: 38; Park et al. 1996: 80; Vaara et al. 2005: 596). Characteristic for these studies is their unanimity in which they pinpoint language, and more precisely the language barrier, as the culprit of organizational misunderstanding. Whereas the studies of Feely and Harzing, and Park et al. emphasize the corrosive effect of the language barrier on both native and non-native speakers, the studies of Marschan-Piekkari et al. (1999) and Vaara et al. 2005 on the other hand focus more on power circuits that arise in the wake of corporate language policies.

In order to get a better understanding of language problems that impede efficient communication, it is necessary to discuss some of the findings of the above-mentioned authors. Their longitudinal case studies have demonstrated that language problems of native speakers mainly consist of miscommunication, attribution and code-switching. The first two phenomena are somewhat intertwined as both allude to the alleged linguistic fluency of the non-native speaker. Miscommunication often arises in situations wherein native speakers wrongly assume that non-native speakers command full linguistic proficiency of the official business language. Needless to say inaccurate attributions create the perfect breeding ground for miscommunication between native and non-native speakers. The biased expectation of the native speaker, however, is bound to be contradicted by the restrictions of reality. And once the linguistic incompetence of the non-native speaker has been discovered, the 'disenchantment' of the native speaker cannot but disrupt the communication as feelings of distrust and dislike affect the business relation.

Moreover, it is very plausible that these negative experiences could grow into individual and even institutionalized prejudices against non-native speakers. Robertson and Kulik in this regard have described the prevalence of stereotype threat in (multinational) organizations. The psychological concept of stereotype threat arises when members of a particular identity group fear that they will be seen and judged according to a negative stereotype about their group. Their anxiety is heightened in situations where they have to perform a task on which members of their group are said to have done poorly. Stereotyped threatened participants often lack the confidence that they will perform well and therefore the stereotype (threat) often becomes a self-fulfilling prophecy (Robertson and Kulik 2007: 24–29). Although Robertson and Kulik have described the effect of stereotype threat on minority groups within the context of the American society such as African-Americans, the elderly and overweight people, they emphatically state that 'members of any group could experience stereotype threat when their identity group is negatively compared with another group' (Robertson and Kulik 2007: 27). The phenomena of stereotype threat could therefore easily be applied to the condition and context of non-native speakers within multinational organizations because linguistic proficiency is very often put on a par with professional inaptitude. This misconception can often assume a life of its own and discredit non-native speakers to a degree that they start to believe that the stereotype indeed reflects a truth about the quality of their job performance. As a result of this negative (self-)perception, the stereotype threat seizes its opportunity. It disrupts the performance of non-native speakers and negatively affects their professional credibility.

Two quotations taken from a case study of Vaara *et al.* (2005) on the merger of a Finnish and a Swedish bank, illustrate the (subjective) interdependence between language competence, self-perception, and power when one language has been chosen to be the corporate language (in this case, Swedish):

> In the beginning it was, of course, a terrible shock [...]. It was really horrible. It felt like [...] half of our professional competence had been taken away when we had to use a language that was not our native tongue. You felt like an idiot [...]. The main thing was to get over the feeling of inferiority.
>
> (Vaara *et al.* 2005: 609)

> In Finland, we lost many potential future key figures because they realized that they would never be able to compete with their Swedish rivals in the organization.
>
> (Vaara *et al.* 2005: 615)

Other circumstances that give rise to misunderstanding and misconception consist of situations where delegations of non-native speakers discuss matters in their own language during negotiations. Another quotation from the above-mentioned case study illustrates this:

> With Finnish as your native tongue [...] you are, in a debate or negotiation situation, in a weaker position[...]. Whether or not this is the case, it feels like it when the other person speaks his/her native tongue [...] But, turning it the other way around, we have this secret language (i.e. Finnish) in which

we can speak pretty freely to each other – in the middle of the negotiation. The majority of the Swedes don't understand one single bit of it.

(Vaara *et al.* 2005: 609)

This switching of codes during times of negotiation and decision-making, however, is often (unjustly) perceived as a manifestation of 'conspiring behaviour' which on its turn triggers a whole new gamut of sentiments of exclusion and hostility.

The case study of Park *et al.* (1996) on United States firms in South Korea zooms in on the problems and grievances affecting non-native speakers. Non-native speakers lose their rhetorical skills when they have to communicate in a language which is different from their own. Even if non-native speakers command the official lingua franca, they are still at a loss when the situation calls for other more decisive and interpersonal skills. Closely interrelated to the loss of rhetorical skills is the concept of face (Park *et al.* 1996: 81). The fear of making a fool out of oneself and/or being regarded as 'dense', may 'force' non-native speakers to keep up appearances. By keeping a low profile and pretending to be in control of the situation, non-native speakers hope to save their face. The context and implications of face-saving strategies will be further explicated through a discussion of experiences of non-native (non-)commissioned officers who participated in an international military exercise on p. 77–78.

All the above-mentioned detrimental effects of the language barrier are undoubtedly the results of the partiality of the language selection between two different linguistic parties. The choice of the official language is in almost all of the situations determined by two tacit but fixed norms: the vitality of the language and the mutual linguistic skills of the parties involved. Reasonably or not, English, to this day, is still respected as the most important language. It has even been stated that the English language becomes of greater importance when the number of nationalities in a company increases (de Swaan 2001). Again, the case study of Vaara *et al.* (2005) on the power circuits in multinational organizations seems to be of value in substantiating this hypothesis. As soon as English was introduced as the new legitimate official corporate language, the tide seemed to turn for the Finnish employees. The Finns experienced the new language policy as a relief and did not waste any time to enact their 'new rights [...] by showing the Swedes their place' (Vaara *et al.* 2005: 615). Whereas the English language re-established the equality for the Finns, the Swedish on the other hand were considerably less enthusiastic about the consequences of the new language policy:

I am a little bit afraid that we are losing some competent people who will become silent, who are not as good (as others) in this language [...]. A lot of culture creation, cooperation and consensus, it is precisely participation in these joint meetings. And if one only sits there and does not understand every nuance or value.

(Vaara *et al.* 2005: 615)

The quotation is not only illustrative of the advance of English as the primary corporate language for most multinationals, a process which is described as linguistic imperialism; it also indicates that English is not yet common ground for everyone (Méndez García and Pérez Cañado 2005: 89). In a meeting between English and non-English speakers for instance, this rule of thumb obviously downplays the non-English-speaking party. Language then installs a distortion in the power/authority balance. Whereas language becomes a means of power for the English speaking parties, it often becomes a shackle for those who do not sufficiently command the English language. A lack of linguistic competence can at worst literally lead to 'excommunication'; for silence is often the last resort for those who, to their own great annoyance, are unable to voice their opinion. Park *et al.* (1996: 87) have described the detrimental by-products of the language selection process as a sense of peripherality and autistic hostility which respectively mean a distancing from the communication network, and an avoidance of communication.

The following section seeks to transpose the findings of the multinational organization to the context of the international military organization. It sketches situations and observations in which language determines the outcome of international military communication.

Language and communication in multinational military cooperation

Because military operations over time evolved into global affairs, the characteristics and hence problems of military organizations started to resemble those of multinationals (van Dijk and Soeters 2008). A participant observation of two commanding officers at Kabul International Airport in this regard confirms the finding that the presence and proliferation of different languages in a multinational operation confronts its members with problems that affect the managerial process (Resteigne and Soeters 2008). The field study exemplifies the (im)practicality of linguistic (in)competence, and demonstrates the powerful position of language nodes within the organization (Feely and Harzing 2003). One of the observed officers was a multilinguist who spoke French, English, German and Dutch fluently. His language proficiency enabled him to receive, influence and transmit information. Whereas the linguistic skills of this particular officer allowed him to become the (in)formal adviser of soldiers from various countries, the other, less linguistically talented, officer experienced great difficulties with the language barrier. His linguistic shortcomings prevented him from taking a proactive stance in communication processes and ultimately condemned him to passively wait for information to reach him (Resteigne and Soeters 2008). In contrast to those who are greatly inconvenienced and impaired by the language barrier, language nodes, like the talented commander, thus often occupy powerful positions within organizations (Vaara *et al.* 2005). They are described as 'gate-keepers', because they can pass or block information between parties. As such language nodes can establish a parallel information network within the organization which either supports or subverts collaboration (Feely and Harzing 2003: 46).

Another field study at Kabul International Airport (see Chapter 14, this volume) illustrates the process of professional incapacitation and isolation as detrimental effects of the language barrier (Feely and Harzing 2003). It relates a situation in which medics at the airport did not sufficiently command the English language and who were therefore deemed unable to provide medical care during an emergency. As a consequence of the poor linguistic skills of the medics, people decided to drive through high-risk territory in order to receive medical support at the German medical facilities at ISAF headquarters. The Spanish medics clearly had trouble translating the medical argot from their mother tongue into English. In order to prevent similar situations, (medical) staff personnel often rely on the service of interpreters (Bos and Soeters 2006: 261–268). But even they at times are not immune to the effects of the language barrier. Two medical examiners, for instance, have written a report about language problems and cultural barriers they and their interpreters encountered in the assessment and treatment of enemy prisoners of war, hired local workers and foreign civilians during Operation Enduring Freedom and Operation Iraqi Freedom (Griffeth and Bally 2006: 258–259). It appeared that although the interpreters were brought up in Arabic-speaking households and were acquainted with Arabic customs, they too sometimes encountered difficulties. The interpreters not only had problems understanding the Iraqi language and traditions, they also had difficulties translating the medical and mental health vocabulary.

The above-mentioned examples demonstrate that language proficiency or a lack thereof, either ease or hinder the wheels of internal and external communication. Through a discussion of a field study which was conducted during an international military exercise in Germany, the final section of this chapter attempts to discover ways in which language (in)competence influences the job performance of key players within international military organizations.

Exercise Kindred Sword: a close look at the implications of multinational military cooperation and communication

Exercise Kindred Sword took place in Lehnin, Germany between 14 May and 25 May 2007. This Command Post Exercise was part of three closely linked Maritime, Land and Air Component training exercises whose aim was to test the combat readiness of the participating units. It was designed to train the command and control elements of the staff of the headquarters of the German–Netherlands multinational corps, (1) GE-NL Corps, in the context of its role as a NATO Response Force.[1] In their effort to sustain stability and peace in times of need, the multinational NRF components depend upon extensive and detailed cooperation within and between the units. It goes without saying that communication in this matter makes or breaks the operational effectiveness of both military exercises and real expeditionary missions. A field study at the (1) GE-NL Corps headquarters offered an exceptional opportunity to observe and analyse how language proficiency influenced the planning, coordination and team work skills of the military representatives of the participating nations.[2]

At the beginning of the field study it became apparent that language appealed to the imagination. The subject triggered people to speak about their own experience. Officers from various ranks and cells showed interest and offered their opinion on international and inter-organizational communication processes. Significant about the majority of these accounts was that although language was always introduced and labelled by the interviewees as a bothersome but bridgeable inconvenience, their experience ultimately tended to tell a more discriminating story. It was as if the recollections of these non-native speakers were intended to make public what the military mind and hence organization was not yet willing to accept or display. That is, that language, and more specifically a lack of linguistic proficiency, touches not only the heart but also the sore spots of military cooperation. It was therefore no coincidence that a Dutch officer, who was part of the CIMIC cell during the exercise in Lehnin, therefore mentioned that the heraldic motto of the (1) GE-NL Corps 'Communitate Valemus' ('Together We are Strong') was not always appropriate. He remembered a situation at the end of his deployment in Kabul 2002 which according to him was illustrative of the communication problems of Kindred Sword.

> When our troops changed guards with 1GNC battalion we noticed that some of the soldiers had changed the caption of their insignias. The official slogan read 'Communitate Valemus' but they had altered it into 'Communicate Problemus'. Hilarious as it was, the joke also unnerved me. It gave me food for thought. It made me think about the motives for their self-mockery or even self-criticism.

The anecdote refers specifically to the language barrier that hampered the cooperation in the (1) GE-NL Corps. Although English was the military lingua franca, the English language proficiency of German soldiers was often so inadequate that Dutch soldiers, in order to communicate more easily, switched to the German language. According to another Dutch military commander working for the 'red force' during the exercise, Dutch soldiers did exactly what most of Dutch citizens naturally tend to do when they meet people who neither speak Dutch nor English: they tried to address their German colleagues in their own language. Similar linguistic strategies of situational code-switching between actors from different countries in a bilateral (business) cooperation have also been described in a case study of a Dutch parent company that runs a holiday centre in Germany (Loos 2007: 37, 44, 50, 54). In anticipation of a prospective rise in German tourists, this particular Dutch organization implemented a German language policy for their (Dutch) personnel. Both situations prove that the readiness to address people in their own language does not solely arise from a demonstration of sympathy or a gesture of courtesy. The choice of language rather rests on the presence of common objectives and the willpower 'to make things work' (Loos 2007: 46, 51; Moelker *et al.* 2007). Efficacy and the corresponding interdependence of key players, apparently form an incentive to overcome cultural and linguistic differences by adapting a language strategy that serves shared interests. Applied to the (1) GE-NL Corps, this hypothesis signifies that Dutch soldiers, because of a lack of English proficiency of their German colleagues, needed to 'shift gears' in order to optimize the cooperation between Dutch and German units. Temporarily abandoning English in favour of German as the unofficial military lingua within the (1) GE-NE Corps, enabled Dutch and Germans to pursue their tasks and attain their goals as a true corps befits.

In the course of time the initial bilateral cooperation of (1) GE-NL Corps, however, has been expanded and transformed into a worldwide affair that encompasses more than 20 NATO member states. It goes without saying that the importance of language proficiency increased proportionately with the amount of participating countries. English could therefore no longer be passed over as the ruling military lingua franca (de Swaan 2001). In multinational teams as the NRF it simply is no longer possible to get round the language barrier by 'switching codes'. In order to partake fully in the organization, members need to acquire a certain level of English proficiency (Crossey 2005). It is then that the language barrier starts to take effect and gets tough on non-native-English speakers. Although the interviews and conversations with Dutch, German, French, Spanish, Italian, Greek, Polish, Norwegian, Finnish, and English (non-)commissioned officers displayed a variety of phenomena that accompanied the language barrier, the interviewees mentioned the loss of face as one of the most feared and poignant effects of linguistic incompetence (see also Park *et al.* 1996; Jones 2005). Significant in this regard was the fact that whether or not people were speaking out of personal experience or had learned from observing the struggle of other non-native-English speakers, each identically linked the loss of face to the public domain and more specifically to meetings and conferences. The below-mentioned quotations come from interviews with respectively a Norwegian officer and a Spanish officer who participated in exercise Kindred Sword.

> Non-native-language speakers are not so much as pushed out of the decision making process by the fluency of native speaking participants, it's more likely that they themselves feel so uncomfortable and awkward talking in the target language that they unwillingly refrain themselves from the communication process. [...] At the end of a meeting for instance, the chairman always asks if everyone agrees with what has been said. Well, this confronts non-native speakers with a problem. If they do not agree, they have to argue why they think otherwise – and this is not an option for those who feel uncomfortable speaking in a second language. But then again, if you agree

with the rest while in fact you do not exactly understand what you have agreed, you might run the risk of having to answer questions before your superiors about matters you do not know of. It's a double trap. What you see is that people keep a low profile in the hope that other's don't address them and don't ask them any questions.

It's hard to express yourself in a new language. It's difficult to learn a new vocabulary, let alone the technical jargon of a particular mission such as during this exercise. [...] I feel ridiculous always needing the help of others. [...] When the telephone rings, I try to be at the other side of the office so that someone else answers the call. I am afraid that when I do pick up the phone, the person at the other end of the line commands even less English or that he speaks in abbreviations and technical argot. I would be at a loss, the conversation would be a disaster. In the beginning it was the same with attending meetings. I didn't feel comfortable with my language skills and therefore didn't dare to speak out in the presence of high ranked officers. My lack of language proficiency even kept me from joining informal meetings. Therefore I sometimes felt that I was missing out on information. But over time, when I became more familiar with my colleagues, I gained more confidence and learned to express myself more often.

The quotes illustrate that, in situations wherein participants considered their language skills to be insufficient, non-native-English speakers rather preferred to remain silent as an attempt to uphold a positive image of role fulfilment (see also Jones 2005: 74). Silence in communication, however, does not always have to be the product of inarticulacy and hence a face-saving strategy. The silence of non-native-English speakers might in certain situations as well be perceived as contextually and culturally defined behaviour (Tatar 2005: 285). In cultures where silence is related to careful thinking and planning, it can function as a reaction to excessive talk and meaningless contributions of others during meetings. Moreover, silence can also be the product of modesty and respect for authority. In this particular instance people remain silent unless they are directly addressed (Tatar 2005: 288–291).

The observations and interviews during Kindred Sword demonstrated that, whereas language incompetence restricts and perhaps even reduces one's voice in the decision making process, language proficiency conversely increases one's hold on communication and information channels (Vaara et al. 2005; Marschan-Piekkari et al. 1999: 430; Park et al. 1996: 86–89). The assumption that native-English speakers in this regard would have a head start on their colleagues is, however, only partially true for the advantage of their fluency paradoxically also happens to be their flaw. Non-native-English speakers repeatedly referred to their British colleagues as examples of an inarticulate and incomprehensible use of language (see also Chapter 6, this volume). A German non-commissioned officer was even strongly convinced that the British deliberately tried to manipulate the communication process by using complex words: 'They tend to outplay the others by their use of English. Language then no longer is used as a tool but as a weapon. The power play doesn't include the Americans. They are more open and outgoing, more social.'

Less hostile but equally critical was the experience of a French officer. He told about the difficulty he experienced understanding his British colleague:

> Speaking the official military language, the British are often harder to understand than non-native English speakers. You could understand single words, but at the end of the sentence I am always clueless about what he was talking about [...]. I would rather prefer to command a German/Dutch type of English than British English.

According to the French officer, the language barrier could be categorized into problems of *hearing* and *understanding*. While non-native-English speakers might cause problems related to hearing because of their bad pronunciation and accent, native speakers on the other hand could create problems of understanding due to the specific use of their grammar, syntax, sense of humour, and – remarkably enough – sometimes their accent too (see also Chapter 6 and 11, this volume). Remarkable in this regard was the fact that these conceptions, perceptions, and theories about native and non-native-English speakers were not communicated and therefore not known to the involved parties. Instead of addressing and giving voice to these language-related sentiments and sensitivities, there was a strong (and implicit) tendency of the military staff personnel 'to beat about the bush' or hush the language matter whenever the subject came up for discussion (van Dijk and Soeters 2008). This evasive behaviour could perhaps best be interpreted as a sensible and tacit strategy to alleviate the consequences of the language barrier. The fact of the matter, nevertheless, is that a cautious approach in this regard will only clutter the channels of clear communication. The language barrier, and not the military organization, as was so carefully intended, will benefit from prudence. Creating a taboo about language problems, after all, will only uphold and not tear down the pillars of miscommunication.

In conclusion, the interviews and the observations tend to reflect a rather ambivalent and even discordant image of the military stance on the influence of language on communication processes and cooperation. Language proficiency of the military lingua franca officially is considered an expected quality of the (1) GE-NL Corps staff personnel. According to the data gathered during the field study, this expectation, however, was not yet fully realized and could therefore, if not anticipated properly, contribute to an unfounded carelessness towards language policies. Negligence could cause the detrimental effects of the language barrier to be overlooked and trivialized. In order to effectuate an efficient communication between headquarters and the theatre of operations, the military therefore needs to be ready for some tough talk on a matter which will not restrict itself to the military exercises.

Epilogue

When all people share the same tongue, language can easily be described as an unrivalled unifier. The opposite, as this chapter hopes to have demonstrated, unfortunately is also true. Language is an unequalled divider as well. It is, par excellence, a factor which can separate and divide relations within and between members of multinational organizations when its 'barrier' is not detected and dismantled in time. In order to make language a potential military resource for effective communication and cooperation, staff personnel should first and foremost become aware of the detrimental effects of linguistic problems. Instead of treating linguistic proficiency as a matter of course, and downplaying the problems of the less linguistic proficient (non-)commissioned officers within the organization, the military should take up the responsibility to manage language matters properly. Communication after all consists of language, and the latter can only fortify the former when the interdependence between both is rightly understood and consequently addressed.

Notes

The author would like to thank the following persons for their support, assistance, and cooperation: General De Jonge, Lieutenant-Colonel Van Rijssen, Lieutenant-Colonel Sampanis, Lieutenant-Colonel DeLaittre, and Lieutenant-Colonel Manzoni. The author would like to give special thanks to Sergeant Platenburg for rendering a ready-made anecdote, and Major Bokodi and Major Kuin for their willingness to share their expertise and companionship. Finally, the author would like to thank Prof. Dr Soeters for his close reading and inspiring concepts.

1 The information described in this section was based on the following web page: www.gnn.gov.uk/imagelibrary/downloadMedia.asp?MediaDetailsID=201621.htm.
2 In the period of 12–17 May a total of approximately 14 face-to-face interviews were carried out with international participants of the multinational military exercise Kindred Sword. The field study could not have been possible without the support of Lieutenant-Colonel Van Rijssen and Lieutenant-Colonel Sampanis.

Part II

Case studies

Chapter 6

The British way in war

The UK approach to multinational operations

Anthony King

Introduction

In 2001, the newly established Joint Doctrine and Concepts Centre[1] published the second version of British Defence Doctrine (Joint Warfare Publication 0–01 2001). In stark contrast with the traditional scepticism of the British military to written doctrine, the publication represented a constitutional statement for the British forces in the post-Cold War era. The document identified six essential elements of British defence doctrine; 'the principles of war, the warfighting ethos, the manoeuvrist approach, the application of mission command, the joint, integrated and multinational nature of operations, the inherent flexibility and pragmatism of British doctrine' (JWP 0–01 2001: 3–1). It also stressed the importance of multinational operations:

> the ability to operate with the armed forces of other nations is an essential quality to be deployed on operations [...]. A clear understanding of the ways in which other nations' armed forces operate and the ability to merge units from several nations into one cohesive force, are increasingly important factors in the conduct of military operations.
>
> (JWP 0–01 2001: 3–8)

However, for preceding generations of British officers the notion that multinationality was a principle that needed to be stated, let alone emphasised would have been extremely strange.[2] It was utterly self-evident that the British fought alongside allies. Almost every famous battle which the British Army has fought on the four continents of America, Europe, Africa and Asia involved a coalition. Waterloo was only one of the more spectacular of these coalition victories. On 18 June 1815, Wellington's army was 67,000 strong but only 24,000 were British. For Basil Liddell Hart, the Napoleonic Wars represented a distinctively 'British way of war' which endured from the seventeenth to twentieth centuries. The Britain Army, principally engaged in colonial policing, operated periodically on Continental Europe as a small, professional force alongside indigenous allies while the Royal Navy protected Britain's imperial interests around the globe. JWP 0–01's concern with multinational operations represents a re-statement of an enduring aspect of British military activity which was only ever subordinated during the Cold War. British forces have historically always engaged in multinational operations. They now prioritise these operations once again.

Britain willingly engages in multinational operations today but these missions raise new difficulties both for British forces and its allies. As the six principles of British defence doctrine reveal, Britain's forces have a distinctive organisational culture. In particular, the warfighting ethos, the concept of mission command and the flexibility and pragmatism of British forces are culturally specific, influencing their approach to multinational operations. It is vital that both British forces and its multinational allies are aware of the distinctiveness of Britain's approach to operations in order to facilitate international cooperation. Drawing on written accounts, observation of British, NATO and EU military practice and interviews with senior British officers, this chapter provides an introduction into some of the distinctive perspectives, understandings and practices which constitute the British approach to multinational operations.[3]

The warfighting ethos

Any consideration of the organisational culture of British forces must prioritise the warfighting ethos at its heart. British forces are actively oriented to high-intensity war-fighting missions which they regard as central to their credibility. They are deeply Clausewitzian in their emphasis on warfighting. The practitioners of limited war in the mid-eighteenth century assumed that it was possible to avoid excessive confrontation in military campaigns. Nations could be persuaded into compliance by mere displays of military force. Carl von Clausewitz utterly disparaged such notions:

> We are not interested in generals who win victories without bloodshed. The fact that slaughter is a horrifying spectacle must make us take war more seriously, but not provide an excuse for gradually blunting our swords in the name of humanity. Sooner or later someone will come along with a sharp sword and hack off our arms.
>
> (Clausewitz 1989: 260)

These sentences have often been misunderstood. Basil Liddell Hart (1933) and, more recently, John Keegan (1993) have taken them as evidence of Clausewitz's bloodlust; he was the 'madhi of the mass' who worshipped slaughter for its own sake. In fact, Clausewitz's point was quite different. He did not disparage limited war. On the contrary, throughout *On War*, he provides numerous examples of very successful limited campaigns. However, he thought it dangerous to believe that the violent dynamic at the heart of warfare could always be appeased. Limited war with few casualties was a highly desirable state of affairs but could only occur if all parties acceded to it. At any point, an opposing nation could precipitate a descent into the familiar vortex of violence culminating ultimately in the absolute struggle of one people against another. To engage in warfare with the belief that it could always be a limited struggle was, for Clausewitz, a dangerous illusion.

During the 1990s, 'post-heroic' interventions into the Balkans have sometimes taken on a caricature of eighteenth-century warfare (Luttwak 1995). The UN and NATO have conducted highly circumscribed operations in the Balkans since 1993 where they have actively sought to avoid any casualties. The United States fought the entire Kosovo Campaign without the loss of a single soldier. The Balkans episode represents only a more general point about current peacekeeping missions. For a significant number of European countries, benign peacekeeping is still regarded as the most desirable form of activity not because it achieves the strategic end state more efficiently but because Western forces simply want to avoid casualties. Yet, while peacekeeping missions in the Balkans were conveniently benign, it is becoming increasingly obvious in Afghanistan and even more so in Iraq that, like Clausewitz's eighteenth-century generals, insurgents are now prepared to sever the arm of sword-waving commanders.

The British armed forces have always taken a Clausewitzian view of warfare but current operational developments have accentuated the warfighting ethos of British forces even more. Consequently, officers have become even more sceptical about multinational operations with forces which prefer to avoid conflict. Britain's warfighting ethos has influenced the attitude of the military towards NATO and the EU in which frameworks many coalitions operations now take place. Although British officers are often deeply sceptical of the United States' use of its military forces, which they, like many others, regard as too 'kinetic', they prioritise US-coalition and NATO operations above all others. They are strongly transatlantic in orientation. It is important to recognise that their commitment to the United States is not ideological; they do not espouse the cultural values of the United States any more than other European officers. The preference for the United States and NATO is a reflection of this warfighting ethos.

Despite this martial bias towards the US and NATO, it would be wrong to suppose that British forces were anti-European in principle. On the contrary, Britain has contributed significant forces to European missions. For instance, the first commander of EUFOR in Bosnia was Major-General David Leakey and Britain, unlike other nations, provided a full battlegroup and brigade headquarters for the Multinational Brigade North West in Banja Luka. The Brigade was de-activated in March 2007 but British presence in EUFOR headquarters is still strong with a British brigadier, with extensive operational experience of the Balkans, acting as Chief of Staff and other important staff posts in the intelligence and operations branches. Significantly, while critical of the ESDP on practical grounds, senior British officers had no ideological objection to it.

> There is nothing to stop us and the French doing work in Africa together. We have the capabilities and the reach [...]. However, it shouldn't be that difficult to do some missions autonomously. In Macedonia in 2001, we did Operation *Essential Harvest* to disarm the Albanian rebels in order to stabilise the region. That was a textbook operation. There was no US involvement. It was done under NATO. It was a good example of what might be possible. And the NRF should be able to do all that.
>
> (British major-general, personal interview, 29 March 2006)

EUFOR's British Chief of Staff similarly emphasised the competence of EUFOR: 'The EU is fine for this mission. It is all about horses for courses, I have no problem with it. But you have to take some of the rhetoric with an appetite suppressant' (personal interview, 22 February 2007). For the Chief of Staff, the grand statements about the ESDP could not be swallowed; Europeans had to reduce their appetites for European military development so that digestibly realistic reforms could be made. However, while the self-interested exaggerations emanating from Solana's office are treated with scepticism, British forces are not averse to European military development. However, they prioritise military capabilities and the professional will to engage in serious operations.

Their warfighting ethos heavily influences the British military's interpretation of their multinational partners. The *Bundeswehr*, in particular, is viewed with dismay by many British officers. It is regarded as a hollow force, constrained by domestic politics, history and a highly educated but timid officer corps.

> Think of Germany. In Cold War days we used to admire them. They had great kit. Their senior officers in the *Bundeswehr* in the early days were still from the German military caste, with experience or fathers with experience in the Wehrmacht and with grandfathers who fought in World War I. But that has gone; they are in danger of forgetting that armies exist to fight.
>
> (British major-general, personal interview, 29 March 2006)

Although the reference to the *Wehrmacht* will be politically unpalatable to German officers given its complicity with Nazism, the major-general's perspective is not unusual. There is a common belief among British officers that as the generation of German officers with Second World War experience retired from the *Bundeswehr* in the 1970s, the force has declined as a significant military entity. Indeed, one British officer with operational experience in Iraq and Afghanistan stated that:

> countries, like Germany, who have no interest in fighting itself should consider financially supporting those that do. Perhaps they should consider giving us their helos [helicopters] if they don't want to fly them a night or into contacts. We could then contract in the pilots.
>
> (British lieutenant-colonel, personal interview, 22 March 2007)

By contrast, the British have been particularly impressed by the possibility of new partnerships with new European and NATO countries. As the cited major-general emphasised: 'I have been impressed with smaller newer nations such as Poland'. Affirming the point, the Estonian company attached to the 3 PARA battlegroup in Helmand in 2006 distinguished itself. The Estonians were initially frustrated by being held back by the Helmand Task Force while they gained experience. However, by the end of the tour in October 2006, the Estonians were not only willing to do anything they were asked but had the confidence of the commanding officer of 3 PARA who tasked them to conduct all but the most difficult missions. On the basis of his experiences, the commanding officer of 3 PARA suggested that 'Perhaps, we should more look to eastern Europe' (personal interview, 22 March 2007). 3 Commando Brigade who took over Helmand from 3 PARA were particularly complimentary about the Danes. Senior officers in 3 Commando Brigade believed that as long as attached multinational forces were given clear missions and no artificial attempt was made to integrate them into existing Brigade units, they functioned very well. A warfighting ethos frames British force's understanding of multinational operations and their willingness of participate in them. With its warfighting ethos, the British are anxious to work alongside nations who recognise the realities of conflict, whatever their provenance. Consequently, they favour NATO over EU missions. The problem for multinational partners working with Britain is not only that Britain oriented to high-intensity operations but their warfighting ethos can often induce arrogance in them, where they are actively dismissive of less experienced multinational partners.

British vs NATO command culture

British forces, like their allies, recognise that in order to conduct multinational operations successfully, a degree of interoperability is essential but this compatibility is not reducible to equipment. On the contrary, forces must be conceptually and practically attuned to each other. NATO has, of course, always disseminated common doctrine and procedure. Since the end of the Cold War, however, as nations have had to cooperate with each other at ever lower levels, NATO has been a crucial agent for convergence. It has actively precipitated the development of increasingly shared doctrine and practices among western armed forces. At the operational level, one of the most significant developments in the last decade has been the development, certification and dissemination of NATO's Guideline for Operational Planning (GOP). In the face of new strategic circumstances in the 1990s, NATO began to develop new methods for operational planning informally in order to deal with non-Article 5 deployments. Out of this initially ad hoc process, the Guideline for Operational Planning (the GOP) emerged in the late 1990s, the most recent version of which was ratified in June 2005. The GOP lays out a single, established structure and method for operational planning, from initial situational analysis to the eventual issuing of the commander's directive. The GOP represents the appearance of common operational concepts and practices. It has been disseminated, formally, through the NATO School and the Joint Warfare Centre and, practically, through NATO operational headquarters.

The GOP envisages a distinctive staff-led headquarters where the Commander's inputs are limited to approving the staff's work and selecting the proposed courses of action. Precisely because NATO is a coalition, it is presumed that a NATO commander will spend far more time than a national commander negotiating with the Supreme Allied Commander and with his subordinate commanders in the assigned multinational forces. Consequently, his staff needs to do more of the work for him; the staff-led GOP system institutionalises this organisational fact. For the staff, the GOP has some distinctive features. The GOP involves five lengthy stages: Initiation, Orientation, Concept Development, Plan Development and Plan Review. Stage II is especially cumbersome, when the staff re-confirms the parameters of the mission through the production of a mission statement. The exhaustive analysis of the mission prescribed by the GOP is essential in a coalition of 26 nations where each must consent fully to the designated mission. The staff must, therefore, ensure that the mission for which they plan accords precisely with the guidance of the North Atlantic Council (NAC). The GOP, then, envisages a specific command culture in NATO operational headquarters; the headquarters is organised as a staff led-system in which the commander has limited inputs but where he has great directive authority. Although certainly exaggerated in NATO, this command culture is evident in the United States, Germany and France.

Although committed to NATO, a quite different command culture exists in the British forces. British command culture emphasises flexibility and pragmatism. As British doctrine emphasises: 'Commanders must be conditioned to think constantly of new ways of approaching an objective [...]. This combination of flexibility and pragmatism is absolutely necessary for the successful conduct of the modern range of military operations' (Joint Warfare Publication 0–01 2001: 3.9). To illustrate the point, JWP 0–01 symbolically invokes T.E. Lawrence (Lawrence of Arabia); 'Nine-tenths of tactics are certain and taught in books; but the irrational tenth is like the kingfisher flashing across the pool, and that is the test of generals' (JWP 0–01: 3.9). Indeed, in British operational doctrine, the pre-eminence of the commander is emphasised at the outset with a quotation from Field Marshal Montgomery:

> I will not on any account be drawn away from first principles: that it is for commanders to make plans and give directions, and staffs then to work out the details of those plans; on no account will I have a plan forced on me by a planning staff.
>
> (Joint Warfare Publication 5.00 2004a: 2–1)

Montgomery's point has been recently echoed by General Rupert Smith, recognised to be one of the most brilliant commanders of his generation:

The operational level commander stands astride the political/military interface with his weight on the military foot. His mastery of the art of war, tested against that of his opponent, links the successful achievement of strategic objective with the actions of his command. He must have a broad understanding of the science of war but it is he, and he alone, who paints the masterpiece.

(Joint Warfare Publication 01 2004b: 5.1)

For the British, the commander actively controls and sculpts his own campaign.

The command culture of British forces is reflected in the planning procedures of British operational headquarters. Thus, Britain, including NATO's British-led Allied Rapid Reaction Corps, does not use the GOP. It has developed its own independent planning process, called the Estimate. This process is closely compatible with the GOP. It employs exactly the same concepts and follows the same logic of the GOP in identifying viable courses of action and selecting the best. However, there are also some notable differences. The Estimate Process is a commander, not staff-led process. In British operational headquarters, the commander plays an interventionist role. This alternative command culture is reflected in some significant differences between the British Estimate and the NATO GOP. In particular, the initial stages of the British Estimate process are conceived and organised differently to the GOP. The first two steps of the Estimate, 'Review of the Situation' (Step 1) and 'Identify and Analyse the Problem' (Step 2), are more streamlined than the GOP. More significantly, in Step 2, the Commander conducts Step 2a, the Mission Analysis, while the Staff performs Step 2b, the Initial Object Analysis. The commander identifies the purposes, tasks and constraints of the mission which he has been given. It is his responsibility to define precisely what his headquarters and the forces under his command must do. His staff meanwhile analyse the enemy and the theatre in which operations will occur. This division of labour is intended to empower the commander in setting the parameters of the mission. The commander takes critical framing decisions independently, channelling the staff effort pre-emptively. It facilitates the production of a coherent plan, informed throughout by the unifying direction from the commander.

The Estimate presumes a high level of competence on the part of the commander and British headquarters give a great deal of latitude to the 'intuition' of the commander. Indeed, in Britain, there has been some criticism of the shackles which even a relatively flexible 'rational' planning procedure like the Estimate currently places on headquarters. These criticisms have been articulated in a number of discussion papers. For instance, in an issue of the Army's Strategic and Combat Studies Institute series, the adoption of more naturalistic planning methods in place of the Estimate process has been proposed. Instead of slavishly following procedure,

naturalistic methods depend on the recognition of the situation as being similar to, or typical of, situations with which the decision maker is already familiar. The decision maker can then envisage a solution to the problem, which based on experience, is probably 'about right'.

(Storr 2002b: 50)

Naturalistic methods, utilising the experience of the commander, are better suited to situations of great time pressure (Storr 2002b: 51). By contrast, it has been claimed by some British officers that, not only do the cumbersome 'rational choice strategies' like the Estimate often fail to produce better solutions, but they can become mere charades, justifying courses of action which have already been accepted (2002b: 50). It is unlikely that 'intuition' will be formally incorporated into British planning doctrine but, in practice, the commander's experience (his intuition) is a decisive factor in the planning process in British headquarters; British forces make institutional room for the 'kingfisher flashing across the pool'. It allows the general to paint his masterpiece. In the GOP by contrast, the staff laboriously analyses the conditions of the mission and affirm all the factors before they can begin planning courses of action properly. It is important that other nations are aware of the distinctiveness of British command culture.

Flexibility and pragmatism

The dangers of the Estimate process and British's commander-led culture are evident. The commander's intuitions could be faulty. He could overlook factors or misinterpret his mission and there is little formal way for the staff to control a mistaken commander. The commander has the authority to frame and, indeed, to drive the planning effort. However, in the British context the commander-led process functions effectively because of the centrality of flexibility and pragmatism to British military culture. The commander can be given precedence in the planning process and latitude in the exercise of his initiative because commanders are trained to be sensitive to direction from their staff. As a result of the organisational emphasis on flexibility and pragmatism, commanders often enjoy relaxed and open relations with their subordinates. Successful British commanders actively look to the staff to confirm and develop their intuitions. This openness between the staff and commander can surprise multinational colleagues. For instance, the current EUFOR Chief of Staff recorded both the different command style of British officers and the reaction of other nations to it:

> There are different national cultures and personality traits. For me personally, I put a premium on the passage of information. I expect people to talk to people and to talk to me – and I will talk to them. In other countries, the Brigadier-General rank has enormous status; it is a general officer rank. People here say 'We have not had a COS like you'. In a US HQ, a Brigadier has general officer status.
>
> (British brigadier, personal interview, 21 February 2007)

At the operational level, British armed forces have a distinctively open command style. It is flexible and pragmatic. This style is effective at the national level where the officer corps is united about a common professional code but it may impair multinational operations, especially for officers used to more staff-led techniques embodied in the GOP where the commander has a more distant relationship.

The flexibility and pragmatism of British command culture is manifested most obviously in the extensive use of irony by British commanders. Indeed, the importance of humour to current military operations is formally recognised by the British armed forces: 'It is highly desirable that they [commanders] have a sense of humour; the importance of this in maintaining morale and motivation should never be downplayed' (Joint Warfare Publication 2001: 7.3). Humour does more than merely sustain morale, however. It is a critical medium of communication across and between the ranks. By means of humour, British forces temporarily bracket their hierarchical and formal military relations with each other allowing them to communicate critical information, beliefs or sentiments which are obstructed by formal rank divisions. Irony is a central resource for British officers when negotiating relations with multinational allies. It is a means of reining in errant commanders and passing unpalatable piece of information around the headquarters. It is crucial to a commander-led system.

Today, one of the British generals most adept at utilising irony, flexibility and pragmatism is General David Richards. As Commander ISAF IX in 2006, General Richards demonstrated great virtuosity in unifying the 37 nations under his command to the mission. He exploited irony frequently as a means of encouraging cooperation. A recent British television programme on General Richards and the ISAF mission usefully recorded the methods he employed to sustain the alliance.[4] The programme followed General Richards as he flew out to Herat to visit the joint Italian and Spanish command of Region West. During the flight, he was interviewed by the film crew. As he explained his rationale for the trip, he began to develop a humorous motif which would be drawn upon recurrently throughout his televised visit. He began by saying, 'I know I'll eat well' but corrected himself for comic effect: 'I'd better eat well, that's the only reason I'm going'. Of course, the real reason for his visit was quite different and was revealed immediately afterwards to the camera crew:

> You do have to massage national and individual egos a bit to make sure they remain together as a team. I am not in any way comparing myself to Eisenhower but I know now why he was considered a great man.

The visit to Herat may have had little obvious operational effect and Richards' purpose was not to give the headquarters any precise guidance. Nevertheless, it was operationally crucial. The aim of the visit was to encourage ever greater levels of commitment and cooperation from the Italians and the Spanish through personal contact with them. The humorous reference to the quality of the food –

in stark comparison to British gastronomy (which Richards implicitly depre-cated) – provided him with the means of stimulating this commitment without causing offence. He was not imposing his authority on the Spanish and the Ital-ians. He staged the visit as if he were a guest, sampling their hospitality, while denigrating British standards.

Within this frame, however, the purpose of Richards' visit became clear. Following a briefing by the headquarters, Richards gave his conclusion:

> I would just like to pass my thanks and congratulations on to other people who are not here. But [I extend] my thanks and congratulations and particu-larly to see such strong joint effort between my two very able commanders. [Sat between the two commanders, he grasped both their arms at this point to emphasise their unity.] Who says multinationality can't work? Well you're making it work. So many, many thanks.

Here, Richards performed precisely the massaging which he recognised as an essential to stimulating multinational cooperation. He flattered the commanders and the headquarters and explicitly thanked them for their efforts. Strictly speak-ing, they were under his command and he had the authority to order them to perform their duties. However, he assiduously avoided such an authoritarian style, preferring to emphasise his indebtedness to them. By stressing his reliance on them – rather than their subordination to him – he hoped to engender the highest levels of performance from them. Of course, implicitly, he was confirm-ing their activities and demanding better cooperation with ISAF HQ but through his self-deprecation, his authority was softened. He concluded his summary by drawing upon the gastronomic motif, thereby conducting professional command relations through the medium of informal, social interactions: 'And now to a good lunch'.

Lunch affirmed Richard's strategy of using informal techniques and humour to promote good multinational relations. Although the commander of NATO's most demanding mission, Richards adopted a genial and relaxed manner at lunch. While NATO forces were facing a number of crises, Richards joked over lunch: 'We are running into a bit of problem – we have run out of vintage [champagne]. We only have normal champagne'. Finally, in the broadcast, having toasted the multinational effort and Afghanistan, he declared, 'Let's call this afternoon a bust'. In fact, while Richards is admired for his flexibility, his staff officers note that he is intolerant of poor time-keeping. Presumably, he was able to perform the arduous role of Commander ARRC and ISAF only insofar as he was strict about time. Yet, during this lunch in Herat, he was apparently insouciant about time. It seems unlikely that Richards had, in fact, become care-less about time under the influence of some vintage champagne. It was rather more likely that he did not actually regard this afternoon drinking champagne with the Spaniards and Italians as a 'bust'. Rather, it represented a crucial infor-mal method of interacting with them in order to unify his command. It is an unconventional approach to command but it is not an unusual one in the British armed forces. General Richards is certainly a fine practitioner of self-deprecation and irony but, in this he represents, only the command philosophy of British forces and the professional culture of the British officer corps more widely. He exemplifies the flexibility and pragmatism of British military culture.

Yet, the use of irony can also be problematic for multinational operations. For instance, in one of the daily ISAF Commanders' Update Briefing in Afghanistan in July 2006, the meteorological officer asserted that the wind would die away in the next few days implying better flying conditions.[5] General Richards turned quizzically to the officer and asked ironically, 'How do you know that the wind will die away? Is that just a case of meteorological intuition?', inducing a laugh from the meeting and from the met officer himself. In fact, Richards point was serious. He was assessing the reliability of the weather forecast, which is vital for military operations, especially in the air, without undermining the credibility of an important member of his staff. British officers recognised the implication but it is uncertain whether multinational partners would always understand the significance of these oblique remarks. They might never recognise the hidden pointedness of General Richards' ironic remark about the weather. Similarly, the British are sometimes insensitive to the subtlety of their irony which is missed by multinational peers.

Indeed, there is evidence that multinational partners sometimes struggle to comprehend British irony. For instance, on a widely circulated cartoon in NATO headquarters, the problems of British irony and understatement are highlighted. Instead of taking the best characteristics of each nation to produce the ideal Alliance officer, the cartoon satirically describes the 'perfect' NATO officer as having the worst characteristics of each nation. Thus, the perfect NATO officer would have the flexibility of the Americans, the humour of the Germans, the humility of the French, the activity of the Spanish and the straightforwardness of the British. British straightforwardness is depicted as a floppy-haired British officer in civilian clothes leaning casually across the desk of a finance clerk. While apparently, chatting congenially with the clerk, the shadow depicts the British officer shaking him by the ankles wringing money out of him. The cartoon is intended to ridicule the elliptical irony of many British officers where apparently deferential comments are tantamount to direct commands.

Of course, the issue of irony is closely linked up with language use. One of the problems with multinational operations is not that the British sense of humour is intrinsically mysterious but that the heavy use of irony requires high levels of linguistic virtuosity to understand what is being implied. It is entirely conceivable that a non-native speaker could comprehend an ironic British comment perfectly and yet completely misunderstand its significance. British forces are often insensitive to the advantages which their native language gives them in certain operations. They do not always allow for non-native speakers and continue to use sophisticated irony where hints and innuendo communicate something quite different to what the actual sentence means. The current

EUFOR Chief of Staff emphasised the language issue. He was critical of British officers who failed to speak NATO English, arrogantly preferring their own rapid and idiomatic cadences. Illustrating the point, he cited a conversation with the current French commander of the Multinational Brigade in Mostar recently who had noted that the absence of English-speaking officers in his headquarters improved communications. Since all officers in Mostar were non-native speakers, none employed colloquial or idiomatic language which was typical among British and American officers.

Of course, it is not only British officers who employ humour and informal interaction in order to encourage cohesion within multinational operations. General Py, as ISAF IV commander, was also a virtuoso at encouraging contributions from his subordinates. He too recognised that he had to persuade not command and his urbane manner proved very successful. However, British humour is an intrinsic element of a flexible and pragmatic organisational culture. This culture, with its emphasis on warfighting, distinguishes the British approach. It is a source of military strength for the British but especially combined with linguistic problems, it can impair British interactions with their multinational partners.

Mission command

During the twentieth century, as the British army expanded in size to fulfil Continental duties, it instituted a directive command philosophy in which subordinates were given specific tasks to perform by their commander with little room for manoeuvre in how to achieve them. This command culture reflected strategic and military imperatives of coordinating mass forces for lineal battle. In the face of changing strategic and operational circumstances from the 1970s, the British Army reconsidered its command philosophy. The Army introduced 'mission command' as a doctrine in the late 1980s on the initiative of General Sir Nigel Bagnall. Mission command quickly became central to the British Army after its formal adoption and is now fundamental to everyday practice. The ease with which this doctrine was adopted suggests that a decentralised command philosophy had always permeated the British Army since the seventeenth century due to colonial experiences and the absence of a centralised general staff (Storr 2002a: 43). In the late 1990s, the Royal Navy (which always institutionalised this approach) and the Royal Air Force also formally adopted mission command as an organisational principle. Joint Warfare Publication 0–01 (2001) defines mission command as 'a style of command that promotes decentralized command, freedom and speed of action and initiative, but which is responsive to superior direction'. Once a commander has ensured that subordinates understand his intentions and they are given sufficient resources to carry out their missions, 'subordinates decide for themselves how best to achieve their missions' (Joint Warfare Publication 0–01 2001: 3–7). Although derived from the German word 'auftragstaktik', JWP 0–01 asserts that 'mission command is the British way of achieving this' (Joint Warfare Publication 0–1 2001: 3–7).

The concept of mission command is not just a philosophy in the British forces but is an active principle which informs relations between British commanders and their subordinates. Commanders actively encourage juniors to take the initiative, while subordinates themselves seek to utilise their autonomy. There is evidence of this approach from the highest to the lowest levels. Thus, in 1999, after Serbia finally capitulated to the NATO bombing campaign and withdrew forces from Kosovo, Lieutenant-General Mike Jackson, Commander ARRC, entered Kosovo and began to conduct a campaign of stabilisation all but independently of his nominal commander, General Wesley Clark, SACEUR. He received his OPLAN for the campaign after he had already established himself in theatre. His independence as a commander, brought up in the British tradition, was most obviously demonstrated when he refused to wrest control of Pristina airport from Russian paratroopers at the request of General Clark with the immortal retort, 'Sir, I am not fucking going to start World War III for you'. His comment perhaps illustrated mission command at its most extreme. Indeed, in reference to the incident, General Wesley Clark has emphasised the distinctive command philosophy of British armed forces:

> In the British System, a field commander is supported. Period. That is the rule. A field commander is given mission-type orders, not detailed and continuing guidance. It is a wonderful, traditional approach, one that embodies trust in the commander and confidence in his judgement as the man on the scene. The American military has always aspired to this model, but has seldom seemed to attain it.
>
> (Clark 2001: 396)

A similar process is evident in Afghanistan. In the course of 2006, the transition of full authority of the operational theatre to ISAF occurred; the US-led Operation *Enduring Freedom* was rolled into the NATO ISAF operation. As NATO assumed command responsibility for Afghanistan, it became apparent that no individual or agency was taking responsibility for significant areas of policy especially in relation to the international relations with neighbouring countries, above all Pakistan. With no direction from JFC Brunssum or from SHAPE, General Richards recognised this lacuna and following his experiences in Africa began to act as a roving NATO ambassador in their region initiating crucial discussions with President Musharraf and other leaders. There was some scepticism towards his approach among staff at JFC Brunssum and, indeed, there have been active complaints by France that this was transforming NATO into a civilian and political alliance. NATO was effectively colonising space which the French believed was rightfully the EU's. Whatever the operational effect, Richards' activities demonstrated the British principle of mission command at work. Like General Jackson, Richards saw himself as acting within strategic guidance to fulfil his mission.

A commensurate independence is evident in other British forces at a lower level. For instance, on entering Um Qasr in Iraq in March 2003, 42 Commando

Royal Marines, independently of higher direction, began to liaise with the local community. While still engaged in serious military operations, they organised football games with the locals to forge links with the town and began to renovate schools in the area. It is regrettable that the initiative taken by British forces at the tactical level in Iraq has ultimately proved futile due to failings at the strategic level. Similarly, in Helmand, the commanding officer of 3 PARA dissociated his battlegroup from the counter-narcotics campaign for which Britain had nominally taken the lead. His forces did not destroy crops or seize opium. Indeed, they were photographed actively handing opium back to locals in order to ensure their continuing support in the struggle against the Taliban. 3 PARA's Commanding Officer followed his mission guidance with a latitude which might be regarded as extraordinary in other forces.

Mission command raises issues for multinational cooperation and, indeed, British officers have been well aware of the problems of organisational incompatibility due to the different expectations about a commander's relations to his subordinates:

> There have been well-described (if slightly sensitive) examples of where forces from other nations have simply not comprehended the freedom of operation which the British practice of Mission Command affords. Conversely, this author (for one) has been more than mildly surprised by the ruthlessly literal interpretation of Mission Command displayed by the *Bundeswehr*, for example.
>
> (Storr 2002a: 47)

Despite the apparent doctrinal coherence between German and British forces regarding mission command, commanders in the *Bundeswehr* are regarded as overly cautious and meek by the British. They follow their mission to the letter so that their autonomy is severely circumscribed. By contrast, while the French are prepared to intervene forcefully, British officers also note that they implement a highly rigid directive command philosophy so that there have been recent cases where the Chief of Defence staff in Paris ordered tactical activity in Africa.

Certainly, some other nations display a version of mission command which is closer to the British. The Dutch seem to be a clear example here where there is a strong culture of mission command (Vogelaar and Kramer 2004). Yet, even here there are some differences. Dutch mission command is part of a much more democratic military culture which includes unionised forces. As Soeters has noted, there is far less power distance in the Dutch military than in Britain (Soeters 1997). Consequently, in the Dutch armed forces, it is not merely that subordinates are empowered to conduct their mission but that they expect to be treated with respect by the superiors; a more egalitarian culture exists. There are some obvious examples of this. For instance, during the German–Netherlands Brigade's tour in Afghanistan, the German commander reprimanded a Dutch subordinate. After the exchange, the Dutch serviceman returned and threw a dog leash into the officer's room, declaring 'You can talk to a dog like that but not to me'. Demonstrating an alternate notion of mission command, such an act would be unheard of in the British armed force where subordinates are empowered but they are expected to defer to commanders. The commander has overarching authority. Mission command in Britain reflects a distinctive national culture so that even when nations all nominally adopt the doctrine of mission command, they, often, operate in quite different ways.

Conclusion

Western forces today predominantly face irregular insurgency warfare prosecuted by guerrilla or terrorist groups in failing states mobilising on ethnic, racial or religious grounds. They are involved in complex stabilisation operations which far exceed the UN peacekeeping of the Cold War and which differ significantly from the lineal conventional warfare for which western forces have trained for two centuries. Small bodies of professional western soldiers from a diversity of nations are operating together on a dispersed engagement space, coordinating military assets and cooperating with non-military agencies. In this context, multinational forces must demonstrate greater expertise and cooperate with each other more closely. In order to facilitate this deeper integration of multinational forces, it has been necessary to develop shared concepts and practices and, over the last decade, a significant convergence of military expertise has occurred.

Nevertheless, national professional cultures endure. Thus, British headquarters, although nominally compatible with their peers, in fact adopt a distinctive modus operandi which reflects British professional culture. Britain's forces are oriented to warfighting above all else and have developed a distinctive command culture in the prosecution of operations. Because command relations in the British forces are open and flexible, commanders are able to take precedence over the staff process in manner which is unusual. Other nations are likely to find the staff procedures of British headquarters disorientating and the apparent informality of commanders even more so. Similarly, the principle of mission command is highly developed in the British forces so that commanders even at a junior level have a freedom of movement which is not evident in all other forces. This creates problems for allies who are surprised by the independence of British commanders and often critical of it. In return, the British are often unconvinced of the commanders of some other forces who are regarded as far too passive.

There is no way of eliminating these cultural differences. The organisational differences between the armed forces are the product of much deeper divergences in professional culture. In his work on professional status groups, Andrew Abbott (1988) has described how these groups cannot be comprehended independently. Rather, professional groups constitute an interactive network in which the constitution of each group is substantially dependent upon its place in the wider nexus. The culture of each group is a product of its struggles and alliances with other groups. For Abbott, there is a distinctive system of professions in each nation which influences the character of each. In Britain, professional status groups are organised on relatively flat social landscape. Professional status groups – even in the public sector – operate substantially independently of the state. They are able to interact with each other relatively freely on a pragmatic basis to their mutual advantage. In France and Germany, by contrast, professional groups, especially in the public sector, are ordered around a centralising state. The military command culture of the British forces is substantially a product of this wider system of professions in Britain. Precisely because British professions are free from centralising state control, military commanders are able to display significant autonomy. Similarly, the hierarchical ordering of the professions around a state precipitates a centralising command philosophy in France and Germany in which subordinates have less freedom of manoeuvre. Just as the professions more widely are tied to a directing state to which they defer, so military commanders are restricted in their actions. The national system of profession constitutes the cultural and institutional framework in which multinational operations take place. These profound cultural and organisational differences cannot be effaced but they must be mitigated for on multinational operations.

The distinctive organisational culture of the armed forces will not disappear in the coming decades, therefore. The most effective strategy for multinational operations may be to accept these differences rather than seek to deny them. Business organisations have confronted a similar problem as the armed forces. As they have globalised, they tried to retain a unified corporate business culture in order to sustain efficiency. In her work on the global city, Saskia Sassen noted the way that the headquarters of major companies are concentrating into a single, enlarged location to synchronise the activities of subsidiaries and alliance partners globally. These empowered headquarters have typically unified themselves around the home nation culture of the corporation. Corporations have effectively sought to implement a lead-nation approach to business, strengthening the unifying nation element. The armed forces seem to be doing something similar especially in high-intensity theatres such as Afghanistan. Lead-nation headquarters and task forces are becoming the norm. The lead-nation principle may not be ideal but it is likely to be the most realistic solution in the coming decades. Multinational forces are likely to be more effective if national forces, capable of cooperating with each other, similarly concentrate themselves into nodes of military expertise rather than by seeking to eliminate the national element in pursuit of an illusory, frictionless supranational organisation. The inevitably enduring frictions of multinational operations can be mitigated through greater self-conscious awareness of cultural differences among the armed forces themselves. National military cultures will remain and, indeed, are likely to be strengthened as professional expertise condenses, but both British forces and their allies may be able to understand each others' distinct military cultures better so that they can unify themselves on the complex missions which they face. Britain's allies may begin to understand that when a British general says that he is calling an afternoon a 'bust', he may, in fact, mean quite the opposite.

Notes

1 The Joint Doctrine and Concepts Centre was founded in 1997 in order to produce and disseminate British doctrine. In 2006, it was re-designated as a Directorate, the Development, Concepts and Doctrine Centre.
2 Interestingly, recognising the new salience of multinational operations, a British RAF officer, Roger Palin, wrote a long and important piece on multinational operations in 1996.
3 The material on which this chapter is based is taken from a research project on European military transformation, funded by the ESRC (RES-000–22–1461) and British Academy, which has been underway since 2003. The interviews cited here were conducted with officers who have been involved with the ISAF mission in Afghanistan, the EUFOR mission in Bosnia or the NRF. In this way, the interviews are intended to give an insight into current British perspectives of multinational operations from the most benign peace-support operations in Bosnia to high-intensity operations in Afghanistan. The chapter cannot claim to be comprehensive. Only the views of British officers are considered. In total, over 200 British officers have been interviewed for this research from the rank of lieutenant to four-star general. The views of NCOs and soldiers are not considered in this chapter. Although multinational forces are now cooperating with each other at a much lower tactical level than ever before, British forces do not integrate below company level and normally below battalion level. Consequently, for British soldiers and NCOs, the issue of multinational cooperation is not of prime military concern. However, the distinctive military culture involving a warfighting ethos, flexibility and pragmatism and mission command is evident among NCOs and soldiers.
4 *The General's War*, directed by Olly Lambert, broadcast 28 February 2007, BBC 2.
5 Fieldnotes, 13 July 2006.

Chapter 7

A regional recipe for success

Multinational peace operations in East Timor

John R. Ballard

Introduction

On 20 September 1999, Major General Peter Cosgrove of Australia embarked the national contingent commanders of his United Nation's force in a small plane and flew from Australia to Dili, the capital of the break-away Indonesian province of East Timor. When the nine men disembarked in the Dili airport they were met by armed Indonesian army troops and escorted past scenes of horrific devastation around the city. Looting and burning were still in progress. The Indonesian government had agreed to the arrival of the United Nations-sponsored international force after the Timorese had voted for independence, but the situation in East Timor remained extremely volatile.

General Cosgrove had elected not to conduct a forcible assault into East Timor, because only the day prior he had successfully negotiated peaceful access to the island province with Indonesian Major General Kiki Syahnakrie, the local commander. Cosgrove was accepting extreme risk by arriving with only the sponsorship of the UN and the endorsement of the regional partners as protection, yet he did so because of his particularly acute sense of the military and political necessities in East Timor at the time. Indonesian forces would still greatly outnumber his troops for several days and the lawlessness of a region subject to the whims of a rampaging militia would pose threats for weeks, yet General Cosgrove's decisive leadership and military skill ensured the success of his unique mission (Ballard 2002).

After General Cosgrove and his multinational force restored a foundation of security to the area, the United Nations deployed a transitional administration team to East Timor under the direction of Sergio Vieira de Mello of Brazil. The team was the foundation for the United Nations Transitional Administration in East Timor (UNTAET) which was designed to develop the organizational, economic, and social framework for a new nation. UNTAET helped the Timorese create a new government, write a constitution, build a baseline economy and hold free elections over the following two years. In May 2002, Timor Leste became the newest free nation on earth.

These UN operations in Timor established a new rule set for modern military action. In many ways the fruition of a decade of multinational peace operations, they were precedence-setting in their use of a regional power to enact a United Nations mandate. They gave appropriate primary roles to other regional military contingents, which greatly aided in mission accomplishment. They also cast a new role for superpower involvement in the world's crises. The upheaval in East Timor was solved through an extremely effective UN intervention, and as multi-national engagement will be the primary context for military intervention in the forthcoming decades, its lessons should contribute much to future military operations. As multinational interoperability is critical to effective command and control and to maintaining partnerships in the modern battlespace, the lessons learned in East Timor should have an important impact on coming command and control arrangements, future training opportunities, developing doctrine, and the policies of the United Nations.

The background to intervention

Neglect and indifference dominate the history of East Timor.[1] Half an island 400 miles north of Australia with a population of only 800,000, it is dry in summer, rainy in winter, mountainous and malaria-plagued. The island remained free from colonization until the early 1500s, when the first Portuguese traders arrived. The Portuguese moved their colonial Timorese capital to Dili in 1769 and settled into an uneasy trading relationship with the Dutch colonists living on the southern end of the island. Poor colonial management led to open conflict between the Timorese and the Portuguese administrators between 1890 and 1915.

The Second World War brought another form of conflict to Timor. Between March 1942 and January 1943, the 300 men of the Australian 22nd and 24th Independent Companies fought along with many local militia to harass and kill Japanese soldiers until being forced to withdraw in January of 1943. The end of the war in 1945 brought a return of the Portuguese and renewed sentiment for East Timorese independence. It also brought some in Indonesia to call for Timor's incorporation into their country as they began their own struggle for independence. East Timor's chance came with the Portuguese "Carnation" Revolution in 1974.

In late April of that year the government in Lisbon fell to a *coup d'état* led by leftist military leaders who sought de-colonization following on the painful con-flicts in Africa. Within weeks of the changeover in Portugal, East Timor developed three separate political movements, each with a different plan for the region's future. The Association of Timorese Social Democrats, or ASDT, favoured de-colonization and independence after political and economic struc-tures were given time to develop in East Timor. The Timorese Democratic Union (UDT), based within the pro-Portuguese elite in Dili, initially sought con-tinued association with Portugal, but turned eventually to favour independence as well. Finally, the third and smallest of the groups, the Timorese Popular

Democratic Association (APODETI) pushed for East Timor's full incorporation into neighbouring Indonesia. Many believe that the APODETI was a product of the Indonesian Intelligence Service (BAKIN), which certainly funnelled funds to the organization.

Faced with popular pressure from within and slow progress towards consensus by other groups, in September ASDT changed its programme to demand immediate independence and its name to the Revolutionary Front for an Independent East Timor (FRETILIN). Even though it enjoyed the bulk of popular support and had made an alliance with the UDT, FRETILIN had also become very threatening to Indonesia. In early 1975, APODETI refused to participate with FRETILIN initiatives and the Indonesian government, through BAKIN, became committed militarily against East Timorese independence. By the summer of 1975, conditions had worsened to the point that the UDT launched a counter-FRETILIN coup in Dili, and on 11 August the airport and the communications centre in the capital fell. Indonesian arrests of FRETILIN leaders began under the guise of freeing the territory from so-called "communist influence".

Instability in East Timor led to Indonesian efforts to restore order, but their actions were seen as aggression by many. The Suharto regime increased the level of effort directed towards pacification and eventually the Indonesian annexation of East Timor became a reality. From 1975 to 1989, East Timor became a closed colony. Although Nobel laureates José Ramos-Horta and Bishop Carlos Belo made the cause of the East Timorese known throughout the world in 1992, it was only the 1998 global economic downturn and the fall of Suharto that made East Timorese independence possible.

The development of military solutions – national strategic interoperability

Decisive changes began in December 1998 when Australian Prime Minister John Downer sent a letter to Indonesian President Habibie pledging support during the special election. In late January 1999, Habibie responded to international concerns for East Timor by offering a referendum to the Timorese people. Still, the scope and mission specifics for any military commitment by Australia in East Timor were very uncertain until the very last days preceding the crisis. Even when the UN brokered talks between Indonesia and Portugal developed a baseline agreement for the East Timor referendum in May 1999, the military mission there remained uncertain.

Australian planners did however start to develop an appreciation of the situation in East Timor and possible military courses of action. Several of these efforts were conducted in conjunction with the United States, including planning team visits and at least one session on conducting information operations. It was commonly assumed that should UN military action be needed in East Timor the US would play a large role and would most likely be the lead for any multinational force used there. This was a valid assumption given the recent history of UN sponsored multinational operations.

The United States also began planning for potential military operations in East Timor. The US Pacific Command's situation assessment team had deployed to Jakarta in January and again in May to conduct initial estimates of the situation. Key members of the 3rd Marine Expeditionary Brigade (3rd MEB) staff, based in Okinawa Japan, conducted mission analysis during May and June. The United Nations Assistance Mission in East Timor (UNAMET) was established to oversee the referendum on 11 June, and by early July full-scale planning for a potential unstable situation in East Timor had been completed at the political-military level in Washington and New York,[2] and had begun in earnest at the military strategic levels all across the Pacific.[3]

Significant US aid had been supplied to Indonesia during the decades preceding the crisis and US diplomatic and economic leverage was believed to exert a strong influence on the government in Jakarta. Through the early months of 1999, Australia, Portugal, the United Kingdom and the United States worked to induce a reduction in the violence in East Timor and stimulate Indonesian efforts to provide security there. Many nations hailed the five-point East Timor peace agreement concluded 21 April between the pro-independence resistance and the pro-integration civilian militias. Then, the United States supported Australia's initiative to develop a UN-mediated agreement between Indonesia and Portugal on East Timor in New York on 5 May. Finally, President Clinton's vocal support for action in East Timor during the Asia-Pacific Economic Conference (APEC) Summit in Auckland, New Zealand was a clear catalyst for UN action. In particular, US participation in the diplomatic effort helped place Australian concerns in a proper global context, as did active support from the United Kingdom.

Originally, the US military planning effort was focused only on the evacuation of key personnel, but over time, it was expanded to include the use of forces in a peace enforcement context, either unilaterally, within a multinational force and/or under the banner of the UN. When US planners had submitted their first concept of operations for review in July 1999, it envisioned that American forces would "force a peace" in East Timor and then turnover the mission to maintain the peace to an Australian-led multinational force.[4] Given a UN sanction, this was not an unlikely scenario from the military perspective and clearly matched previous patterns of US force employment. It was considered likely enough in July that the prospective US commander, Brigadier General John Castellaw, was placed on a two-day notice to deploy.[5] Unfortunately, at the time, no government envisioned that Australia might become the lead nation for an initial intervention in East Timor. This planning error would adversely impact the eventual construction of General Cosgrove's multinational force, to be known as the International Force in East Timor (INTERFET).

At the time these planning efforts were underway, Australia was modifying its military command structure as a part of a move towards more joint solutions common within many western nations. As a consequence, a new military head-quarters was created, Australian Theatre, which was to play a key role in the development and execution of military action in East Timor.[6] Under headquarters, Australian Theatre (then commanded by Air Vice Marshall Bob Treloar, RAAF), the commander of the 1st Division, Major General Cosgrove was slated to command any major deployment of forces as the Commander, Deployable Joint Force Headquarters (DJFHQ).

General Cosgrove was well suited to the task that he would find in East Timor for several reasons.[7] First of all he was a combat veteran who was well familiar with the rigors of small unit operations. Secondly, he was a graduate of some of the best military schools; he had received a solid education in current joint operational thinking as well as a strong understanding of military doctrine from his time as a student at the US Marine Command and Staff College in Quantico, the British Army Staff College in Camberley, the Australian Joint Services Staff College and the Indian National Defence College. He was well respected by commanders in the region and had the trust of both the Australian Chief of Defence Force and Prime Minister.

General Cosgrove and his headquarters had previously participated in a multinational exercise named *Rainbow Serpent* in 1998 and been scheduled to conduct a bilateral exercise with US forces, named *Crocodile '99*, which helped pre-stage personnel, forces and equipment that would be important for success in East Timor. Perhaps as important, through such exercises many regional planners had come to form bonds of mutual respect and real trust with their Australian counterparts.

Initial operations in East Timor

US and Australian support for the Timorese began on 28 August, when Admiral Dennis Blair directed American naval forces be positioned in adjacent waters to assist the execution of Australia's operation *Spitfire*, a service's protected evacuation of personnel from East Timor. The USS *Mobile Bay*, an Aegis cruiser, and USNS *Kilauea*, a logistics support ship, were soon lying off the coast of Dili harbour. The presence of two US ships contributed to the deterrent effect for the evacuation and signalled US commitment to future operations, if required. At the same time, American liaison officers deployed from Okinawa to Brisbane to complete multinational planning. Unfortunately, the post-referendum violence in East Timor continued unchecked for several days, into September.

The results of the popular consultation were announced by the United Nations on 3 September. The Security Council condemned the violence that occurred before and after the vote and called on the government of Indonesia to provide appropriate security in the region. Unfortunately, the days following the completion of the referendum witnessed the worst violence the East Timorese had experienced since the 1975 Indonesian invasion. After discussing the problem with Prime Minister Howard, President Clinton decided that external force would be required to stop the violence in East Timor. On 8 September, with the level of violence still increasing, the UNAMET staff decided to leave East Timor. In view of the devastation wrought by the militias, a five-member Security Council team was dispatched by Kofi Annan the next day to assess the problem, and in response, on 15 September the UN Security Council authorized its resolution 1264, which put into effect

> the establishment of a multinational force under a unified command structure with the following tasks: to restore peace and security in East Timor, to protect and support UNAMET in carrying out its tasks and, within force capabilities, to facilitate humanitarian assistance operations.

The resolution also authorized the nations participating in the multinational force "to take all necessary measures to fulfil this mandate".

Admiral Blair had deployed a Pacific Command Planning Liaison Team (PPLT) to Brisbane, Australia on 10 September.[8] By that time the 3rd MEB staff, under General Castellaw, had developed a series of scenarios in case President Clinton directed a US military presence in East Timor. US forces established a headquarters in Darwin and also manned an office within the Australian Theatre headquarters building. A US Air Force Expeditionary Group provided daily cargo and personnel lift from Darwin and US strategic lift (under the operational control of the US Transportation Command) provided large-scale movement of multinational troops and equipment as member-nations identified such requirements.[9]

INTERFET began its operation, codenamed *Stabilise*, on 20 September with the extremely delicate, permissive insertion of forces negotiated by General Cosgrove.[10] Thereafter, the force quickly began to execute Cosgrove's "oil spot" concept of providing security in East Timor by establishing a base of operations in Dili and then expanding its control first to the eastern part of the island and then back to the western border area between East and West Timor. Cosgrove's concept was based upon a very good intelligence appreciation of the region, and the INTERFET staff developed effective reconnaissance and surveillance and solid battlespace awareness so that when Indonesian or militia activities failed to match expectations, Cosgrove had the information he needed to move decisively. He did just that on 3 October, moving into the western border region as his main effort ahead of schedule to take advantage of an opportunity to isolate the militia from its support. Once operations began, General Cosgrove identified heavy-lift helicopter support as a critical requirement and General Castellaw ensured that such capability was provided by elements of offshore Marine Expeditionary Units.

Of much greater import within the interoperability arena was the US communications and intelligence support provided to the INTERFET commander. In particular several key assets, including Trojan Spirit, were located within Dili to facilitate command and control for the American contingent of INTERFET. A full, joint-capable, US node within the INTERFET headquarters enabled excellent fusion of information with Australian sources and gave General Castellaw full voice, data, NIPRNET and SIPRNET access from any of his four command locations.[11]

The deployed Australian forces included robust communications at higher headquarters levels, but other multinational forces did not deploy such capabilities forward. This created a gap in command and control coverage that only the US could fill. General Cosgrove asked for and General Castellaw provided a Joint Task Force enabler communications package from the Marine Expeditionary Unit to supply immediate command and control capability for multinational forces in the eastern regions of East Timor. Later this temporary capability was replaced by elements of the US Army's 86th Signal Battalion.[12]

Operational interoperability and responsive command

At the operational level, the key interoperability challenge was the integration of differing national force elements into a cohesive multinational force. This challenge is significant in most modern operations, but was greatly compounded during operation *Stabilise* due to the extremely short preparation time and extended period over which nations were deciding upon their force commitments. General Cosgrove's headquarters did not have to manage the strategic level coordination for this team-building effort,[13] but it did have to take the contributions, once identified, and place them into a realistic and operational multinational framework. The INTERFET commander did this with many techniques, but some deserve specific mention.

Use of operational regions

Because of the differing tactics, equipment and national objectives of the force elements allocated to INTERFET, the entire force was not operationally cohesive, which is often a reality of modern multinational operations. The key is to properly task every force element available and to effectively share scarce resources for the good of the entire command. INTERFET did this exceptionally well. Once the centres of gravity were evident, the staff managed the forces available to develop a strong "Dili Command" foundation for INTERFET overall, and focused the combat power of the force in such a way as to maximize the effectiveness of each national component. Thus, the Australian "Multinational" 3rd Brigade was placed in the west, the 3rd Royal Australian Regiment in Oecussi and the Thai Joint Task Force, Philippine Battalion and Republic of Korea Battalion all in the east. This assignment of Thai, Philippine and ROK areas of operations not only satisfied national command concerns, but also acknowledged the focus of the Thais on humanitarian assistance, which was the primary mission requirement in the areas assigned to them, and the ROK contingent's need to maximize force protection during a critical period back at home (Ryan 2000).

Not only did this regional employment concept take best advantage of the strengths of each national contingent, it also paved the way for the eventual turnover of responsibility to UNTAET and its use of national regions within the United Nations framework. This concept is certainly not new; it had been used during previous interventions in Somalia, Haiti, and Bosnia. But the decision to employ it was a conscious act and deserves recognition as the best fit in the circumstances of the time, made operationally effective through strong leadership and effective staff work.

Use of doctrinal sources

Some nations eschew doctrine and many officers never read it. Yet there is no doubt that doctrinal sources were used and did aid the development of a workable multinational structure for INTERFET. The US Joint Publication 3–16, *Multinational Operations*, and the *ABCA Multinational Operations Handbook* were both used by planners prior to the deployment into East Timor. In particular, the roles and responsibilities generally ascribed to a "lead nation" were key drivers. Another telling example of the use of developing doctrine was the focus INTERFET made on effective use of a civil–military operations centre (CMOC) in East Timor.

Employment of liaison officers

Liaison officers have done critical service throughout history and did so with great effect in East Timor. Australia decided to link liaison officers to INTER-FET units as early as possible, normally from arrival in Darwin or Townsville, and this policy won great reviews from the units supported. Not only did this linkage permit INTERFET units to gain a better appreciation of Australian procedures, but it also established such rapport that several liaison officers deployed forward with the units they had greeted. A team of liaison officers also was established in Dili to support the national element commanders within the force. This group facilitated the national component commanders' forum and visitors from the contributing nations. A third type of liaison was established in the field with the ASEAN national contingents. In these cases the Australian liaison officers were also accompanied by a communications detachment. This dual conduit concept provided a tool for the INTERFET commander to transfer vital information between Dili and the supported national contingent headquarters, even on occasions when the information was particularly sensitive.[14] An acknowledged shortfall in almost every recent military operation is a lack of trained linguists – this was certainly true in the case of East Timor. This can really only be solved through the development of trained linguists and professional liaison personnel – a goal which is a fiscal challenge for most countries, given the large number of probable languages needed, the time required to master some languages, and the cost of sending personnel off for the months it takes to master language skills.

National commanders meetings

General Cosgrove took the liaison task to heart so well that he personally performed several actions designed to aide the cohesion of his force. Among these were visits to contingent areas of operations, weekly commanders' meetings and the development of a number of social functions designed to improve multinational cohesion. Cosgrove's weekly national contingent commanders' meetings clearly fostered a greater level of understanding and sensitivity among the group of officers assigned the difficult duty of leading their nation's forces within the INTERFET structure.[15]

Multinational command integration

Thailand's General Songkitti Jaggabatara served as both a national command element commander and General Cosgrove's first deputy.[16] Under many circumstances this "dual-hatting" might have been a contribution to multinational cohesiveness, but during operations in East Timor the complexity of both roles did not mesh well together – primarily due to what Alan Ryan has insightfully called "divergent operational cultures" (Ryan 2000: 10). The key issue is ensuring centralized control of the entire multinational while facilitating the execution of assigned tasks by the national elements using their own doctrines and procedures. General Cosgrove alleviated this problem operationally by employing operational regions, but it remained an issue for multinational staff effectiveness. Alan Ryan has recommended integration of the national command elements (NCE) within the main multinational headquarters, and although General Songkitti needed such integration to function fully as a deputy, integration of the NCEs within a multinational structure is probably a bridge too far in interoperability for most nations today. Most security analysts and military leaders agree that this is an area that deserves improvement.

Multinational exercises and national cooperation

No multinational force can operate effectively on such short notice without a foundation of trust. Some degree of trust can be founded on common mission goals, but trust is much more durable when it is also based upon previously developed, mutual, professional respect. It was this kind of trust, which powered the "ANZAC" components of INTERFET and fostered the strong relationship that existed between the Australian, New Zealand, United Kingdom and American elements of the multinational force. With the use of Ghurka troops within the UK contingent, this special trust was given particular value in the East Timorese context, as non-white, regional partners. This trust also made for very fluid information transfer among the member states of the "Five I's" – the English-speaking nations of Australia, New Zealand, United Kingdom, Canada and the United States. Significantly, it was among the "Five I's" that the bulk of information was communicated within the multinational force. Consequently, the force commanders relied on those nations as the backbone for their multinational command and control.

Joint operational synchronization

Another operational strength of INTERFET was its ability to plan and synchronize the application of the capabilities of the separate services of the contributing nations. Several nations, including Australia, New Zealand, and the United States, deployed elements of land-, sea- and airpower to East Timor. Due to the dominance of short time-scales and demanding space and geography challenges, General Cosgrove had to employ fairly robust levels of joint capability to accomplish many of his primary tasks. Heavy-lift helicopter support, amphibious shipping and fixed-wing air-transport support were all key to the initial stages of the operation. Although the requirements for joint synchronization varied over time, there can be no doubt that joint planning and execution was an important factor in INTERFET's operational success.

The transition to UNTAET

The near-fatal seam in command transition that marked operations in Somalia during UNOSOM II in 1993 served as a shocking wake-up call around the world. As a direct consequence, operational commanders in Haiti, Bosnia and Kosovo focused hard on developing criteria and processes for the transition from combat operations to stability operations. In the case of INTERFET, the transition from initial stability operations to the establishment of UN operations under UNTAET was accomplished remarkably smoothly by General Cosgrove and his staff, using steady-state pre-conditions, a desired end-date, measures of effectiveness for security, and phased execution over a three-week period to ensure continuity of effort. This smoothness was largely the result of the regional employment strategy of INTERFET and the phased arrival of UN forces. In any case, the transition process will certainly stand as a model for future multinational operations under a UN mandate.

The selection of the UNTAET military commander, given the crucial role that General Cosgrove had played in INTERFET, was originally somewhat contentious. Several regional nations had indicated the desire to provide the peace-keeping force commander, but there were both political and military criteria that seemed to limit the selection of the UNTAET military chief to one of the major force contributing nations already in East Timor. As the then serving deputy of INTERFET, Lieutenant General Jaime de los Santos of the Philippines had both familiarity with the situation on the ground in East Timor and the commitment of a major force supplying nation as clear attributes, plus his selection would do much to ensure continuity of effort through the transition from INTERFET to UNTAET.[17]

In addition the Philippine military was adept in the peacekeeping skills needed in East Timor. In many ways, UNTAET's peacekeeping tasks (still under Chapter VII of the United Nations Charter) were even more challenging than the peacemaking mission that had been assigned to INTERFET. General Cosgrove had the full authority to authorize the use of deadly force to confront militia threats in East Timor from the first day of his arrival. The military forces assigned to INTERFET were employed in the specific hard skills for which they were trained by their providing nation – infantry combat, reconnaissance, close air support and the employment of indirect fire (mortars and artillery). INTERFET had full warfighting offensive and self-protection capabilities. UNTAET military forces were also authorized under Chapter VII authorities, so they also had full warfighting offensive and self-protection capabilities, but they were intended to be employed in an environment that was relatively free of threats and to focus more on local security and state building than conventional combat tasks that were not considered typical for most military forces. UNTAET military forces had to extend the helping hand of humanitarian assistance, but always retain the capability of employing the mailed fist of combat when necessary.

In January 2000, the UN focus of effort in East Timor began changing to facilitate the transition to UNTAET's primary nation-building tasks, but episodes of combat continued and safety remained the primary concern of Mr Vieira de Mello, the United Nations Transitional Administrator in East Timor. Incidents near Suai, Oecussi, Mahata and Passabe early in the year seemed to demonstrate serious, though last-ditch, efforts by the militia to exert power in East Timor. Meanwhile, humanitarian assistance efforts had succeeded in assisting the return of thousands of East Timorese to their homes, but the overall situation remained far from certain. Riots even broke out on one occasion in Dili as locals trying to enforce new rules were confronted by gangs of youths opposing the return of order (Patterson 2000).

On 23 February, the UNTAET military contingent commander, General de los Santos, assumed full responsibility for the population and security of East Timor from General Cosgrove. By skilfully employing proper planning processes and successfully transitioning its efforts from establishing peace and security to maintaining the peace in East Timor in a time driven fashion, INTERFET truly exceeded most expectations for its period of service in Timor. It also executed the military force transition to UNTAET flawlessly, region by region. General Cosgrove returned to Australia as a true national hero.[18] Benefiting from his service under General Cosgrove, de los Santos continued much of what worked so well during the INTERFET period, to include maintaining a close working relationship with Mr Vieira de Mello and also pressed to shift military actions to focus more on supporting long term development.

On 11 April, General de los Santos and the commander of the Indonesian army forces in West Timor signed a Memorandum of Understanding covering security, boundary crossings, the passage of refugees and the provision of humanitarian assistance along the border between East and West Timor. This memorandum set the essential conditions to normalize local relations over the border area – an essential element of security and economic prosperity for the Timorese. Luckily, the Indonesian government honoured the conditions of the memorandum allowing a return to stable cross-border activities over time. Unfortunately, even after the agreement was put into effect, on 20 June, the UN High Commissioner for Refugees (UNHCR) and other aid organizations had to suspend their activities in three camps in West Timor following threats and intimidation against staff by militia groups. Until the militias were brought under control neither the Indonesian government nor the UN management in Dili could effectively bring an end to problems in the westernmost sector of East Timor.

Thai Lieutenant General Boonsrang Niumpradit[19] assumed command of UNTAET from General de los Santos on 21 July 2000, and largely continued the same security policies started under INTERFET, yet with an eye more attuned to the increased role of the Timorese in security policy (Niumpradit 2002). Still, the transition was another of the most important parts of the long-term service of UNTAET and the two commanders managed to turn over all the key elements of information without a reduction in efficiency. Unfortunately, and highlighting the danger that still confronted those serving in East Timor, only six days following General Niumpradit's assumption of command, on 24 July 2000, the UN suffered its first combat-related death of a UN peacekeeper in East Timor. Private Leonard William Manning, a New Zealand soldier was killed during an exchange of gunfire with an armed group near the still untamed border with West Timor.[20] Only two weeks later, on 10 August, a second UN peacekeeper from UNTAET's Nepalese contingent, Private Devi Ram Jaishi, was killed during another exchange of fire with militia in Suai, close to the area where Private Manning was killed.[21]

These tragic deaths showed the world that the situation in Timor, though much improved, would not be completely calm until a regular Timorese security force was capable of managing the western border. On 6 September 2000, three employees of the UN High Commissioner for Refugees (UNHCR) were killed by pro-Indonesian militia gangs in Atambua, West Timor. Following that attack, the UN decided to evacuate all of its staff members from West Timor and suspend all humanitarian efforts in the region. Two days later, the UN Security Council responded to the deteriorating security situation in West Timor by adopting resolution 1319 and calling on Indonesia to take immediate steps to disarm and disband militia in the border area. By the fall of 2000, Indonesia had greatly reduced its operations near the border, but militia strife and criminal violence beyond its control called for an increase in Indonesian diligence.

On 12 September 2000, the East Timor Transitional Cabinet approved the creation of an East Timor Defence Force (ETDF). The ETDF was to consist of some 1,500 troops drawn from the ranks of former FALINTIL pro-independence guerrillas and supplemented by an equal number of new reserve members. Though external security was not much of a concern outside the border region with Indonesian West Timor, the formation of a defence force was another integral step towards self-governance. General Niumpradit retained command of the multinational force until 31 August 2001, when he was succeeded by Lieutenant General Winai Phattiyakul, a fellow Thai, who commanded the UN forces in East Timor until independence the following year.[22]

Interoperability issues existing for other nations – the tactical level

Though most of the crucial issues existed at the operational level of war, the operations in East Timor also presented several interoperability solutions at the tactical level that deserve study. One of these was the functioning of the multinational battalion from New Zealand that operated in the border region around Suai. The New Zealand battalion was formed around a Kiwi core unit from the 1st Battalion, Royal New Zealand Infantry Regiment (1st RNZIR), which was activated for operations in East Timor on 20 September, deployed to Townsville on 12 October and moved into Suai during the week of 21 October (Nelson 2000). For these Kiwis, this was a hugely significant event – the first time since the Korean War that a battalion group was deployed for operations. Once deployed, they quickly became a capable tactical force.

In East Timor the battalion operated within an Australian brigade structure, while integrating a Canadian company, a platoon of Irish Rangers, Australian communications and intelligence assets, and eventually a Fijian company, finally swelling to over 1,000 personnel (Nelson 2000).[23] Its area of operations, surrounding the devastated town of Suai, encompassed nearly 1,700 square kilometres, yet even with the elements of six nations operating within a very lean tactical headquarters, the battalion conducted operations very successfully. The battalion, along with its sister Australian battalions within the 3rd Brigade was assigned to the critical border region with West Timor, where the militia threat remained significant through the operation. Within the area of operations it faced off against some 200 armed militia. In addition to security patrols, the battalion repatriated over 30,000 refugees and responded to five live-fire incidents.

Several keys to the successful integration of multiple nations within a tactical unit are in evidence. First, the traditional working relationship and common equipment base of Australia and New Zealand made for easy integration of the battalion within the brigade structure and the commanders all had similar backgrounds and educational experiences. Second, the common language and similar heritage was a critical aide to successful cooperation at the company level. Third, the battalion staff conducted command post exercises with the Australians to ensure communications and command procedures worked efficiently.

Finally, the professionalism of the soldiers made development of normal operating procedures fairly easy.

At the tactical level, technical issues can often be the root of operational problems. Equipment provided from New Zealand was functional, but outdated. It was augmented by Australian resources and in a more specialized way by US logistics support, particularly heavy-lift helicopters. It essentially conducted operations in a very austere environment with few, if any, technological advantages over its adversary, yet did so effectively across all the nations involved because of a common command, control and communications foundation. In one respect, the experiences of the 1st RNZIR make a case for minimization in technology where multinational operations are to be conducted at the tactical level.

Warfighting imperatives

Lessons taken from operation *Stabilise* include multinational warfighting imperatives applicable to UN-directed peace operations in many other circumstances. The multinational structure in East Timor was both interoperable and operationally effective and observations from East Timor can and should reorient ongoing developments and should be used by future UN staff and commanders to leverage combat power while minimizing the confusion inherent in modern, multinational military operations.

First, future commanders must maintain cooperation across the levels of war. Through the concerted and timely efforts of politicians, diplomats and military leaders across the globe, the right conditions for intervention were developed without causing more bloodshed in East Timor. General Cosgrove was then able to inject the proper use of force at the operational level, to avert conflict with the Indonesian forces during a period of significant uncertainty and yet still establish momentum for INTERFET's success. Multinational forces were melded together in a variety of ways to meet mission requirements while retaining respect for the character of each national contribution. This degree of success across the levels of war is unique. The multinational force employed in Iraq in 1990 did not transition completely through combat to desired end-state; the operational command structure used in Somalia in 1993 cracked; the multinational force employed in Haiti lacked strategic cohesion; the coalition operations in Bosnia and Kosovo experienced a high incidence of discord at the operational and strategic levels and even recent operations in Iraq and Afghanistan have suffered from a lack of cohesion. This was not the case in East Timor because missions were adapted to match both the national interests of the forces involved and the regional threat.

Developing responsive operational command is a requirement driven by the uncertain nature of these operations. They are more difficult than traditional combat operations because traditional military tools are used in ways that require more deftness and understanding than hitting power and range.

Multinational forces will remain ad hoc; national sensitivities and cultures must be accommodated; the "enemy" will remain more situational than human. "Measures of effectiveness" and "rules of engagement" aside, battling against insecurity and instability will always be frustrating. The only reliable response against such friction in peace operations is command and control flexibility.

Dynamic leadership is irreplaceable, and it starts with national commitment in multinational peace operations. Australia stepped up to lead INTERFET, even on short notice and General Cosgrove commanded the multinational force with great skill. The United States strongly supported the international effort, yet did not dominate decision-making or diminish the right regional leadership. It is vitally important that the US learn the value of being an equal member nation in such efforts. General Castellaw was a supportive national component commander and the US contribution was appropriate. Operation *Stabilise* showed both how important it is for all nations to serve as equal partners and the long-term benefits accrued from regional partnerships.[24]

Operation *Stabilise* and the UN operations that followed it also showed the value of training, exercising, and developing doctrine to support multinational peace operations. The training exchanges among the nations involved, the exercises such as *Rainbow Serpent* and *Crocodile*, and the doctrine such as the *ABCA Handbook* were all immensely helpful during execution. Most officers interviewed in East Timor commented on the increased levels of trust and "make-do" attitudes that resulted from having worked together previously. In an era when budgets are tight and many politicians do not understand that the real value of these activities far exceeds the immediate benefits, multinational training and exercise opportunities still deserve strong support.

Operation *Stabilise* also reinforced the relevance of joint approaches at the operational level. Even given that the geography of East Timor drove planning towards land–sea–air solutions, it is clear that joint approaches contributed much to the effectiveness of the campaign. Without a joint perspective, General Cosgrove could not have executed his deployment under uncertain conditions as well, nor could he have adjusted as decisively from his "oil spot" strategy to quickly focus on border operations when the opportunity arose.

Nations must continue to work the technical interoperability problem. As the United States moves farther a field, towards ever more digitized systems, it must understand the real costs of the widening gap with its friends and allies. The natural trade off for the US is increased commitment as a lead nation when it can ill afford to do so, or the maintenance of a suitable suite of multinational command, control, communications, computer and information technology that can meet the requirements of lower intensity peace operations with a variety of multinational partners. Elsewhere, other likely regional partners should continue efforts to standardize systems to at least the data interchange level. This is the least important of our several priorities, yet only because professional military personnel will find a way to make things work – if they have trust in the operational and strategic elements of the mission.

Future success in military operations will also require a greater understanding of and facility with the coordination required among the national and international organizations that engage in the world's affairs. Cultural sensitivity and diplomacy will be required in new ways and in greater strength – particularly on the part of military commanders. And, the historic fundamentals for success in a more uncertain and more complex age will remain as they have been for centuries, firmly rooted in leadership, professional skill and discipline.

Finally, we must understand that modern military operations remain costly – in real human terms. Member states of the multinational force expended huge amounts of national treasure in East Timor. This treasure must be measured in terms of regional stability, military operations tempo, and equipment and personnel readiness. INTERFET personnel died bringing freedom to the people of East Timor. Even in modern *peace* operations, uncertainty, pain and death exact a high price. This is well recognized by the people of the contributing nations, and it should never be forgotten.

Notes

1 For historical details, see Dunn (1996).
2 A political-military plan for East Timor had been developed by planners within the US Department of State and passed on the United Nations staff. Interview with Dr James Schaer, US Department of State, 10 January 2000.
3 Source: US Forces INTERFET (USFI), *Operation STABILISE After Action Report*, 11 February 2000, p. 2.
4 Interview with Brigadier General John G. Castellaw, USMC, Camp Smith, Hawaii, 18 August 2000.
5 Ibid.
6 Changing the national command structure at this key juncture caused some significant confusion.
7 For additional information see his autobiography (Cosgrove 2006).
8 The mission of the JTF-TSO ships was to escort transports and be prepared to serve as "lily pads" for helicopters during an evacuation. USFI *After Action Report*, p. 3.
9 National contingents from Thailand, the Republic of Korea and Jordan were transported with US lift support; key supplies were also given to Australia.
10 The deployment was preceded by reconnaissance and surveillance operations conducted by the Special Air Services, which facilitated General Cosgrove's confidence in executing the intervention.
11 NIPRNET is unclassified internet communications; SIPRNET is a classified means.
12 The battalion maintained a communications node in Baucau throughout the INTERFET deployment.
13 Strategic coordination was accomplished by Bob Treloar's Australian Theatre headquarters in Darwin, and by the Commander Australian Defence Force, Admiral Chris Barrie, and his staff in Canberra.
14 In other words, putting a "person in the loop" facilitated delicate communications requirements. Interview with Squadron Leader Sharyn Philpott, INTERFET Liaison Officer, 24 July 2000.
15 These officers were tasked with both national command responsibility (as a primary duty) and the mission of working within a coalition structure. Such tasks often can conflict and require sensitivity to the needs of all parties.

16 According to his official biography, General Songkitti Jaggabatara had previously served as the Thai Attaché in Jakarta and the Director of Intelligence on the Army Staff. Online. Available on: www.schq.mi.th/history/Gen_Songkitti_history.pdf.

17 General de los Santos replaced General Songkitti Jaggabatara as the full-time INTERFET deputy commander in 2000. According to his official biography, General de los Santos had previously served as commanding general of an infantry division and Superintendent of the Philippine Military Academy. See: en.wikipedia. org/wiki/Jaime_de_los_Santos.

18 In July 2002 General Cosgrove was promoted to the rank of General and assumed the position of Chief of the Australian Defence Force; he retired from active military service in July 2005 and published his autobiography, *My Story*, in 2006.

19 According to his official biography, General Niumpradit had served as the Director of the National Defence College (NDC), the Director of Joint Operations, Supreme Command Headquarters and the Director-General, Office of Policy and Planning in the Ministry of Defence. Online. Available on: http://mail.mod.go.th/etmr/boon-srang.html.

20 Source: "New Zealand soldier found mutilated in East Timor", *Reuters*, 28 July 2000.

21 From the United Nations Daily Highlights, "Annan Expresses Condolences for Soldier Killed in East Timor" dated 11 August 2000. Online. Available on: www.hri.org/news/world/undh/2000/00–08–11.undh.html.

22 According to his official biography, Lieutenant General Winai Phattiyakul had served the Director of the Directorate of Joint Intelligence, the Supreme Commander's Military Assistant for Foreign Relations, Chief of the Office for Thai–Myanmar Border Security Coordination, and Deputy Director of the Course Director Division, Army War College. Online. Available on: www.unis.unvienna. org/unis/pressrels/2001/sga776.html.

23 Eventually, as UNTAET assumed control of the assigned region from INTERFET, the Canadian company departed and was replaced by a Nepalese company.

24 It also showed the military ANZUS alliance to be valuable even long after New Zealand ceased to be a full participant.

Chapter 8

An unusual bi-national military cooperation

The case of Turkish–Gambian relations

Abdulkadir Varoglu, Mehmet Cakar and Nejat Basim

Introduction

Military cooperation for training is a conspicuous and widespread phenomenon between nations today. It started when the first regular armies appeared and has been in existence since time immemorial; however, such cooperation reached its zenith in amount and intensity during the Cold War. Then, the United States as the primary constituent member of the North Atlantic Treaty Organization (NATO) and the United Kingdom, France, (the former West) Germany as secondary powers in the anti-communist part of the world (the so-called "free world") regularly provided military training to the other members of their camp through military cooperation agreements under various names and forms. On the other hand, the rival group, namely the Warsaw Pact, led by the Soviet Union, as well as various other communist countries (China, Cuba, North Korea, Vietnam, etc.) and other non-communist but anti-West countries had their own web of military cooperation.

Military training cooperation involves a flow of knowledge and experience in armaments, weapons systems, warfare tactics and strategy, communications technologies, and military organization methods from the main core or secondary core countries (USA, UK, France, USSR, China, etc.) to non-core, or peripheral, countries. Such inflow of knowledge and experience is referred to as "structural transfer". In time, as non-core countries acquire and build up knowledge and experience, they too begin to provide similar training to other periphery countries. In other words, periphery countries may act later as core countries in "structural transfers" to other periphery countries.

Turkey and the Turkish Armed Forces (TAF) are a case in point. Turkey has been at the receiving end of structural transfers in the military field for the past two centuries; however, since the end of the Cold War in 1989, it is fast becoming a provider of structural transfers while still continuing to be a recipient at a decelerating pace.

Turkish military training cooperation with foreign powers dates back to 1793 when the Ottoman Sultan invited French, British and Swedish military advisers (mostly French) to reorganize the Ottoman military machinery along Western lines; an initiative which was later called *Nizam-i Cedit* (New Order) (Berkes 1978: 93). The military machinery of the empire which was then in rapid decline became a testing ground throughout the nineteenth century for Western military models, continuously infusing reorganization ideas and warfare techniques. By the First World War, the (Ottoman) Turkish military was a hybrid of various systems and ideas. This structure continued in the aftermath of the First World War when the Ottoman Empire disintegrated and the present Turkish Republic was founded on its ruins. The Republican Army mostly retained its inherited hybrid form but gradually assumed a peculiar national mould until after the Second World War. As the world entered the Cold War from 1947 onwards and Turkey sided with NATO, in line with military cooperation agreements there began an intensive influx of American military know-how and experience as well as armaments into the Turkish Armed Forces, together with the armed forces of other free countries.

Besides, the US was not only giving economic and military aid but also provided know-how for the reform of the state and the industrial structure of Turkey (Usdiken 2004). To support the process financially, the US provided extensive funding which enabled the training of Turkish government officers in agriculture and education in the USA. The diffusion process of foreign managerial knowledge and practices were seen as the core of the modernization process and the transfer of such capabilities as the driving force of economic development in Turkey (Usdiken 1997).

Throughout the Cold War period, Turkey, like many other countries in the free world, received military aid and training from the core or secondary core countries. By the 1990s, based on this infusion of knowledge, experience and capability as well as self-created knowledge and experience, the Turkish military was finally well-equipped to provide such training and aid to less-equipped countries in terms of military institutional capacity.

Today, Turkey, as a member of the United Nations and the NATO alliance, shares its military knowledge and experience with other countries on a bilateral or multilateral basis. Such improved cooperation among countries correlate with the recent changes in the global security environment in which the Turkish Armed Forces (TAF) actively participates in initiatives to secure peace and stability.

Turkey, through the TAF, has so far signed military training and technical cooperation agreements (the so-called "Framework Agreements") with 47 countries, and military cooperation agreements with 43 countries. Under such military training cooperation agreements, the TAF has provided various training to more than 20,000 military personnel from 94 countries at home, and to more than 90,000 military personnel of 16 countries abroad (Anatolian News Agency, 2 January 2006). In addition, during the 1990s, the TAF provided military equipment to friendly and allied countries that gained their independence in the Balkans, the Caucasus and Central Asia; an area of immediate interest to Turkey both geographically and culturally.

The Turkish–Gambian cooperation, began in 1988 when the Gambian delegation at the Islamic Conference Organization contacted their Turkish counterparts for this purpose. Following the negotiations, an agreement for military training and technical and scientific cooperation was signed.

The Turkish–Gambian military cooperation is rather unusual: first, it started relatively earlier than similar relations of Turkey with Azerbaijan, Georgia or Macedonia, for instance; second, Gambia does not necessarily lie within the geographic area of immediate national interest for Turkey, but is encompassed in Turkey's wider interest in world peace; third, this cooperative relation is not formed under any global (UN) or regional (NATO etc.) umbrella organization; and finally, it was not initiated by Turkey as in the cases with Georgia, Albania or Azerbaijan. What is more striking in the case at hand is that Turkey, once a periphery country and the recipient of structural military cooperation, has now assumed the role of a regional core, or a secondary core in its relations with another periphery country. Thus, the flow of military knowledge and experience between two non-core countries is the substance of the relations between Turkey and Gambia.

This study aims to investigate reasons for and outcomes of military cooperation between Turkey and Gambia with a special emphasis on its sociological aspects as well as its implications for international relations. The study specifically examines the following two questions: (1) whether and to what extent cross-national structural transfer is possible among periphery countries, i.e. whether such transfer will be restricted only to the military sphere; and (2) whether such transfers will lead to isomorphism among the institutions of the partners.

Theoretical framework

There are two theoretical aspects involved in the relationship between Gambia and Turkey, i.e. the structural transfers between countries and the isomorphism of organizations.

Djelic (1998: 66), who has studied the diffusion of US industrial structural regulations after the Second World War in France, West Germany and Italy, concludes that the spread of a large-scale cross-national transfer of practices follows a three-step process. First, on the national level, a traumatic disruption should bring a sense of crisis and a questioning of pre-existing institutional and structural arrangements. Afterwards, a redefinition of the geopolitical environment, and particularly the emergence of relationships of asymmetrical dependence, should turn the foreign model into an available model. Here, the foreign model can emerge as either familiar or superior. Finally, a binational "modernizing" network, sharing similar and compatible objectives, should create a bridge between the two countries. The modernizing network consists of a small group of individuals within the respective national environments who hold and control key positions of institutional power. In addition, cross-national organizations and national institutions located at the intersection of state and economy within the receiving country are particularly important (Djelic 1998: 66).

Defeat in war, military occupation, colonization, the collapse of a regime and its dominant ideology, or a deep economic crisis are examples of traumatic disruption (Djelic 1998: 67). Such conditions lead to the displacement of the former political elite and the questioning of the former social, political and economic structures. Such a line of questioning leads the new political elite to conclude that a national crisis exists and therefore strongly encourages them to undertake major transformations.

According to Djelic (1998: 68), the elite in the receiving country should be ready for change and the model should be relatively familiar or perceived as superior. The external model should be readily available and there should be frequent contacts between the recipient and donor countries. In these terms, the geopolitical system in which the recipient country is embedded and particularly the asymmetric dependency come to the fore.

It could be argued that in the international arena, there are dependency relations between countries and these relations particularly have effects on the organizations of these countries. Nation states adopt certain organizational practices in order to preserve their current status or advance their interests in the world system. Transferred organizational techniques may lead to the emergence of new organizational processes referred to as "the best practice".

Organizational techniques are considered soft and social technologies (Arias and Guillen 1998: 110). Organizational structures, forms, or practices like the management of human resources could be given as examples of such social technologies. The international transfer and diffusion of organizational practices through institutional borders is a complex activity in terms of geographic, cultural and institutional differences between recipient and donor countries. Further, such international transfers may involve covert economic and political interests of external powers (Usdiken 2004). In other words, transfers of organizational practices are characterized by various degrees of dependencies between states, implicit nationalist aspirations and competitions (Kipping et al. 2004).

Transfer of organizational techniques and practices is well known in the military arena. For example, NATO is an organization that diffuses and transfers organizational practices to member countries (and at times non-member countries) through its agreed procedures. Military training cooperation is a platform available for sharing experience and transferring military practices between countries.

The transfer of organizational practices and training cooperation between two sides may lead to the homogenization of the organizations. Such homogenization of organizations is best defined by the concept of isomorphism (DiMaggio and Powell 1991). Isomorphism is the process by which an organization comes to resemble other organizations in the same organizational field.

DiMaggio and Powell (1991: 67) suggest that three mechanisms lead to institutional isomorphism: coercive, mimetic and normative. Firstly, coercive isomorphism stems from formal or informal pressures on organizations by other organizations upon which they are dependent and from the expectations of their society. The most typical example is governmental regulations and laws that force organizations to conform to common legal norms. Mimetic isomorphism, on the other hand, arises from the need to overcome organizational uncertainty. Particularly when organizations are uncertain about the way to proceed, they imitate and copy each other more frequently. They copy perceived successful organizations in order to minimize cost and use time efficiently. The attempts of Japan's modernizers in the Meiji era (DiMaggio and Powell 1991) and also the efforts of the Ottomans for imitating Western organizational "best practices" in the late nineteenth century are examples of this sort. Finally, normative isomorphism emphasizes the diffusion of rationalized models and practices between organizations through formalized education of professionals and their job networks. Professionals and the related professional culture (e.g. military) easily comply with them and further standardize the work methods and techniques through organizations and thus cause a kind of diffusion in their networks (Varoglu *et al.* 2006).

The emergence of nation states gave rise to the monopolization of setting the rules of legitimation and institutionalism by the state (Guler *et al.* 2002: 212; Arias and Guillen 1998). While states are transferring and implementing organizational practices and innovations to get ahead in the international arena, they also boost diffusion of such practices inside their own territories. States encourage organizational changes and push coercive isomorphism by legislation, regulation, licensing and permissions.

Arias and Guillen (1998), on the other hand, criticize previous studies on international transfer of organizational practices for their uni-dimensional emphasis on transfer from developed countries to the developing ones; according much attention to multinational corporations, while disregarding the core role of the state apparatus, and neglecting the international relations context (dominant countries, superpowers, dependent and developing countries, etc.). They suggest that a comparative historical analysis as Immanuel Wallerstein's (1974) world systems approach should be made.

In Wallerstein's (1974) approach, the world economy is a dynamic system that changes over time, but, what persists is the enrichment of the core (Northwestern European) countries at the expense of the peripheral economies. While criticizing the modernization theory, Wallerstein also offers alternative explanations. Dependency theory is one of the building blocks of Wallerstein's approach which contributes to his conceptualization of the dominance of core countries on the periphery.

Similarly, Jepperson and Meyer (1991) maintain that the modern world system has stratification among nations. The stratified world system involves dependency relations between the core and periphery states, mostly in the political, economic and military fields (Danziger 2004: 305). In political dependency, the dominant country uses the advantage of factors such as its power in international relations and its political institutions. In economic dependency, the core country uses its dominant economic and financial structures through the apparatus of economic aid. In terms of military dependency, the threat to use military power, military protection, training cooperation and transfer of resources could be given as examples. For instance, in the Cold War period, South Korea was dependent on the USA in the political, economic and military fields and faced North Korea which was supported by the USSR and China.

In such cases, financial and technical support is transferred to the recipient country externally and unilaterally. On the other hand, organizational transfers tend to increase in multitude and greater frequency when developing countries are dependent on the core countries and experience dire needs in basic infrastructure investments and technical expertise (Arias and Guillen 1998: 120).

Relations between the core and periphery countries, especially those in the Third World, are sometimes referred to as "neo-colonialism". This term refers to the ongoing dependency of the Third World on their former colonial masters. Through military support, transfer of technology, foreign aid, loans and economic interventions, former colonial relations are continued under various new forms. Dominating core countries usually act through the invisible elite of the recipient country, multinational corporations or international regulatory agencies such as the International Monetary Fund (IMF) to accomplish their transfers in the dependent periphery countries.

An analysis of the Turkish–Gambian relations

The military cooperation between Turkey and Gambia has been going on for 16 years. The initial content of the cooperation was logistical support from Turkey to Gambia. In 1991, a gendarmerie unit from Turkey was charged with the task of establishing and training the Gambian National Guard. The Gendarmerie force in Turkey is a police force in charge of security in rural areas. Like the Gendarmerie in Italy or France, the Turkish Gendarmerie is accountable both to the Ministry of Internal Affairs and to the Turkish General Staff, signifying a matrix type dual line of command. In 1999, the Turkish–Gambian military cooperation was expanded to provide training to the entire Gambian Armed Forces including Army, Navy and Air Force, and to establish the Training Command of Gambia. Since 2000, the Commanding Officer of the Training Command has been a Turkish Gendarmerie Colonel.

In line with the agreement, 137 Gambian officers and 5,000 other military personnel have been trained by Turkish military instructors in Gambia since 1991. In the meantime, 60 officers and NCOs received Turkish-language education and military training at Turkish military institutions. Normally the lingua franca is English. Gambian military personnel trained in Turkey were also familiarized with the Turkish language, culture and business environment in Turkey, and some of them, after retirement, got engaged in commercial activities between Gambia and Turkey. Trade between the two nations now exceeds a modest volume of US$10 million annually.

To get more information on the day-to-day Turkish–Gambian military cooperation, in addition to the secondary data from the Turkish Gendarmerie Command, interviews were held with 12 officers and non-commissioned officers from Turkey and Gambia who had been involved in the activities as trainers and trainees. A brief interview was also conducted with the officer in charge of the African desk at the Turkish Ministry of Foreign Affairs.

The Turkish–Gambian cooperation can be analysed from three specific perspectives. The first is Gambia's dependency on foreign economic and technical aid that has a significant impact on the nature of her relations with Turkey. It can be observed that Gambia has offered diplomatic support to Turkey in the international arena in exchange for Turkish aid and military training. Such reciprocity may be attributed to the post-colonial trauma of Gambia, the collapse of regime and recent secession from Senegal. After the colonial period, there was a lack of regulated institutional environment, particularly in education, the national economy and the state apparatus. Such lack of institutionalization was accompanied by inadequate capacity in industry and trade, problems of infrastructure, inadequate technical education capabilities, and an unstable political environment.

The second basis of Turkish–Gambian cooperation is a climate of trust between the two countries created by a binational modernizing network. While Turkey with its technical expertise and operational capabilities is a competent partner, it is also disassociated from colonial powers, particularly in the sub-Saharan Africa. This relationship should not be considered as an example of Wallerstein's dependency model because Turkey has never been a core (colonialist) country, even though Gambia was at the periphery.

The third basis of the Turkish–Gambian cooperation is the religious and cultural similarity felt by the people of both countries. Due to religious affinity (94.7 per cent of the Gambian population is Muslim) especially after the first interaction in Gambia, there seems to be warm relationships between both sides. On the other hand, Turkey is perceived as a familiar model of development by Gambians.

Role of dependency

Although Djelic's (1998) general model was developed for understanding the industrial organizational practices, her approach can also help us to understand the Turkish–Gambian cooperation case within the framework of dependency. Sub-Saharan African countries with a colonial background like Gambia face some post-colonial problems, such as lack of good governance, etc. (Noorderhaven and Tidjani 2001). Gambia is also dependent on foreign aid. Such problematic conditions consequently determine the nature of Gambian foreign affairs. As in the case of Taiwan–Gambia relations, Gambia may lend diplomatic support in the international arena in return for foreign aid (Baker and Edmonds 2004).

With reference to Djelic's traumatic disruption and national sense of crisis conceptualization, Gambia needs the transfer of organizational practices and techniques so as to overcome its organizational insufficiencies. In that sense, Turkey has expertise in the military, technical and organizational fields. As it is expressed in various interviews done with the Turkish officers, the cost of such Turkish military assistance to Gambia is around 10,000 dollars annually.

It can also be argued that Gambia and the sub-Saharan peninsula are important for Turkey in terms of political support in the international arena. For example, Turkey, like Austria and Iceland, is competing for temporary membership in the UN Security Council for the 2009–10 period and needs support from other countries. Another example of political support from Gambia involves the recognition of the Turkish Republic of Northern Cyprus (TRNC). Like many of the sub-Saharan countries, Gambia is a member of the Non-Aligned Movement and the Greek Cypriot Administration, which is also a member of this movement, periodically protests the Turkish military presence in northern Cyprus, calling it an occupation.

Gambian president Yahya Jammeh stated in 2005 that Gambia was ready to recognize the TRNC as a sovereign state (*Hürriyet* 2005). Following that statement, the Greek Cypriot Administration protested to Gambia (*Sabah* 2005). However, this protest was rejected by the other Non-Aligned countries on grounds that the Greek Cypriot Administration is no longer non-aligned, but a member state of the European Union. In recent years, children of senior civil servants in the sub-Saharan African countries have been enrolling in the TRNC universities which are strongly subsidized by Turkey as it is the case with the entire northern Cyprus.

The third example of foreign diplomacy relations with Gambia is that they supported the Turkish candidate for the election of the Secretary General of the Organization of the Islamic Conference against the Arab majority. The fourth example is that Gambia provided diplomatic support to Turkey when, in 1988–89, the Bulgarian administration tried forcibly to change the names of Bulgarian citizens of Turkish origin.

One incidental outcome of the Turkish–Gambian military training cooperation was the 2005 military coup attempt against the Gambian president and the government which was stopped by the Presidential Guard organized and trained by the Turkish military. The swift action by the Presidential Guard to foil the attempted coup was later associated with the training and discipline earlier instilled by Turkish military advisers, as thankfully stated by the President of Gambia in the opening ceremony of the Parliament and at the Gambian Armed Forces Academy.

The relationship and dependency model between Turkey and Gambia is significantly different from the relationship between Taiwan and Gambia. Taiwan provides large-scale aid to Gambia (Baker *et al.* 2004). The rationale behind it is that Taiwan has established technical missions in various developing countries where it receives political recognition. Taiwan's aid programme to developing countries has been driven largely by its desire for greater international recognition. By the end of 2002, fewer than 30 countries formally recognized Taiwan, most of which were small, poor countries that were not included in the sphere of Chinese economic investments and thus went after securing Taiwanese foreign aid and investments in return for their recognition of Taiwan. As such, they play a critical role in lending credence to Taiwan as a sovereign nation, and not as a province of mainland China. Both China and Taiwan compete with each other using their aid packages in Africa. Recognition of either one by the aid-recipient African country automatically leads to the cessation of aid from the other. That happened for Gambia too.

Cultural and religious similarity

There is also a religious similarity between Turkey and Gambia based on historical relations and cultural sympathy. The first factor is that, until the second half of the nineteenth century, Ottoman Turks blocked western colonization attempts in the region (Kavas 2005). Gambia and Turkey both have predominantly Muslim populations, and are in frequent contacts under the umbrella of the Organization of Islamic Conference.

The cultural ties between Gambia and Turkey also have roots in the history of Africa, especially in terms of Muslim religious orders. West Africa has three dominant religious brotherhoods (different interpretations of Islam) which are Qaddriyya, Tijanniyya and Sanussiyya. Adnani (2005) states that while historically Qaddriyya was more sympathetic to Turks, Tijanniyya stood more opposed. In addition, Qaddriyya brotherhood was the sole supporter of Ottoman forces in the wars against the French occupation in 1830 in North Africa (Adnani 2005). Darboe (2004) states that Qaddriyya brotherhood is the common, more tolerant and accommodating type of Islamic interpretation in the region. The secular way of life that characterizes both countries is another case of similarity that both sides seem to be aware of.

In addition, as other studies (e.g. Soeters et al. 2004, 2007) that examine the international peacekeeping operations and compare the perception of death in different nations show, Turkish military personnel are more comfortable working with partners from Muslim and Mediterranean countries and those with more or less collectivist cultures. Also as Wasti (1998) states, the applicability of Western organizational practices of, for example, human resources management are not very compatible with Turkish ones. These findings imply that Turkish societal characteristics are relatively much more in line with non-western counterparts. The cultural comparison study of Noorderhaven and Tidjani (2001) for African countries may support the conclusion that Turkey and Gambia have similar values.

Organizational cooperation

In 1988, Turkish officials were approached by Gambians; later the Gambian President was invited to Turkey. At the same time, the Ambassador of Gambia to Saudi Arabia was accredited to Turkey. For three years, the relationship was based solely on military logistic support. In 1991, upon a Gambian request to train the National Guard, a team composed of four officers, one NCO and one civilian was sent to Gambia. The first group was not well-informed about the scope of the mission and the first problem they faced was the lack of military training materials. At the same period, Nigeria was training the Gambian Land Forces; the UK was providing training to the Police and Israel was having talks to sell weapons. Turkish personnel were shown great respect by Gambian military personnel and local people. In 1993, the temporary status of the mission was changed to a permanent one. After the military intervention in 1994, the other countries left Gambia, and Turkey started to support the training of fire fighters and civil servants too. In addition to basic military training, Turkey also provided courses on map reading, border protection, narcotics, criminal acts and crime scene investigation, and custom duties processes. At that time, the only English-speaking person was the Gambian assistant to Turkish officers. Then, Gambian authorities decided to send some officers to Turkey for language training. Turkish personnel tried to learn the local language, not for training purposes but for communicating with locals.

Turkish personnel emphasized the following points during the interviews:

> At the very beginning, none of our Gambian counterparts had any idea who we were and where we were coming from. Some of the Gambians were calling us "Barbary (Moor)" as they learned from their English colonialists. Collectivism (team building) was very easy in military training, and a high power distance existed (we were called boss for a while) in cultural terms. From time to time, we felt ourselves as the only decision makers. They were expecting directions from us. Then, it was easy to train them in the autocratic-benevolent style of Turkish officers.

Nobody showed any displeasure toward the Turkish presence nor showed any hostility to Turks. In the eyes of our Turkish respondents, Gambians were very easy going and took life very optimistically. The slogan everywhere is "no problem in Gambia". They were feeling at ease in terms of time management and did not like to be pushed around. Soldiers were eager and willing to learn. They had no problems with physical adaptation to the requirements of military training. The military career and officership were viewed as a professional job. Gambians did not feel much affection to the military in the way Turkish people feel toward the Turkish army.

The characteristics of the Gambian leadership are important to understand the effectiveness of Turkish–Gambian military cooperation. Ba Banutu-Gomez (2003) states that Gambian government officials have a five-dimensional leadership practice: (1) Traditional African Leadership Practice, (2) Shared Vision, (3) Accountability, (4) Patriotism, and (5) Willingness and Openness to Change. The most important one among these is the Traditional African Leadership Practice (TALP) which is the bond between these leadership practices. TAL practice is the transfer of leadership information, customs, or beliefs from one generation to another.

Ba Banutu-Gomez (2003) states that TAL practice is the root of African society which nurtures and nourishes African society through valuing family, respect for elders, consensus, community life, collaboration, communication, teamwork and team credit, consultation, roles and purposes and advice. The core of TAL practice is consensus. In Africa, decisions are made through consensus. Ba Banutu-Gomez (2003) maintains that in making decisions through consensus, one does not need to worry about time or how quickly decisions are made; but how the leader is able to listen and to get everyone on board.

During the interviews, Turkish officers stated that such emphasis and efforts of Gambians on consensus created various hurdles for the fast decision-making requirements of military tasks. It was perceived as time consuming by the trainers. On the other hand, as Darboe (2004) states, advice is also important for Gambians who rely on seniors in the workplace and elders in the society for advice. This practice strengthened the expert power of Turkish trainers in Gambia and facilitated the construction of respect and trust towards Turkish military personnel. Then, the transfer of foreign organizational practices and aid became easier in all aspects of cooperation.

Isomorphism

The Turkish–Gambian military cooperation appears to have led to both mimetic and normative isomorphism. While the will of the Gambian military organization to model the Turkish prototype fits the mimetic isomorphism, ongoing training expertise caused the creation of professionalization, which fits the normative isomorphism. For example, on a television programme, a Gambian Infantry Company was doing a physical exercise by singing well-known Turkish folk music in an excellent way.

The formal training programme applied by Turkish officers and the established structures seem to produce an institutionalized system through isomorphism processes. For example, the military training units established and run by the Turkish Gendarmerie are visited periodically by the leaders of West African countries during diplomatic assemblies held in Gambia. This example shows the diffusion of cognitive legitimation of the new organizational form in the institutionalization process. In fact, it is possible to state that this process could be observed in other sub-Saharan African Countries like Senegal, the Republic of Congo and so on.

Conclusion

The Turkish military mission left Gambia in 2005, leaving behind a Turkish military officer at the Ministry of Defence as an adviser, but the relationship between Gambia and Turkey still continues. The initial objective was to cooperate on military training, then it turned to encompass a wide range of business relationships including technical and commercial activities. This was made possible through having human resources interoperable in language, environment and philosophy. Turkish multinational corporations have not made any investments in Gambia. Rather, small and medium-sized firms prefer to have commercial relationships. Agreements, especially for training projects with the Turkish Gendarmerie, were signed with other sub-Saharan countries too. Among these countries Senegal signed in 1998, Burkina Faso in 2001, the Republic of Congo in 2005 and Ethiopia in 2006.

During the past 15 years, more than 5,000 military personnel were trained by the Turkish military even though the number of soldiers was always less than 2,000 at any one time in Gambia. This shows that the ultimate aim is not only to provide military training but also to convert this relationship into real cooperation. This binational relationship is much different from the tasks performed by the TAF in Bosnia, Kosovo, Albania or Afghanistan in terms of the initiatives taken by Turkish authorities. Officers and NCOs were always in contact with locals and they felt that it was a real mission to help a friendly country rather than creating colonial or neo-colonial relationships or being part of a larger UN or NATO mission.

In 2005, representatives of sub-Saharan countries offered to sell petroleum to Turkey in return for high quality Turkish goods, so as to have an alternative to Chinese goods in the sub-Saharan Africa. Further, Turkey provides food aid to sub-Saharan countries to ease starvation; its amount reached $3.5 million dollars in 2005. Turkey also contributes military and police officers to the UN missions in Sierra Leone, Congo, Sudan, Ivory Coast and Liberia. After the Turkish military mission in Gambia was ended, other sub-Saharan countries indicated their desire to have similar Turkish training mission in their countries.

The answer to the question whether the cross-national structural transfer is possible between peripheral countries through military cooperation programmes is affirmative for the Turkish–Gambian experience. It started with military applications and was later extended to other areas. The answer to the question whether this transfer would create an isomorphism among organizational processes and structures is also affirmative.

Chapter 9

Towards transnational identities in the armed forces?

German–Italian military cooperation in Kosovo

Maren Tomforde

Introduction

The multinational character of military contingents and the diversity of cultural environments that the armed forces have to deal with, have become predominant features of today's military activities. Such conditions demand a high level of intercultural competence of each individual involved. When deployed abroad, troops interact with up to 40 other partners from all over the world (Schmitt 2004: 103). Camp Warehouse in Kabul (Afghanistan), which hosts more than 30 nations, is a good example of a truly multinational military setting. These multinational arrangements have to meet a number of diverse challenges both on an operational and sociocultural scale: for example, next to operational challenges, actors also have to deal with multiple cultures and have to successfully operate under increasing diversifying and demanding conditions. Anthony King (2005: 332) stresses in that regard:

> This is a new and important development. Today, the armed forces are concentrating on certain key, specialist units that are best adapted to the current strategic environment and these units are being drawn into ever closer integration with other similar units from other member states. The armed forces of Europe are becoming transnational.

One aim of this chapter is to examine, based on the empirical example of German–Italian cooperation in Kosovo, to what extent military personnel is becoming *transnational* in the true sense of the word and how military identities and boundaries are renegotiated in novel ways. The term "transnational" generally stands for relations between individuals of different states, in contrast to international relations, which refer to contacts between states, governments, or organisations. Transnational are generally those organisational structures and relations, which are independent from any nation state in particular. In migration theory, "transnational" is used for a type of movement where connections are kept both with the former country of origin *and* new state(s). Assimilation into the new society is not a priority due to the fact that close ties continue to be maintained with the country of origin and among individuals from that state who might be spread all over the globe. Transnational migratory movement is not unidirectional but can go back and forth and even involve further countries. People usually do not have an overriding feeling of obligation or loyalty to the nation states involved but are rather deeply connected to their own group of reference. Diaspora groups such as the Jews, Armenians, Chinese, Hausa or Afro-Americans are a good example for true transnational communities (see also Kokot *et al.* 2004; Basch *et al.* 1994; Bhabha 1994; Appadurai 1991).

In the context of armed forces, "transnationalism" does not imply that national identities become irrelevant, or that national armed forces relinquish their sovereignty to one *supranational* military such as a "European Army". King (2005: 333) stresses the contrary:

> There is no evidence to suggest that the national identity of personnel will become irrelevant or that the sovereignty of member states will be subsumed to a higher authority. [...] Specialist military units are co-operating with each other ever more closely but their national identities and their nation-state's control over them remains a manifest reality.

Therefore, when investigating multinational cooperation, the level of transnationalism and nature of military identities/cultures need to be analysed to better understand processes and challenges of multinational military integration. Yet, so far only little is known about processes of identity making and boundary drawing among multinational forces. In general, with a few exceptions, academic research activities dealing with multinationality have only been taking place since the 1990s so that a research gap needs to be closed (Gareis *et al.* 2003: 16; see also Soeters *et al.* 2006; Hagen *et al.* 2003). It becomes crucial for military organisations to comprehend how military personnel from all ranks manage cultural diversity instigated by the necessity of international cooperation between the various national contingents and by the relations with the other actors in the theatre of operations. Major questions are: how do armed forces cope with the challenges connected to the shift from purely national roles to increasing multinational tasks in intercultural missions? What kind of challenges are encountered by military personnel during missions and for which reasons? How are the soldiers prepared for intercultural encounters? What do mutual perceptions look like? What kinds of implicit and explicit self-concepts exist? And, last but not least, what are the main constraints *against* and the main prerequisites *for* a truly deep integration in multinational theatre?

Data

On the basis of a comparative German–Italian case study, this chapter explores the intercultural challenges with which soldiers are confronted in multinational cooperation. How soldiers cope with diversity within multinational task forces, and how their identities and military cultures are transformed due to that inter-action are also explored. In collaboration with social scientists from the Depart-ment of Peacekeeping Studies, University III in Rome, the German–Italian cooperation in the Multinational Brigade (Southwest) in Kosovo was studied by questionnaire as well as by means of numerous semi-structured interviews and anthropological participant observations in the summer of 2005. Results from the qualitative research are at the centre of attention here. To better understand the processes of the constitution of (transnational) identity and culture during peacekeeping, the chapter looks at the individual level of soldiers' practices, problems and ideas and puts these into the larger frame of peacekeeping.

Military culture

In the field of sociocultural anthropology definitions of culture have been widely questioned and disputed in the past decade. It is argued that rather than remain-ing wedded to a concept of culture as a conceptual structure comprised of representations of reality to orient, direct, and organise action in systems, we should understand culture as a constant flux of continual re-creation of "living, experiencing, thinking, affectively engaged human beings who follow [...] particular lifeways" (Rapport and Overing 2000: 96). The concept of culture should thus be strongly related to *practice* in order to combine the perceiving and the acting agent. In other words, it is necessary to openly acknowledge the important relationship between symbolic meaning and practice, between mind and body, between actor and action, and between concept and performance (Barth 2002: 35; Rapport and Overing 2000: 97; see also Bourdieu 1977). Anthropologist Tim Ingold (2002: 330) also argues for a revision of the word culture, opting for the verb "culturing", which he argues places a stronger emphasis on cultural practices than on culture as a delimited "object". This (new) approach to cultures or to "culturing" that emphasises social action as a central constituent of any cultural phenomenon, is also useful for the assessment of military cultures.

At first glance, all military cultures have many aspects in common; yet, at second glance they are also very unlike in many ways. The military creates a common professional military culture and a common military mind as Slovenian sociologist Ljubica Jelušič (2003: 356) puts it: "The military is tied to distinct goal, mission, and methods of executing a particular mission. It is the product of intraoccupational socialization, which provides a homogenisation of values or occupational minds." Basic military and auxiliary trainings as well as daily work experiences, the so-called "practicalities of real life", socialise an individual into the military organisation. This military socialisation process is similar around the globe: the "old self" is deconstructed in favour of a personality who shares military values and who is willing to subordinate and commit her- or himself to military rule, even in times of danger. Discipline, hierarchy, strict organisation, bureaucracy, comradeship, trust, loyalty, importance of uniforms and other military symbols are part of the peculiarities of the military profession worldwide. All soldiers construct a new identity and are initiated into a new status and social roles (Soeters *et al.* 2003: 250). They learn military ways of "walking, talking, and thinking" as well as of channelling and controlling emotions. A so-called "culture of discipline" forms one important aspect of military principles that are always and everywhere the same. The basis for this common military culture around the world lies in the "historical model of the Prussian corps" (Ben-Ari and Elron 2001: 284). Practices and information about military techniques were and still are exchanged in joint classes at military academies, joint trainings and missions around the globe. Cultural practices such as customs of hail and farewell, parades and ceremonies, as well as military symbols such as uniforms and badges are exchanged on a large scale (Ben-Ari and Elron 2001: 286). Historical continuity is further guaranteed by means of sharing the same physical space during multinational missions and immediate, daily encounters within the camps. Even informal ways of behaviour are partly similar in most military organisations: for example, for soldiers around the globe joking and jesting is an important way to cope with work stress and the tough sides of army life (Ben-Ari and Sion 2005).

However, not all military cultures are completely alike. Of course, variations exist between the countries, and also between various types of military organisations such as the army, the air force, or the navy (Soeters *et al.* 2003: 237–238). Armies can, for example, represent different concepts of "strategic culture", work ethos or concepts of time (cf. Longhurst 2000). Next to common, historical military roots, all armed forces also have their particular military identities, micro-traditions, doctrines, styles of leadership, training practices, work concepts, etc. as they are also inherent organisations of the societies and nations they belong to. These features characteristic of national cultures and sovereign armies need to be recognised and shaped when encountering mixed units and multinational structures. This is the ambiguity and ambivalence multinational settings and actors are confronted with. In other words, increasing integration in multinational headquarters, staff organisations and military units is a more demanding challenge for military personnel than purely national tasks are because cultural particularities of participating soldiers of other nations have also to be taken into consideration.

It goes without saying that it is easier to standardise technical equipment, regulations, and organisational structures than to achieve a common perception of vocabulary, work results and concepts of time (Lang 2001a: 42; 2001b: 757). Of course, due to these and other challenges not all missions run smoothly or effectively at all times. On the contrary, more often than not, institutional and intercultural differences between military organisations account for challenges and problems in international collaborations.

Intercultural differences are minimised and integration enhanced if some (or all) of the following *prerequisites* are met (see also Gareis *et al.* 2003: 78; Prüfert 2002: 257; Triandis 2002; Oliver and Montgomery 2000):

- Clarity and unity as regards the purpose of the multinational unit as well as an overarching aim, which serves as a guideline for all activities.
- Legal framework agreements and a formal structure, which subdivides the overall task into subtasks to which all members of the group can relate.
- Common language.
- Formalised working processes, which clarify what can be expected from the other and what is expected from them in return.
- A good communication system that provides all the information necessary for a successful integrated working process.
- Clear acknowledgement of the double function of multinational military bodies: military tasks *plus* integrative mission tasks.
- Awareness of aspects of cultural interaction including self- and xeno-perceptions; military leaders should act as mediators between their own troops and those of other nations.
- Personal interactions of the soldiers involved, covering all ranks, arms and specialisations. It is essential that people become acquainted with each other on a personal level.
- A standard, permanent cultural, evaluative and organisational pattern to solve problems in a multinational unit.
- Common activities as positive social interaction to foster integration and multinational contacts; e.g. sports competitions are moral builders and provide the basis for positive competition.
- Joint sleeping quarters.

As far as successful military cooperation goes, the most important conflict arises from differences between national military traditions and sovereignty on the one hand and demands of deepened, multinational integration on the other. It is also Eyal Ben-Ari's and Efrat Elron's (2001: 298) contention that the feeling of belonging to a nation state is not minimised, but on the contrary intensified during multinational military missions. For example, in joint meetings, flags of each participating nation are put on the table or on Power Point slides instead of a single, joint flag replacing the others.

Not only are national identities and cultures stressed, in daily practices during missions they are also represented in a simplified way omitting national varieties and differences. As the discussion of research results below shows, national cultures are for example represented by means of national foodstuffs such as pasta for Italy or beer for Germany. In the following, it will be shown that these simplistic representations of national cultures enable the formation of national in-groups on the one hand, but also the demonstration of national values and identities to the "out-group" on the other. This kind of boundary drawing does not impede, however, the constitution of a multinational peacekeeping identity existing *next to* national, regional, or service identities.

Case study: German–Italian cooperation in Kosovo

In summer 2005, the Headquarters (HQ), the Headquarters Company (HQ Coy), and the Multinational Logistic Unit (MLU) of the Multinational Brigade Southwest (MNB SW) in Prizren, Kosovo were mainly staffed by German and Italian military personnel. These two nations were in principle contributing equally to the functioning of the multinational headquarters. The organisational structure of the HQ MNB (SW) was similar to those of other corps staffs and headquarters within NATO (in peacetime).

The HQ MNB (SW) was structured according to the principle of deepened integration. At the time of research, the headquarters was led by a German Commander, an Italian Deputy Commander, an Italian Chief of Staff (COS), assisted by a German Press and Information Officer (PIO), a German Legal Adviser (LEGAD), and the various divisions. These divisions were either headed by a German or an Italian with deputies belonging to the other nation. Due to the lack of qualified personnel available, the Italian side could not, however, provide staff for several positions, which where left vacant. As Italian officers claimed, too many specialists were involved in other missions, especially in Iraq, so that these positions were only given second priority. Nonetheless, politically, the mission in Kosovo was as important for the Italian side as for the Germans. Three positions in the Headquarters were staffed by two Austrian and one Spanish officer. Due to linguistic and other cultural similarities, the two Austrians defined themselves as belonging to the "German side" while the Spaniard identified himself with the Italian side of the Headquarters. The main task of the MNB (SW) was to guarantee a secure environment for all (ethnic) groups, to prevent ethnically motivated, violent uprisings and to enable a peaceful and sustainable development in Kosovo.

As far as the context of the Multinational Brigade is concerned, the Headquarters, the HQ Coy and the MLU were staffed by Germans and Italians in more or less equal numbers. However, the Headquarters was located in Camp Prizren, which hosted, in addition to the MNB (SW) the German and Italian National Headquarters, 1,800 German military personnel belonging to the German troops of the contingent. The Italian troops, more than 2,000 in number, were located in Camp Aguila in Pec, which is about $1\frac{1}{2}$ hours' drive northwest of Prizren. The Multinational Logistic Unit (MLU) was in Camp Airfield, not far from Camp Prizren. In the following section, daily life in Camp Prizren as well as in neighbouring Camp Airfield, where the German–Italian Logistics Unit was stationed, is analysed in terms of sociocultural practices, arrangements and understandings. These shape (and are shaped by) (sub)cultural structures of the armed forces deployed in multinational peacekeeping missions.

Daily life in Camp Prizren

Due to its German national contingent, Camp Prizren was, despite its multinational headquarters, a truly German camp with a large majority of German military personnel, German buildings, German equipment, German streets, sidewalks and street-names, mainly German food, etc. Even the German road-traffic regulations applied so that an Italian could theoretically get a German parking ticket if parking in front of the headquarters for example. Italian soldiers lived separately in their own barracks, which were provided by the German contingent. All in all, the *spatial setting* was dominated by the German forces, while the Italians had built small national enclaves within the camp such as "the Italian mile" with two Italian espresso bars and an Italian *baita* (house, restaurant) which also had an open outside space with tables and chairs. The German service members not only liked to visit the "Italian mile" for a cappuccino, but also the *baita* – the only official open space within the camp to relax outside in the sun. Due to a rigid, "Prussian work concept" and an expected military behaviour that is respectable and honourable at all times, it is unthinkable to find such open leisure areas in any *Bundeswehr* camp. Unofficially, German leisure areas are, instead, hidden behind the barracks to maintain the image, also for German society at home, that the German soldiers are always strictly and dutifully following their mission tasks. Qualitative as well as quantitative research results show that Italian service members did not understand this contradiction between German "official" behaviour aimed at an image of constant diligence and the "unofficial" behaviour of relaxing secretively behind the German barracks or at the Italian *baita*. German service members, on the other hand, had little understanding for the relaxed work and time concepts of their Italian comrades who would, for example, not go into their offices at a fixed time in the morning, but only when work actually needed to be done. Further misunderstandings occurred due to different operational styles of both nations. Germans follow the principles of "Auftragstaktik", focused on the *work process* and on subordinates to reach a task through an independent, self-governing work style. The Italian operational style is much more focused on the *outcome* of an undertaking, assigning a more leading role to the superior who is informed about all stages of the working process. Both the German and Italian service members thought their own operational styles to be more efficient and misunderstood the principles underlying the work procedures of the other side. Despite these differences, of which only a few examples can be highlighted here, German and Italian soldiers very much appreciated the multinational cooperation in Prizren. Survey results show that the majority of the German (73.6 per cent) and Italian soldiers (72.6 per cent) considered the cooperation between the two nations to be "very good" or "good". Also, 89.4 per cent of the Italians and 86.5 per cent of the Germans were convinced that they could trust their partner and rely on the other nation in times of crisis. For both sides, social networks – formal and informal – were seen to be crucial for good and successful cooperation.

In their everyday routines, German and Italian military personnel interacted in many different ways and on many different levels, both formally and informally. In the Multinational Headquarters, they jointly convened formally each morning for multinational staff meetings to update each other on most important tasks and organise future operations. Due to some English-language deficiencies both on the German and Italian sides, the communication process in these meetings did not always run smoothly so that some of the decisions and information had to be re-discussed in the national meetings held immediately afterwards. Thus the lack of functional communication and multinational structures can strengthen a tendency towards (informal) national networks and can have, in the end, a disintegrating effect. Unofficial networks serving national interests can disrupt the functioning of the formal organisation charts and chain of command. These networks can thus pose a threat to good mutual cooperation and understanding. Despite some difficulties, German–Italian integration was good, even though the MNB (SW) did not manage to provide the basis for deep integration in every aspect. German and Italian service members accomplished their assignments by sharing responsibilities, and also came together after work on a regular basis, inviting each other for tasting either German or Italian specialities, such as beer or pasta. Through these mutual invitations, good relationships between Germans and Italians were built, and strong reciprocal ties established (cf. Mauss 1923–1924).

Despite this clearly positive example of good formal and informal cooperation, various challenges had also to be met by the multinational forces. For example, Italian servicewomen and servicemen had arrived prior to German soldiers and were also going to stay longer than their German comrades as German military personnel are deployed for four months and the Italian term is six months. As a consequence, organisational conditions added to the fact that both nations constituted a separate contingent with its own time frame and psychological phases connected to the different emotional stages of deployment (see Tomforde 2006a). In addition, for the Italians the mission in Kosovo, in comparison with other operations abroad (e.g. Iraq), was considered to be a minor task while for the Germans the Kosovo mission forms a major part of the out-of-area military involvement of the *Bundeswehr*. Interestingly enough, the Italian participation in the war in Iraq did not seem to be much of a topic in conversations between Italian and German service members as it was realised that participation or non-participation depended on political decisions made by their governments, which they, as soldiers, not always shared.

More importantly, majority–minority differences within the German-dominated camp as well as different structural conditions of both the German and Italian contingents accounted for challenges, which had to be met next to those already known for other examples of multinational cooperation: e.g. lack of a clear common task profile, varying language capabilities, priority of national (legal) systems over multinational rule sets, lack of opportunities to meet on a formal and informal basis, and thus existing prejudices and stereotypes about the other partners. Also, no joint pre-mission training had taken place that could have facilitated the development of mutual trust and a joint mission identity. Ljubica Jelušič and Bojan Pograjč (2006 and chapter 10 of this book) have shown for the trinational Italian–Hungarian–Slovenian Brigade (Multinational Land Force, MLF) from Udine (Italy), which took over the MNB Headquarters in Prizren in fall 2005 after the German contingent had returned home, that joint pre-mission training adds to better multinational understanding and successful deep integration at all levels.

It goes without saying that it is always an intricate endeavour to judge the *efficiency* or *success* of multinational missions. What is efficient, what is success and what can be seen as a failure? For example, judged from the outside, German–Italian cooperation in Kosovo was a success as mission tasks were fulfilled and no major incidents happened. Both sides valued the cooperation. Survey data highlights that the majority of the Germans (87 per cent) and Italians (74 per cent) would decide again to work in German–Italian headquarters or units.

Looking at the true integration level that was reached, however, one can say that this mission was not an overall success, but not a complete failure either. Although for a number of different reasons outlined above, national identities and boundaries were clearly maintained *inside* Camp Prizren, *outside* the Camp both German and Italian service members displayed a multinational peacekeeping identity. For example, German and Italian soldiers did not necessarily greet each other within the camp boundaries. However, once outside the site, Germans and Italians would heartily greet each other on the streets of Prizren or when patrolling the roads in Kosovo. Also, German and Italian military personnel changed their national uniforms to that extent that they added badges of the MNB (SW) or soldiers from both nations wore name tags with the German *and* Italian flags. Even if some of the soldiers did not interact daily with members from the other forces, they viewed multinational cooperation as an extra added-value to their job and held other UN, NATO or EU military partners in high esteem. In a way they were proud to be part of a multinational body and grateful for the opportunity to work multinationally. By participating in the mission, German and Italian servicemen and servicewomen felt initiated into a "global peacekeeping community", which has the important responsibility to provide the grounds for peace processes in former war areas (see also Tomforde 2006b). Indeed, already the mere fact that more than one nation is contributing to a peacekeeping mission is a message of non-alignment and even-handedness conveyed to the (multi-ethnic) populations of conflict regions. Soldiers are very much aware of the fact that their daily multinational cooperation symbolises neutrality and is meant to set a good example of multinational/multiethnic integration for the conflict and war ridden host cultures (see also Rubinstein 1998: 190). From this viewpoint, the effectiveness and legitimacy of multinational military operations do not only rely on military skills but also on the symbolic role the armed forces themselves represent and play (Chapter 14, this volume). In other words, military forces during peacekeeping missions indeed *perform* in a multinational *theatre* in the real sense of the words. As Eyal Ben-Ari and Efrat Elron (2001: 277) astutely put it: "it is the very multi-nationality of peacekeeping forces – and their constant visibility to the opposing forces – that signals the forces' neutrality and impartiality."

Daily life in Camp Airfield

In the nearby "Camp Airfield", located on a former, desert-like airfield, living and working conditions were harsher and in many ways different from the main Camp Prizren. There, both Italian and German service members lived together. Theoretically, they were also supposed to work together in the field of logistics. This cooperation was, however, made difficult by national rules and legislation. For example, Italian soldiers were not allowed to drive German military vehicles as the Italian driver's licence is not accepted under German law. German personnel, on the other hand, could not drive Italian cars as these were not fitted with seat belts – a requirement according to German regulations. Many such rules hindered cooperation on a technical level. However, soldiers of both nations helped each other as equal partners, which provided for good work and personal relationships. In spite of the fact that soldiers (mainly NCOs and enlisted personnel) from both nations were not fluent in English or the other nation's language, many good personal contacts developed between Italians and Germans. People started not only to improve their English, but also to learn Italian/German.

After work, soldiers convened in their common recreation room to cook and drink together. "Pasta and beer parties" were held on a regular basis to introduce each other into the main aspects of their respective national cultures, but also to improve mutual understanding and cooperation within the Camp. Just like in Camp Prizren, these pasta and beer gatherings were part of an informal, reciprocal network maintained by German and Italian soldiers in which national identities as well as a new, joint transnational peacekeeping identity were stressed.

As Camp Airfield was much smaller and less well equipped with recreational facilities than Camp Prizren, both Germans and Italians developed a bi- or even transnational "Camp Airfield identity", distinguishing them from personnel working in the much larger Camp Prizren. By maintaining a Camp Airfield identity, soldiers could strengthen cohesion and camaraderie within their in-group in the Camp and make the harsher living conditions tolerable. This specific identity stood out from the mere German/Italian identities and underlined the uniqueness of the Camp Airfield experience. By means of this special identity, people could be proud of belonging both to a special unit, coping with hard conditions as well as belonging to a transnational military body.

Cohesion among Italian and German military personnel was strengthened as people were in personal contact with their international comrades. Attempts were even made to learn, on a rudimentary level, either German or Italian for daily use with comrades from the other nation. As a result of these structural conditions and sociocultural practices, relationships were characterised by motivation, trust, and understanding of the other. People had a joint task to fulfil, bonded in order to make living in the Camp bearable and interesting, and lived the identity of a minority group belonging to a transnational military body.

Conclusion

> Multi-national peace-keeping forces as organizations are characterized by an inherent tension between national and transnational belonging.
>
> (Ben-Ari and Elron 2001: 271)

Military sociologists Charles Moskos, John Williams and David Segal (2000: 5–6) assume that participation in multinational missions diminishes soldiers' ties with the nation-state and alienates them from national structures. Eyal Ben-Ari's and Efrat Elron's (2001: 298) contention is, on the contrary, that the feeling of belonging to a nation state is not decreased, but rather intensified during these missions abroad. The general conclusion that can be drawn from this chapter is that the truth lies in between: national identity is retained and in some cases and settings even enhanced, *but* at the same time multiple new identity structures related to multinational peacekeeping missions are constituted. As identities are not primordial but rather negotiated situationally and flexibly (cf. Hannerz 1992: 230–241; Dumont 1986: 25–30; Barth 1969: 10–18), peacekeeping soldiers can display both their national identities and multinational or even transnational identities at the same time.

It is through concrete interactions and sociocultural practices found in peacekeeping missions that (new transnational) identities are constituted, negotiated and played out on a situational basis. Research data shows that this is only partly the case. Indeed, daily interactions and sociocultural practices during multinational operations bring differences between cooperating military forces in the foreground. But, and most importantly, they also have a socialising effect. It is my contention that multinational service members are, step by step and to varying degrees and at differing paces, initiated into a truly transnational peacekeeping identity and subculture that exist next to national ones. Each deployment adds to further experiences that are passed down from one comrade to the next, from one contingent to the other. In total, each mission plays an important part in socialising the military personnel into today's new, transformed "global" armed forces mainly involved nowadays in missions of multinational character. Just like employees working for international companies or, also, civil servants working for the European Union, soldiers become accustomed to international cooperation and integrate these (new) multinational tasks into their self-perceptions (see Trondall and Veggeland 2003: 75–77). Multiple military identities and alliances that are supplementing national allegiances are the result. A truly transnational peacekeeping habitus ("we are all the same, working towards the same aims") is developing that can help to overcome obstacles hindering integration such as language problems, lack of clear tasks, structures aimed at integration, prevailing prejudices or stereotypes. People thus see a deeper meaning in what they do and show a high level of commitment to multinational structures. Working in peacekeeping operations is seen to be more significant and interesting than the sometimes monotonous military service in their home countries. Many soldiers are convinced nowadays that one has to have participated in at least one mission abroad in order to talk about multinational missions, which have become so central to today's armed forces. Despite existing differences and challenges that have to be met, there seems to be a broad acceptance as well as support of multinational structures. The soldiers we interviewed were convinced that they served the important transnational goals of stabilisation of conflict areas and peace. This shared meaning of peacekeeping missions as well as a common military culture form the basis for a new transnational military identity that is gradually developing next to its national counterpart (see also King 2005: 331; Evetts 2002).

Chapter 10

Diversity versus effectiveness in multinational units

Italian, Hungarian, and Slovenian cooperation in the multinational land force

Ljubica Jelušič and Bojan Pograjč

Introduction

Nowadays military organizations have many studies, handbooks and guidelines concerning the use of equipment, technological integration of troops in operations, military hierarchy, rules of engagement, and assigned tasks to the deployed units. There is still a lack, however, of professional rules concerning the training of professional soldiers to execute their tasks with empathy toward the local population; of education about different culture patterns and historical events of the armies involved in the military operation; of studies on communication and language diversity of the troops and regions where the operation is carried out. These aspects form the qualitative side of military effectiveness. They are important for the mission outcome and for the satisfaction of the soldiers who perform their job within the multinational military formations.

The multinationality of military formations

Multinational military formations exist in many forms of varying permanency (Klein and Haltiner 2004). Some units are in standing military formations, whereas the others are ad hoc structures, formed to fulfil an assigned task in a mission, and reshaped after or abandoned after the completion of the task. Synchronization of the activities of these units requires cultural, operational and institutional compatibility. The effectiveness of the units is a result of the synchronization on all three levels, and it is a long-term process. Cultural compatibility includes the political decision-making of forming and deploying units, and is subjected to the current political life and distribution of power in each country. Although Rules of Engagement (RoE) exist and specify when to deploy military units, real-world crises often require politicians to make immediate deployment decisions about unforeseen events. This means that military personnel, no matter how well-trained and operational they are, depend on an agreement among the political leaders of each contributing country.

Most European countries have military units deployed in peace operations outside of the home country's borders. After the Cold War, the logic of national defence was transformed into international defence of national interests. The aim of the new missions is to provide protection from terrorist attacks, international crime, human trafficking, and similar threats. These new operations always occur in a multinational setting, which may or may not affect the operational activities of deployed military units. Usually, the command, staff and officers from the contributing nations collaborate in a multinational headquarters, and then transmit the internationally agreed tasks to their national units, who execute these tasks.

Multinationality is a prominent political and military feature of NATO and EU countries. Even great powers like Germany have expressed their readiness to accept the multinational character of military formations as a fact. Slovenia has an armed force of 7,228 troops, of which 3,077 were deployed abroad in peace missions in the past ten years. For Slovenian military personnel, deploying in multinational units has become common. Slovenian soldiers have no other choice but to join forces with other nations. As a consequence the education and socialization process within the military must stress the new reality of being deployable in a multinational framework. The military should try to minimize national feelings and patriotism and to transfer loyalty from the nation state to the international politico-military organizations and to the military headquarters of the multinational force.

The restructuring of the Slovenian military for multinational operations

Adapting the Slovenian military to meet international requirements for peace operations abroad was not easy or short for many reasons. The Slovenian Armed Forces (SAF) was formed while gaining independence[1] in 1991 and its territorial force character had been the basic reason of its successful stopping of the attacks from the "multinational" former Yugoslav People Army during the June–July 1991 armed conflict. The newly formed Slovenian military was defined as a defence force that was not supposed to move beyond the state borders. Generations of Slovenian soldiers had been trained in the former Yugoslavia, where they had to serve in the military (compulsory or professional service) outside the borders of the Republic of Slovenia, in other former Yugoslav republics. This de-territorialization of military service socialized conscripts in the cultures and languages of other Yugoslav regions. Although the working language was Serbian, conscripts kept their own languages (Slovenian, Croatian, Macedonian, Albanian, etc.) for personal conversations in their free time. Being part of units of conscripts from different cultural settings helped young men to understand the cultural distances, and to disregard social differences in order to make military cohesion possible. Most Slovenian soldiers, however, hated this feature of military training. For many of them it was a reason to express the conscientious objection against military service. The new Slovenian military respected such feelings and its founders tried to avoid all characteristics that would look like the former Yugoslav military. Although military service was friendlier towards conscripts in comparison to the former Yugoslav army, the motivation to serve in the military nevertheless rapidly decreased and, in 2001, the number of conscientious objectors reached one-third of the age cohort.

In 2002, politicians decided to end conscription. The last draftees finished their compulsory service in 2003. The decision to end the draft was made under pressure from the Slovenian public and to answer the political demand to have a constabulary force ready to contribute to peace support operations (PSO). Conscripts and reservists could not indeed be deployed outside the country and therefore were unable to contribute to the major missions of the military. International deployments began in 1997 with a medical staff platoon, serving in the operation ALBA in Albania. In the past ten years the number of deployed soldiers participating in peacekeeping operations dramatically increased, reaching its highest number (977) in August 2007. Since then, the military has been confronted by the same problem that formerly kept Slovenian people out of the former Yugoslav military – multiculturalism. The Slovenian military that had carefully tried to form its identity of serving-at-home (soldiers trained near their hometown) during the period of conscription (1991–2002) transformed its culture into one of deployments abroad (Bosnia-Herzegovina, Kosovo, Lebanon, Afghanistan, Syria, Sudan, Congo). Learning how to cope with multiculturalism became important again, although in more complicated circumstances, where languages and cultures are more foreign than the Slavic speaking former Yugoslav military.

In order to adapt to the new situation, the SAF underwent a substantial restructuring. A new unit was formed in 1996 called the Battalion for International Cooperation. This Battalion, composed of volunteer soldiers, was designed to participate to international missions (peacekeeping, manoeuvres, bilateral and multilateral exercises, training outside Slovenia), while the other units would serve only within Slovenia to defend the borders. The Battalion for International Cooperation became the elite and best-equipped unit in the military.

Slovenia asked for NATO membership in 1996, but the application was rejected at the NATO Madrid Summit in July 1997. The political attempts made in 1996 to show the readiness of Slovenian politicians and the military to carry out the Alliance obligations did not satisfy NATO's requirements.

Beside the initiative to form the Battalion for International Cooperation, there are at least two additional important multinational moves worth mentioning. Slovenia announced its readiness to contribute to the Multinational United Nations Stand-by Forces High Readiness Brigade. The trilateral cooperation of Slovenia, Hungary, and Italy was initiated in the Foreign Ministers' Statement in 1996. This political forum served as the framework to form the Multinational Land Force Brigade (MLF) as a common three-state military formation.

The multinational land force

The Agreement to form the MLF was signed in Rome by the defence ministers of the three contributing countries on 18 April 1998. The organization of the MLF was negotiated over a period of three years and formally agreed in a Memorandum of Understanding, signed in Rome on 12 July 2001. The MLF is a brigade-level forma-tion with a permanent integrated command structure, established on the organi-zational principle of the lead nation (Italy) without standing troops. Troops are assembled at special request, and must be identified at the end of the year for the next year. Italy, as a lead nation, contributes the commander of the formation and a brigade-level command with the majority of the posts occupied by Italian officers, and the remaining by individuals from other two nations. The home basis of the HQ is Udine in Italy. The working language in HQ is English; the official languages are the three languages of the contributing countries (Italian, Hungarian, and Sloven-ian). The level of integration has two dimensions, HQ and units. The HQ operates as integrated structure (its members work together on permanent basis in Udine); the units are not integrated, created as separate national modules by countries pooling their resources on an ad-hoc basis for a single operation. The MLF can be deployed as a humanitarian, peacekeeping, conflict preventing or interposition force.

Data and methods

The MLF unit was the subject of different surveys because of expectations that it will serve as an experiment to study the interoperability of the three-nation armed forces. In 2001, three research teams from the three cooperating countries joined their efforts in a common project, analysing the sociological problems of the unit, such as personal and work relations, military traditions, organization methods of different parts of the unit, disciplinary aspects, integration level, and officers' coping with differing cultural backgrounds of the force members. The results of the study were published in the book *Sociological Aspects Concerning the Relations Within Contingents of Multinational Units*, edited by Gianfranco Gasperini (Italy), Beno Arnejčič (Slovenia), and András Ujj (Hungary) in 2001.[2] The survey method consisted of a structured questionnaire, completed by all officers who took part in the MLF exercises.

The officers had different levels of international experiences. Italian officers belonging to the Julia Alpine Brigade had direct experience in international mandates and multinational missions (Gasperini *et al.* 2001: 84). Slovenian offi-cers belonging to the Military Police and the Battalion for International Cooper-ation had limited experiences from SFOR assignments. Hungarian officers had experience from service abroad in UN, SFOR, and OSCE missions.

The second study was devoted to the historical perspective of the MLF polit-ical and military development in comparison to other European multinational units. The study was conducted by Bojan Pograjč (Slovenia) and published in his BSc thesis at the University of Ljubljana in 2006.

The third empirical study called *The Social Analysis of Slovenian Military Cooperation in Peace Support Operations and at the International Military Headquarters*,[3] was conducted among Slovenian MLF staff members (officers and NCOs) after finishing their deployment in the 2006 KFOR mission. In May and June 2006, the researchers[4] from the Defence Research Centre (DRC), Faculty of Social Sciences, University of Ljubljana, conducted semi-structured interviews. All interviewed respondents were deployed at the Headquarters Brigade South-West in KFOR in the 2005–2006 rotation as part of the Italian contingent in HQ that had two leading nations, Italy and Germany. The empirical findings of the correlation between cultural diversity and military effectiveness of multinational units rely on a secondary analysis of the conclusions, published by Gasperini *et al.* (2001), Gasperini (2004), Pograjč (2006) and the analysis of primary sources, collected in interviews in 2006.

Results

Cultural and organizational problems of the MLF at the beginning of its manning

During its formation in 2001, the MLF encountered several problems typical for multinational military formations (Gasperini 2004; Gasperini *et al.* 2001). Respondents of the 2001 MLF survey stressed the controversies between the working language (English) and the official national languages of the component parts (Slovenian, Italian, and Hungarian). Difficulty in understanding each other at the beginning of the unit formation led to feelings of marginalization and self-marginalization among some officers, especially from the Slovenian and Hungarian contingents. The respondents stated that the Italian operational procedures were a problem for the two other parts, given the historically different army styles (Slovenian and Hungarian). Slovenia as non-NATO member at that time maintained traditions from its territorial defence history. Hungary as the country invited to join the NATO in 1997 was at the beginning of an internal restructuring based on NATO standards.

The level of unit integration was very low. It reflected the limited amount of experience the military personnel had from previous cooperation in multinational formations. Italian soldiers had a long tradition of cooperation in NATO structures. Hungarian soldiers brought very important knowledge from UN peacekeeping and SFOR operation. Slovenian officers had very little experience in multinational operational settings at that time. The MLF survey found integration obstacles between officers and soldiers, officers and NCOs, and field officers. They thought misunderstandings between the three nations could be avoided with improved English-language capabilities. It would eliminate, according to them, the misunderstandings and possibility of an atmosphere of mutual distrust. Improved language skills and increased joint experiences were thought to be the main solution for achieving a higher integration level (Gasperini *et al.* 2001: 193).

Although members of the MLF staff were carefully chosen, they had to over-come prejudices and professional shortcomings in order to establish functional relationships, while deployed at the MLF home base in Udine.

Personal and professional relationships among staff members depended on mutual understanding due to the language barriers and historical prejudices. The first members of the MLF staff from Slovenia were officers and NCOs who were personally motivated to gain new military experiences. They had little experience operating in international military frameworks, and despite their knowledge of the English language, they had problems with the military vocabu-lary, especially the English NATO standard expressions (STANAG vocabulary and procedures).

There were some historical concerns, expressed mainly by Slovenia, during the political establishment and manning phase of the MLF. The Slovenian public and media questioned the credibility of forming a military unit with Italy due historical memories from of the Italian occupation of Slovenian territory before and during the Second World War. Some attention focused on the name of the Italian unit about to lead the MLF organization. This unit, Julia Alpine Brigade, with its home base in Udine, was known to some Slovenian war veterans as the executor of cruel military attacks during the Second World War in Slovenia. The Slovenian government respected the public feelings by asking Slovenian sol-diers who were selected as candidates for HQ in Udine to express their personal historical feeling about the cooperation with Italian unit. Candidates with per-sonal reluctance or prejudice towards Italy were excluded from a job in the MLF. The Slovenian officer who ran the selection process for the MLF staff, said in the interview:

> The officers who cooperated in the common exercises with Italians and Hungarians were candidates for MLF staff functions. I told them – anybody who has some historical problems that would be an obstacle for his coopera-tion with Italians and Hungarians at the exercises or during the operation are asked to step out. They don't need to cooperate in this project.

The respondents, interviewed in 2006, reported that they never experienced or felt any pressure from their military collaborators regarding these historical questions. They never researched the historical origins of the lead nation unit. During our survey, they admitted that they were not familiar with the content of the military museum of the Julia Alpine Brigade in Udine, but promised to visit it after returning to the staff offices there.

Lead-nation principle and forced adaptation

The lead-nation principle of organization is very common to structures where one great military power invites small countries to contribute troops in accord-ance with their ability. Small countries would, on the other hand, rarely organize multinational units in which they would take the role of a lead nation. This task belongs to bigger countries that are financially/economically sound enough to form battalion- or brigade-level units, and that have enough personnel to develop the main structure of unit. Small countries may take crucial, but out-sourced tasks in such units. Soldiers from small countries are expected, no matter how important are their duties and how well performed they are, to surrender specific cultural expectations, professional standards, and discipline codes to the lead nation.

One key aspect for the integration of small countries units relates to the amount of responsibility that they can undertake. Small countries usually join military operations in which their units are too small to take their own area of responsibility. They contribute their national modules to bigger units which are able to organize transport, logistical support, build the bases, and organize the retreat in case of emergency. Because they are not able to be fully autonomous in the field, they must be ready to fulfil the given tasks in a professional way, but they can hardly influence the methods of assigning the tasks to the soldiers participating in the mission.

On the other hand, the lead-nation principle helps in establishing uniformed rules of engagement and codes of behaviour, necessary for achieving a higher level of military effectiveness. The MLF structure followed this pattern. The Slovenian and Hungarian members of the MLF staff cooperated in Italian-led activities, such us organizing training, exercises and events of the formation, but, initially, rarely proposed initiatives to transform the Italian procedures to the needs of the two additional components. This caused some discussions about the unit uniformity. On the one hand, some, mainly Italian officers, were in favour of developing specific organizational principles and integration procedures for the MLF Brigade. Slovenian and Hungarian officers, on the other hand, preferred using NATO standard integration procedures, given that the costs for implementing them would be smaller. After 2001, a search for more international integration procedures began. Developing NATO experience among Hungarian troops and convergence to the same knowledge level among Slovenian troops helped to favour the NATO identity. The 2004 integration of Slovenia to NATO and the growing self-confidence of Hungarian soldiers gained from their NATO experiences helped to reach a final decision, i.e. if MLF is supposed to be a unit on call for NATO purposes, it must be established according to NATO integration standards. The development of this decision shows that the structure of multinational units is a product of turbulences and internal debates, and not always a clearly perceived goal from the beginning of the unit. One Slovenian officer described this process in the interview:

> There were hard times at the beginning. We did not know each other. So, we adapted to the lead nation principles of the Italian military. But we recognized through time that Italians were also changing. If we had some suggestions, they would accept and respect them.

Language in everyday work and language in risk situations

There is a general expectation, that there should be one official language to guarantee effective communication flows within the mission (Szvircsev *et al.* 2007). In order to achieve the maximum effectiveness, there should be also one official language in every multinational military formation. Usually, the units that are formed within the NATO framework or which were established to cooperate in NATO missions tend to have English as the official language. English communication is also a good choice in units where constituent parts are very weak in speaking or understanding the language of the lead nation. If we turn back to the example of the Italian–Hungarian–Slovenian MLF Brigade, we see that its founders agreed to have English as official language, because it was very difficult for Hungarian and Slovenian officers and NCOs to speak Italian fluently enough to communicate on all practical issues. So, despite the fact that Italy is the lead nation, English was chosen as the working language for all three nations. This decision was very operational – the MLF was supposed to be deployed under NATO or EU request; therefore it was important for staff personnel to be integrated not only within the HQ, but also as a possible unit under NATO command. Therefore, in this respect, the nations constituting the MLF were very equal.

In 1997, when the unit was formed, Italian officers were more fluent in military terminology and NATO abbreviations practices, because they had plenty of experiences from past NATO operations and activities. Slovenian and Hungarian officers lagged behind in this respect. The survey carried out by Gasperini *et al.* (2001) confirmed the higher level of English-language capabilities among Italian officers and the rather poorer English of Slovenian and Hungarian officers, at least at the level of officers' self-perceptions. This problem influenced the effectiveness of training, common exercises, and mutual understanding within the officers corps of the MLF. Practical exercises demonstrated that converting to English was difficult, but it was not the only reason for slowing down the development of unit readiness. Usually, lead-nation officers tended to communicate among themselves in Italian because it was more convenient to make decisions quickly, rather than first share the information in English with their Slovenian and Hungarian counterparts and then decide. As everyone's English improved, the need for Italian officers to speak their own language while working with the two other groups decreased. One Slovenian officer described the Slovenian integration through improved English-language capabilities as:

> We had to break the ice two times. First, with English knowledge, and second, with presenting our military experiences in the international circumstances. So, it was not enough to have the knowledge, it was more important to push it through and make it evident. We lacked the experiences in rhetoric and self-confident appearances.

The Slovenian and Hungarian officers and NCOs, who joined the MLF Head-quarter in Udine, stayed there to work and train together for two or even four years. The Udine HQ is not only the MLF home base, but also the home base of the Julia Alpine Brigade. According to the survey among Slovenian participants in the HQ functions (conducted in 2006), the majority of the HQ activities cannot be fulfilled without entering into the network of the Julia Alpine Brigade, be it in logistical, communication, or training aspects. Although the MLF staff members use English as the working language within the MLF HQ, they some-times experienced problems with Italian military personnel outside the MLF framework at the same base. They realized that the only effective communica-tion with them had to be in Italian.

Therefore, Slovenian officers decided, that in order to make the everyday life in Udine easier (in some cases they also have families there), they should learn Italian before coming to Udine or during the initial stages of their work. When we talked to them in June 2006, they mentioned the importance of English as the working language, but mainly for cooperation in MLF staff activities. For pur-poses of effective work in Udine they stressed the importance of basic know-ledge of the Italian language. They adapted to the situation of being under a lead-nation command by improving their English and learning the second lan-guage, Italian. Working effectiveness was the primary goal over maintaining cultural differences.

They did not report similar tendencies in learning the third language in the unit, Hungarian. With relation to their Hungarian colleagues, they developed another pattern of behaviour. They tried to learn some basic expressions in this language or they tended to learn the trilingual expressions of some words to express some empathy towards their Hungarian colleagues. Nobody has learned Hungarian in order to increase military or everyday work effectiveness yet.

We mentioned that some members of the MLF HQ were deployed in KFOR, in the German–Italian Brigade Headquarters South-West, first in 2004 and in rotation November 2005–May 2006. They served in this capacity as individual officers and NCOs. English was the official mission language. As members of the Slovenian Army and of the MLF structure they found themselves in a special contradictory situation. Being members of the MLF they had high sympathies for the Italian part of the HQ working problems. On the other hand they could cooperate quite well with German staffers, whom they found culturally and organizationally more similar to themselves. Some of the Slovenian soldiers even understood German expressions, due to their primary-school German-language classes.

When emergencies occurred, Slovenian soldiers realized something surprising for them: although they were all supposed to communicate in English, German staffers would switched to German to discuss the situation among them-selves and Italian staffers would do the same. After a while, all staff members would switch back into English. The lesson Slovenians learned was that emer-gency cases may cause language set-backs. In such cases, it is good to have a basic knowledge of the languages of the lead nations within the HQs.

In emergency cases, Slovenian military people felt more tightly connected with their MLF comrades with whom they had previously trained while working in Udine and in common exercises. These ties even evolved through the operation into a specific MLF military identity. Although for an observer just a piece of tissue, the emblem of the MLF unit they wore on their uniforms became within the HQ Brigade South-West a real form of symbolic identity and differentiation.

MLF/KFOR members were dispersed throughout the HQ into different functions and, from an operational point of view, were not supposed to directly cooperate with each other. In fact, they kept their MLF ties, exchanged all news, information and emotions. In our qualitative survey in May–June 2006, which was conducted immediately after returning ceremony in Udine, they expressed a growing enthusiasm to continue their common work with their comrades in Udine. The mission seemed to have contributed to their interpersonal integration and operational effectiveness.

Military traditions and civil–military relations

The end of the mission was for the Slovenian members of the MLF/KFOR mission a new lesson in civil–military relations. They described the ceremony in downtown Udine in which they took part together with their families and where the inhabitants of Udine welcomed the returning troops with great respect and celebrations. The military parade from the barracks to the city centre respected the everyday life of the city (public transport was not stopped), and many citizens attended the ceremony. When Slovenian respondents spoke about the ceremony in our interviews, we realized that they were amazed by the public acceptance of the military tradition, and by the way in which citizens of Udine greeted their soldiers from international missions as heroes.

The soldiers and the audience sang the Italian anthem together with the military orchestra, which was a surprise for the Slovenian participants. Such ceremony would hardly happen in Slovenia. Those interviewed said that the SAF has not developed these remarkable military ceremonies yet. Beside, the public would probably view a military parade downtown as a militarization of the civil society. Searching through the recent history of the SAF, we found that the last open public manifestations of the SAF dated back to the conscript times. These were usually organized when conscripts arrived at the military barracks and after three weeks when they celebrated the end of their initial training stage in the military with an oath. In some towns, this ceremony was organized in the city centres. After 2003, when the SAF became an all-volunteer force, such public appearances were never organized again. The SAF instead organizes "open-door days" where citizens are invited into the barracks, but reciprocity is not assured. Local communities invite the military only when they need some logistical or cultural support from it (cooking at public manifestations, tents for local needs, military orchestra to play at festivities, etc.).

Conclusion

The Italian–Hungarian–Slovenian MLF Brigade was formed to carry out peace support operations within the framework of the Petersberg declaration, including combat tasks. It has never been deployed as a whole unit, but has many experiences in deployment exercises. The cooperating military organizations have tried to improve interoperability and assimilated standard NATO integration procedures. Some parts of it are currently transformed into the European Battle Group. Based on the data we collected among participants of the MLF activities, we may conclude the following.

Cultural differences in military formations are not obstacles to a unit's effectiveness if the unit successfully formulates the organizational principles, procedures, and integrative standards. In the case of the MLF, the solution was to adapt NATO standard operating procedures. Members of the unit must be encouraged and personally motivated to respect cultural differences and overcome historical prejudices. Improving working language skills can help to solve integration and communication problems. However, it is not enough to improve personal relations and create social networks among soldiers. Military units from small countries, or from countries contributing troops to a larger lead-nation unit, must also learn some basic expressions in the lead-nation language (if it is not English) in order to overcome the expected chaos in crisis events, when people under stress tend to switch back to their mother tongue. If military personnel are supposed to work at the multinational headquarters within the country of the lead nation, they should also learn the language of the civilian environment.

At the beginning, the cultural differences between Italian, Hungarian, and Slovenian members of the MLF were an impediment for achieving more rapidly military effectiveness. With years of common exercises, improving language skills, and common staff deployment in peace operations, however, these cultural differences lost their disintegrative character and instead became a source of mutual understanding. The MLF Brigade, now partly the EUBG, will still have to demonstrate if the achieved level is enough for deployment in EU crisis response operations.

Notes

1 Slovenia declared its independence on 25 June 1991. It was immediately followed by an armed attack from the Yugoslav Peoples' Army. The war was finished after ten days of clashes and the signing of the Brioni Peace Declaration; Slovenia achieved internationally recognized independence in January 1992.

2 The survey was executed by the Military Centre for Strategic Studies in Rome, the Centre for Strategic Studies at the Slovenian Ministry of Defence, and by the Office for Strategic and Defence Studies of the Hungarian Ministry of Defence.

3 The Project is led by Ljubica Jelušič and is sponsored by the Slovenian Ministries of Defence and of Higher Education, Science and Technology under programme CRP MIR 2004–2010.

4 The researchers Jelena Juvan and Ljubica Jelušič asked questions on the tasks of respondents in the MLF and at HQ Brigade South-West; the characteristics of organizational culture in the MLF (symbols, rituals, military tradition, discipline, common trust), language problems in the MLF and at HQ Brigade South-West, personal and professional relations in the MLF, impact of the deployment on the MLF culture, impact of the joint training on the MLF cohesion and integration. The respondents described their experiences on these topics in accordance with their own personal duties during the permanent work at the MLF staff in Udine and during their mission in Kosovo. Some respondents were deployed in Kosovo as MLF members twice, in 2004 and 2006. The interviews partly repeated some research questions, conducted by Gasperini *et al.* in 2001, in order to find the differences over time.

Chapter 11

Swedish–Irish cooperation in Liberia

Erik Hedlund, Louise Weibull, and Joseph Soeters

Introduction

Today international commitments have become the core of operations conducted by the Swedish Armed Forces (SAF), and Swedish military units, in cooperation with military forces from other nations, are increasingly active in international, peace-promoting and humanitarian tasks.[1]

Therefore, the ability to cooperate successfully, in the widely varying social and cultural environments in which Swedish troops may be committed, places increasing demands on knowledge and awareness within the field of cultural competence and cooperation (Andersson 2001; Blomgren and Johansson 2005; Blomgren 2007; Johansson 2001; Hagen *et al.* 2003, 2006; Klep and Winslow 2000; Berggren 2005). Cooperation in Military Operations Other Than War (MOOTW) not only involves military units, but also, to an increasing degree, police forces, NGOs, civil authorities and the civilian population (Gareis *et al.* 2003; Blomgren and Johansson 2005, Callaghan and Schönborr 2004). Despite the fact that politicians,[2] military officers, and researchers have repeatedly stressed the importance of an improvement in social and cultural awareness, this field of study has not yet become a priority issue for the Swedish Armed Forces.[3] In order to better prepare Swedish officers and soldiers for future missions – apart from appropriate training – there needs to be more research focusing on Swedish experience in various operational theatres.

This chapter aims to analyse the social and cultural strains between Swedish and Irish troops in a Quick Reaction Force in Liberia. More specifically, we want to illustrate (a) how perceptions of the Irish developed and spread within the Swedish contingent, before and during the mission, (b) how these perceptions changed over time, and (c) how Swedes were regarded by the Irish and locally employed Liberians.[4]

Background

In September 2003, after 14 years of bloody civil war that claimed between 150,000 and 200,000 human lives, the UN Security Council decided to establish a multinational peacekeeping force, the United Nations Mission in Liberia (UNMIL). UNMIL's task was to support the ceasefire agreement and the peace process and to protect the civilian population and UN personnel.[5] The 15,000-strong force that came from countries such as Pakistan, Nigeria, Ethiopia, Bangladesh, Ireland, and Sweden was also tasked with beginning the disarmament process and assisting in national security reforms, including national police training and the formation of a new, restructured military.

The first Swedish deployment to Liberia was in February 2004 (LA 01). The Swedes became part of an integrated Quick Reaction Force (QRF) with Ireland as the lead nation. The QRF did not have its own Area of Responsibility, and its task was basically, at short notice, to provide support to other UN forces anywhere in the country, in the event of violent upheaval and attacks by insurgents. Another task, exclusively for this mission, was guaranteeing safety and public order during the trial of Charles Taylor in Freetown, Sierra Leone.

The Swedish contribution was a 230-strong, fully equipped, mechanised infantry company, while the Irish contribution was a reduced mechanised infantry battalion of about 430 personnel. Both had their own support, maintenance, and administrative personnel. Since Ireland was the lead nation, the Commanding Officer (CO) of the complete contingent was Irish. It was not until the middle of the second deployment (LA02) that Sweden provided the Second-in-Command (2IC) of the contingent; according to Swedes, this did much to improve Swedish–Irish cooperation.

The Battalion was deployed on a headland just north of Monrovia close to the once luxury hotel, Hotel Africa, with beautiful views over the sea. Although the Battalion was physically integrated in a shared camp, a small road divided the national contingents' respective areas. In addition, there was almost complete separation of tasks, except for the HQ and planning sections, a common communications centre, and some medical facilities. Each country had its own guard and patrol duties, maintenance section and also its own logistic facilities in terms of food, accommodation and leisure time (welfare). The camp bar was run solely by the Irish and the only shop on camp was run by the Swedes. There were significant differences in the standard of accommodation, vehicles, and equipment. The Irish lived in air-conditioned tents, while Swedes lived in air-conditioned containers with dehumidifiers. Swedish vehicles and equipment were much more modern and in better condition than Irish vehicles and equipment.

Despite the fact that the QRF has received much praise for its efforts (Almén and Sörensen 2007), cooperation and integration between the Swedish and the Irish have not been perfect and without their complications. As early as the first Swedish mission, cultural friction emerged and the road between the two contingents became more social than physical (Sjöblom 2005). The Swedes felt that the Irish kept a much more hierarchical distance between soldiers, NCOs, and officers. Irish commanders often made decisions themselves, without consulting subordinates. The Swedish military doctrine of "auftragstaktik" (mission command) (Vogelaar and Kramer 2004), which places greater responsibility for how tasks are dealt with at a lower operational level, was not socially or culturally interoperable with the more hierarchical structure of the Irish. There were also basic differences in ideas on what constitutes a task and how it should be completed. If Swedes are generally encouraged to use their own initiative, it is not the case among Irish. The Swedes also felt that the Irish had less restrictive rules and norms concerning alcohol consumption, socialising with the local population, and visiting prostitutes.

In general, Swedes had a relatively negative view of Irish behaviour. A later study – of the third mission in Liberia (LA03) – (Weibull and Johansson 2006) showed that Swedish perceptions of the Irish, acquired during the first mission, were basically unchanged, i.e. Swedish perceptions of the Irish were still largely negative. Almost half of the Swedish respondents (46 per cent) said that they had experienced conflict with Irish personnel, while approximately one third (34 per cent) did not share this experience. Individual appointments seem to have played a role here; e.g. it appears that everyone in the Battalion staff experienced conflict with the Irish, whereas figures for the maintenance unit were much lower – about a quarter (26 per cent) and in the infantry company just over a half (52 per cent). The study also contained questions about Swedes' perceptions of cooperation with the Irish in general: 11 per cent were very positive and 7 per cent very negative. The majority of answers, however, were in the middle of the scale, with almost equal numbers saying they were either fairly positive or fairly negative (42 per cent and 40 per cent respectively).

When Swedes were asked which factors they considered to have the greatest influence on the climate of cooperation in multinational units (Weibull and Johansson 2006), respondents cited good language ability and a common position and policies concerning relationships with the civilian population; i.e. areas emphasising communication and a common view on ethical issues. As far as language ability was concerned, Swedes generally considered themselves to be quite good. A few mentioned that the Irish accent was occasionally difficult to understand. Others even had a tendency to think they were better than the Irish ("sometimes the Irish aren't very good at ordinary school English!").[6]

Data

Semi-structured, individual interviews and, to a limited extent, participatory observation (Gellner and Hirsch 2001) were mainly used to collect data for this study. Twelve people in the Swedish group (ten privates, one reserve officer, one officer), selected by our point of contact during pre-deployment training, were the project's main respondents; they were interviewed three times: first, during pre-deployment training, second, five months into the deployment (August 2006) and finally, six months after their return home (May 2007).[7] On our first visit to Camp Clara, five additional Swedish respondents were interviewed, including the Second-in-Command (2IC) of the contingent and the

Press Officer. During our second visit (October 2006) 12 Irish personnel (ten privates, one NCO and one officer) and six local employees were interviewed. A total of 35 interviews were conducted. Each interview lasted about 45 minutes to $1\frac{1}{2}$ hours; all interviews were recorded and transcribed. The respondents were men and women between 21 and 45 years of age. The interviews of locally employed Liberians took the form of two group interviews. All Swedes and locally employed Liberians were interviewed by the Swedish co-authors. Irish personnel were interviewed by the Dutch co-author, the aim being to allow them to feel that they could talk freely about the Swedish. The two one-week visits to Liberia also allowed us to gather data via informal conversations and to get a better picture of the working conditions and the physical environment.

Results

The emergence and spread of perceptions

During the pre-deployment training, which lasted approximately two months, there was almost no formal information given about the lessons learned from previous missions in Liberia. Despite this, there was a widespread and common image of the Irish, which indicates extensive informal learning. In some cases this informal learning seems to have started as early as basic military training and come from unit officers who had served on previous missions. For those who were particularly interested, information about the Irish could be obtained from an unofficial, independent website. This website, which was available for the duration of the Liberian missions, included a discussion forum where experiences from Liberia were discussed – including opinions about the Irish. However, the most influential informal learning channel was the pre-deployment training. Here, respondents testify to an extensive transfer of informal information and knowledge. For younger soldiers in such a situation, the most important and most respected sources were soldiers with previous service abroad, especially in Liberia.

Meeting places

At platoon level and below the main meeting places for daily job-related contacts with the Irish were the shared communications centre and the vehicle repair unit. There was no real operational cooperation except for a few long-range patrols. During their spare time, the social contacts between Swedes and Irish were effectively non-existent because there were no natural meeting places in the camp. The camp pub, which was run by the Irish, was only frequented by a few Swedes and they tended to sit at a table by themselves in the outer areas of the premises. The Irish sat in larger groups, talking noisily in order to make themselves heard above the crowd and the background music. The Swedes described a sense of not feeling welcome, not feeling at home, and not being comfortable in the noisy, raucous atmosphere. The bar was more like an Irish party or carnival than a place for Swedes and Irish to meet and socialise with each other.

In other words, the lack of meeting places meant that the Swedes and the Irish had no opportunity to deepen their knowledge and understanding of each other.

Perceptions of the Irish

Before the mission

Before the mission had even started, the Irish were generally viewed as being disorderly and rowdy. However, some Swedes had more moderate opinions, differentiating between different battalions[8] and acknowledging individual differences among the Irish as a group. That said, there was a general and widely shared opinion that the Irish were inclined to start a party and drink alcohol as soon as the opportunity presented itself.

> The guys who were down there before us, they were rowdy – trouble-makers. They say that certain Irishmen are damned good and some are bad, it depends a bit on who they send out there too. They hit the bottle a lot more, the only thing they did in their spare time was to drink an awful lot.

The Irish were also said to have visited prostitutes, despite the fact that this was forbidden.

Even though the general view of the Irish was negative and emphasised perceived deficiencies in many areas, there was general recognition of their professional ability to carry out their military tasks: "Everyone I have met has been very professional; many of them have been on international operations before."

During the mission

Swedish perceptions of the Irish before the mission remained more or less unchanged after six months of living in the same camp. However, during the mission new issues emerged, which indicated social and cultural differences between the Swedes and the Irish. According to Swedes, Irish soldiers generally seemed to be less well educated, working-class and potential criminals, who basically had to choose between joining up, being unemployed or going to prison: "on the other hand, they are people who would either have been in jail or been unemployed". This compares with the Swedes who had all completed high school. Many had completed extensive vocational-training programmes or had started or completed university or college education.

Swedish officers and soldiers are recruited for positions based on their skills and interests. According to Swedes, this contrasted with the Irish situation, where the skills and interests of ordinary soldiers are not taken into account; they are simply posted into vacant positions: "Nobody has looked into what skills they might have from civilian life and what they would like to do. They're just put into a position." This, combined with the fact that many of the Irish were professional soldiers who had been ordered to deploy, contributed towards a comparatively lower degree of motivation, will and ambition to do a good job.

> So, you see, they're not volunteers – so both their morale and their will to be here is not as great and the obvious result is as you might expect – they would rather stay in camp than go out and complete an assignment.

Swedes, on the other hand, saw themselves as being extremely motivated because they wanted to experience as much adventure as possible during their six-month mission.

Nor were the Irish regarded as organising their activities with the same degree of advance planning as the Swedes; instead they seemed to take things as they came, which, according to Swedish views, led to a certain amount of disorder and chaos. This *laissez-faire* mentality differed considerably from the Swedish model.

> I think they deal with assignments as things come up, which in itself isn't the wrong kind of attitude, because there are examples where units with that approach have managed much better when things go to pot. But this is typical of the things that we've reacted against here – things that are very difficult for Swedes to understand.

In addition to comments on the Irish *laissez-faire* mentality, another constantly recurring topic of conversation among Swedes was – in their view – the lack of hygiene procedures among the Irish. "Well, take a look in their canteen, you can go in there and compare the level of hygiene in their compound and ours. All right, it works, but not much more than that." The Swedes were obviously proud of their hygiene procedures, which included washing their hands with soap and water, then disinfecting them with "alcogel" before and after meals and after going to the toilet. Swedes were also very proud of their higher standard of accommodation, living condition, and their much better organised part of the camp. The stricter order of things in the Swedish part of the camp led the Irish to call it "Little Germany".

However, if there was one thing about the Irish that irritated Swedes more than anything else, it was their attitude towards rules and regulations.

> Well, we follow the rules fairly stringently, the Irish don't. The Irish have a tighter set of rules, but they don't seem to care too much about following them. They don't give a damn about how violations are dealt with.

The Irish did not see themselves as rule-breakers in the true sense of the words; they felt that certain actions, which were contrary to rules and regulations, showed a conscious, positive flexibility and empathy. Unlike Swedes, they would, for example, give away money and sweets to children and adults who gathered at the camp gate; they would regularly allow locally employed civilians to take food from the camp, without the gate pass required by the rules and regulations. Even the locally employed civilians commented on the Swedes' lack of sympathy and flexibility, when compared to the Irish.

> When we are working, it saddens us to see Swedes throwing away food and burning things that we are badly in need of. But, if you don't have a gate pass, the Swedes won't let you out. We realise they have their orders. The Irish are different, they're more flexible. We can take food and other things out, we don't need a gate pass. Tell them to change their policy. If the Irish can, the Swedes must be able to as well. They're so restrictive. A rule is not a bible.

On the other hand, Swedish policy was to keep strictly to rules and regulations, so as not to encourage corruption and also to maintain security in the gate area. For them, as far as gifts were concerned, it was the job of aid organisations such as the Red Cross which dealt with humanitarian activities.

Two other breaches of regulations that irritated Swedes were, firstly, that the Irish definitely did not keep to the regulation "three-can rule" concerning alcohol consumption and, secondly, that they were rumoured to slip away from camp to visit prostitutes. Swedes would joke that, as far as the Irish were concerned, the "three-can rule" meant three cans at a time. However, some respondents showed a certain degree of understanding for the fact that the Irish applied some rules (e.g. those governing alcohol consumption) differently from the Swedes.

> A lot of it lies in that fact that it's their job. This is normal; it's what happens in everyday life, like. So therefore they don't think this thing with alcohol is a big deal. They've got a lot more spare time down here in camp. They only get to go home once a year, while we can go home three times in seven, eight months. They can have time off for one week in camp and I can understand if they go to their pub three evenings a week. So I can understand if they go on a binge here a bit more, while we can go home and do it.

As far as visiting prostitutes is concerned, it has been difficult to find first-hand information to confirm that such visits took place. However, rumours that such visits had taken place during earlier missions were rife.[9] Swedes, on the other hand, distanced themselves completely from anything having to do with prostitution: "and then, you know, they visited prostitutes. That's something that's blacklisted – both in Swedish rules and regulations and in the Swedish mentality. So that feels really very strange."

The Irish saw themselves as being very sociable and easy to get on with; they had the "gift of the gab",[10] something acknowledged by both Swedes and locally employed Liberians. "The Irish are more relaxed when they talk to the Liberians. The Irish soldiers are very sociable." In interviews, locally employed personnel said that Swedes ought to be more flexible, more sociable and show more interest in talking to them, if only to gain access to important information.

> Communication is important. For example, if I've got something I want to say, maybe I won't say it because we can't communicate. Liberia is a friendly country. If they go to a more hostile country, they're going to have to learn to be more flexible with civilian employees. It's the only way things will work. If I don't want to talk to you, I won't. Then you lose access to information. I have lots of information that might be useful to them, but they don't ask.

Locally employed Liberians also described Swedes as being somewhat awkward and socially shy: "Swedes aren't so keen to be friends. You can see in their faces that they want to be friends, but they don't quite know what to do." Another cultural difference mentioned was the importance and influence of religion on relationships between Irish men and women in camp: "They're Catholics so then there'll be a bit of a difference in how they associate with girls and that. They don't talk to them, they're not allowed to be billeted with the girls; they're a bit stricter that way." However, we saw no evidence of this. On the contrary, during our two visits to Camp Clara Irish men and women socialised regularly together in the pub.

From the preceding, it is clear that Swedes had a lot of negative opinions about the Irish. Interestingly enough, however, the reverse was not true: from interviews with Irish respondents, it appeared that they did not have the same problems with Swedes. On the contrary, they thought the Swedes were good soldiers, good guys, and that there were little or no problems in Swedish–Irish cooperation. They also openly admitted that they envied the Swedes for their better equipment and living and working accommodation ("our government could learn from that"). In other words, the problem seems to have been predominantly a one-way – on the Swedish side – rather than a two-way problem.

To summarise our findings we can say that Swedish soldiers' perceptions of the Irish before the mission basically remained unchanged during the mission, although new aspects were added during the six months that they shared camp. Most of these perceptions can also be seen as negative. A positive exception was that, although Swedes saw Irish soldiers as people who might otherwise be unemployed and/or potentially criminal, they were still regarded as being relatively competent as professional soldiers.[11] Another was that the Irish were considered very sociable and easy to get along with, despite the fact that they were also seen to be disorderly and to overly enjoy drinking. These partly contradictory views indicate that Swedish perceptions of the Irish were largely based on prejudice and stereotypical opinions.

Some of the more obvious cultural differences between Swedes and Irishmen in the results of this study were ethical issues such as attitudes towards alcohol, prostitution, and flexibility (or otherwise) when it comes to following rules. There were also other obvious differences in aspects of hygiene, working and living conditions, motivation and attitude to work performance, and differences in social competence.

Discussion

How can we understand and explain the primarily negative Swedish perceptions of the Irish? It is obvious that these perceptions were mainly stereotypical (Allport 1954) and were created and spread through informal learning (socialisation) before the mission, in particular during pre-deployment training and especially from veterans with previous service abroad. According to Säljö (2000) and Lave and Wenger (1991), the creation and transfer of perceptions in an informal, cultural, and communicative process can be described as a form of "word-of-mouth" learning. The force of this learning process was strengthened because the Swedish Armed Forces have not implemented any formal procedures for the continuous evaluation of lessons learned from previous Swedish–Irish cooperation. Instead, the perceptions and preconceptions, which developed among soldiers and junior officers during the first mission in Liberia, became institutionalised and remained largely intact. This phenomenon was also observed in a study of the German–Netherlands Brigade in Kabul (Hagen et al. 2003).[12] When this perception of "them and us" has been established, it becomes very difficult to change. This remained true despite the fact that a majority of respondents described how they actively tried to take information they received about operations in Liberia "with a pinch of salt" and deferred forming an opinion of their own until they arrived in the theatre.

One reason for the creation of negative perceptions before deployment, their remaining intact and, to a certain extent, becoming even more unfavourable, may be that there were no continuous, extensive, and planned integration efforts in line with recommendations derived from the contact hypothesis (Allport 1954). The Swedish and the Irish effectively lived separate but parallel lives in the camp. Such a situation provides an ideal condition for a division into "in-group" and "out-group". Furthermore, there is often a tendency for the "in-group" to overestimate their own performance,[13] while underestimating the performance of the "out-group" (Festinger 1962; Merton 1968). The initial negative perceptions and the lack of contact could also be factors contributing to the fact that they did not evolve according to the so-called "acculturation curve" (Hofstede and Hofstede 2005), but instead, strengthened during the course of the mission.[14]

An additional factor which could have played a role is the strong polarisation that can arise in binational constellations (Earley and Mosakowski 2000; Søderberg and Wedell-Wedellsborg 2005). Binationality is the worst of all compositions when compared with near homogeneity or heterogeneity. If the two parties are culturally similar, there is a particular tendency to emphasise individual and distinctive characteristics and identity a phenomenon that Ignatieff (1998), inspired by Sigmund Freud, described as the "narcissism of minor difference".[15]

During our two visits to Camp Clara, it was not difficult to see that the Irish consumed more alcohol than the Swedes, who hardly visited the noisy pub and, when they were there, kept to the prescribed "three-can rule". For the Irish, the bar was something of an oasis, where the rules that prevailed were those of the carnival, a clearly demarcated place to let off steam and behave in a way not permitted by everyday social conventions (Da Matta and Green 1983; Da Matta 1991; Bakhtin 1984).

The main reason for the Swedes being irritated by the Irishmen's drinking sessions did not seem to be the fact that the Irish tended to drink considerable amounts of alcohol – well beyond the "three-can rule"; even Swedes are known to drink a bit too much – for example when on holiday in such places as the Canary Islands and Mallorca. Nor was the main cause of Swedish irritation security-related. It was rather linked to concepts of the workplace and professional ethics. Swedes firmly believe that work and alcohol do not mix. This is not the case for the Irish, who come from a culture where one often goes to the pub for a pint at lunchtime.

Another area of contention, which is also linked to moral values, was prostitution. It has not been possible to prove that the Irish visited prostitutes to any great extent. However, according to rumours, there was a "heck of a lot" of coming and going through the main gate at night, especially during earlier missions.[16] As is the case with alcohol, Sweden has chosen an alternative path on the issue of prostitution, compared with other countries in Europe. This path includes, for example, a recent law criminalising clients, but not prostitutes. So, Swedes have a different approach to prostitution, which in all probability had a negative influence on their perceptions of the Irish. Or as a Swedish general said: "The Irish have no problem with prostitution, but they do with abortion; whereas the Swedish accept abortion, but not prostitution." The Swedes were also very proud of how tidy and well-organised their area of the camp was compared with the Irish area and often made fun of the obvious differences. They often pointed out the Irish lack of hygiene when it came to meal times and using the toilet and suggested that the minor epidemics of eye inflammation on the Irish side could have been a result of inadequate hygiene. The differences in living standards, organisation, and hygiene between the Swedes and the Irish could possibly have been a manifestation of different national, cultural, and historical characteristics. One distinguishing factor between the two countries is that Sweden, since at least the 1960s, has been a country characterised by the modern ideal and the need for order and cleanliness (Gaunt and Löfgren 1984) in a way not reflected in Ireland. Not so many decades ago, Ireland was a relatively poor country where many families lived in cramped and, by Swedish standards, not particularly hygienic conditions.

The Irish and Liberians – and Swedes themselves – testified to Swedish shyness and difficulty in making contact and small talk with strangers in an easy, natural manner. This is an observation that often comes up among Swedish ethnologists (Daun 2005; Arnstberg 1989). For example, Daun states that Swedes' social insecurity manifests itself in their becoming tense and anxious before they meet strangers. This insecurity could explain why Swedes tended to keep a certain distance and never got to know the Irish or the Liberians particularly well. They kept to themselves, the safe and the familiar (Gullestad 2002).

Apart from the explanations and causal connections outlined above, there are two additional aspects that we would like to highlight for future studies. The first aspect concerns the fact that Swedes both were, and considered themselves to be, well-educated and belonging to a well-established middle class, while the Irish were described more as working-class "ruffians" with all that this implies in terms of behaviour and interests (Bourdieu 1984). In other words, it is likely that part of the explanation for the differences in behaviour between the Swedes and the Irish is linked to social-class differences.

The second aspect concerns differing conditions and principles in terms of the organisation of work between a professional army and a temporary force consisting of volunteers and civilian men and women. Swedish soldiers volunteer for international service and there is stiff competition for the available slots. They are in the theatre of operations normally for a six-month period and during this period they want to get as much as possible out of the six months. The mission is a break in their everyday life and takes on the nature of an adventure. On the other hand, the Irish, as professionals, are regularly obliged to deploy on international missions and probably have a more routine outlook on such missions. As long-term professional soldiers, they have perhaps less inclination to constantly perform to the best of their ability. On many occasions moderation may be good enough. In other words, within the Swedish–Irish camp, the motivation, expectations, and willingness to produce maximum performance during the mission were quite different. Furthermore, the Swedes had more leave periods when they could go home, party and meet friends and loved ones, while the Irish had fewer leave periods and opportunities to leave camp. Instead, they spent almost all of their free time in the camp. All in all, these different circumstances probably had quite a significant impact on people's motivation and attitude towards work and free time.

Conclusion

In spite of everything, the Swedes thought that they and the Irish had a great deal in common.[17] However, despite this view, there were noticeable domains of cultural friction at Camp Clara. This raises the question: How would cooperation work between Swedes and personnel from a country where the cultural, social, and educational differences were even greater? The QRF in Liberia never faced any particularly threatening situations and it would have been interesting to see how Swedish–Irish cooperation would have worked on really demanding operational tasks. However, in preparation for future international operations, there seems to be a real need to open a dialogue with partner nations about ethical issues, operational approaches, policies, and HR issues in order to achieve some sort of harmony. It would also be a good idea to establish procedures for feedback and the continuous evaluation of experiences gained from cooperation with other nations.

Notes

1　At present there are about 1,000 Swedish men and women in some 15 locations around the world involved in peace promotion and security tasks; the ambition is to double this number.
2　The former Defence Minister, Ms Leni Björklund, emphasised the importance for Swedish officers on international missions to be able to "understand and interpret their operational environment" and that subjects such as "the arts, history, the science of religion and cultural anthropology" should perhaps be included in officer training (www.folkochforsvar.se/files/RK%202006/Leni%20Bjorklund060117.pdf.).
3　In pre-deployment training, carried out eight weeks before deployment, personnel are given very limited information on the specific cultural conditions in the mission area, but no information whatsoever about the nations they will cooperate with.
4　This case study is part of a larger research project, completed by Erik Hedlund and Louise Weibull, including both the 5th Swedish Liberia force (LA05) and the 14th Kosovo force (KS14). The research issues that this study aims to address are: (1) What perceptions do Swedish troops have of military partners and local actors before their tour of duty? (2) Do these perceptions change during and after the mission – and, if so, how and why? (3) How are Swedes regarded by other nations in overseas operational forces and by local actors?
5　The DDRR-process; Demobilisation, Disarmament, Rehabilitation, and Reintegration.
6　Previous studies have confirmed that, in an international context, language knowledge plays a lesser role in deciding which countries people prefer to work with, when compared with shared moral values. In the field of Nordic cooperation, the lack of language knowledge among Finns is sometimes mentioned. However, this has not reduced the will and ability of Swedes to work with Finns. On the contrary, Finland is considered to be a country that people would particularly like to work with, a view borne out by Swedish experience in Kosovo (Weibull and Johansson 2006). Results from a comparative survey of officers from nine countries (Boene 2001) showed that Swedes gave a relatively high rating to cooperation problems arising from ethical differences.
7　One respondent returned home early and was replaced by someone holding the same appointment.
8　The Swedish and Irish units rotated at different times.
9　Swedish contingent commanders stated that only a few individuals were guilty of visiting prostitutes.
10　If someone has the "gift of the gab", it means that he speaks in a persuasive and interesting way.
11　Compared to other non-western nations, the Irish were considered to be a crack unit.

12 It was also among lower-ranking Dutch officers that the most negative attitudes towards Germans were found and spread in the German–Netherlands Brigade in Kabul (Hagen *et al.* 2003).

13 One part of the current research project (not yet published) deals with Swedish self-perception; here it is clear that Swedes have a very positive image of themselves when compared to their perception of the Irish.

14 This might be seen as a "near-neighbour phenomenon", meaning that neighbours who live close to each other, but without close contact, tend to fabricate and interpret each other's activities negatively.

15 Of particular interest is the very positive Swedish view of the Irishmen they cooperate with in Kosovo; this has become clear in the part of the study that involves a group of Swedes in KFOR (not yet published). The situation in Kosovo is generally much more multinational.

16 It should be noted that this sort of contact with the local population was contrary to both Swedish and Irish regulations.

17 One Swedish soldier said: "They're about the same as us. The difference isn't enormous; we're Westerners after all."

Chapter 12

Accidental neighbours

Japanese and Dutch troops in Iraq

Jan van der Meulen and Hitoshi Kawano

Introduction

For somewhat more than a year, Dutch and Japanese soldiers worked side by side in Al Muthanna, in the south of Iraq. Accidental neighbours, but not quite so: given the turbulence of post-Saddam Iraqi society, both countries took pains to select a relatively safe region for stationing their troops. During the time their missions coincided, the contingents worked together in formal as well as in informal ways. Across the board these contacts were rather selective and not very intensive. On the one hand this reflected the physical separation of the two military camps. On the other hand and more important, relationships were limited because of differences in task and mandate the two national contingents were faced with – as a direct outcome of political processes at the respective home fronts.

In this chapter we will shift back and forth between Dutch and Japanese perspectives. First we will address in some detail the ways in which both countries arrived at the decision to join the Stabilisation Force Iraq (SFIR). Thereafter Japanese–Dutch cooperation per se will be the focus, in the context of the tasks both countries had taken upon them. These tasks were only partly overlapping, one of the main reasons why, as we just alluded to, mutual contacts were not that extensive. Nevertheless, some interesting and relevant observations can be made on 'cooperation lite'. Taken together these help underline the thrust of our argument in this chapter, which is about the degree to which national defence and security policies put their stamp on the operational whereabouts of multinational missions. This particular point will be elaborated even more emphatically in the third section, which tackles the issue of how to deal with risks. In fact, this seems to be a core issue for any nowadays military deployment – not just with regard to the two accidental neighbours we are talking about in this chapter. In the final section we will offer some concluding observations on national preoccupations in the context of multinational missions.

Political decision-making

Neither in Tokyo nor in The Hague, was the decision to join SFIR an easy one. In principle governments in both countries took a positive attitude towards UN resolution 1483 (22 May 2003), which called upon 'the willingness of member states to contribute to stability and security in Iraq by contributing personnel, equipment and other resources under the Authority'. In Japan as well as in the Netherlands, however, a number of political sensitivities stood in the way of any kind of routine decision-making. Especially in the former country, the constitutionality of sending troops to Iraq, stirred a heated debate. In fact, this was the next round in what, since the end of the Cold War, had become an ongoing deliberation about which new roles the Japan Self-Defence Forces (JSDF) should and could perform. For the Dutch the issue was not a constitutional one, but definitely a matter of difficult political and military calculation: the wish not to be seen as part of an occupation force had to be balanced with the will, if necessary, to show a robust posture.

The Hague: no occupation

On 17 March 2003, the Dutch government ventured its political support for the imminent American–British invasion of Iraq, but declined to make any kind of military contribution. For the latter there would not have been the sort of massive majority in Parliament, which in the Netherlands traditionally is looked upon as a prerequisite for troop deployment. The political backing-up of Operation Iraqi Freedom was motivated by a mixture of principle – Saddam's violation of numerous UN resolutions – and pragmatism: the wish not to be estranged from the policies of the UK and the US. This position was not without its adversaries and it has become more and more contentious in retrospect. For the moment however, it succeeded in constituting a political consensus, which later that spring helped pave the way for joining SFIR (van der Meulen and Soeters 2005: 547–550).

In itself the latter decision typically befitted Dutch defence and security policy as it evolved since the beginning of the 1990s. Contributing to the international lawful order, had become the constitutionally legitimated core business of the military, alongside the more traditional task of protecting and defending the interests of the state. Whether in the context of short-term humanitarian assistance or of long-term nation-building, soldiers had been practising peace missions around the world. At the time (spring 2003) Dutch contingents were part of the Stabilization Force (SFOR) in Bosnia and Herzegovina as well as of the International Security Assistance Force (ISAF) in Afghanistan.

On 6 June 2003, the Dutch cabinet, a coalition of Christian democrats, conservative liberals and social liberals, headed by prime minister Balkenende, decided to contribute to the stabilization force for Iraq by deploying a battalion of marines together with a mix of supporting units. The legal basis for this deployment was found in UN resolution 1483. Not in the least as a result of its own pressure, the government claimed, the resolution had a preamble in which an explicit distinction was made between the two countries constituting the Coalition Provisional Authority (CPA), i.e. the US and the UK, and the rest of the countries contributing to SFIR. While the former two had the status as well as the responsibilities of 'occupying powers', the other nations, though within the command of the CPA, could and should not be looked upon as belonging to an occupation force (Klep and van Gils 2005: 470, 471).

This latter position served a psychological function with an eye to public debate in the Netherlands but it also had formal implications in the field. Legally speaking, it limited the role of Dutch troops (and of the other non-occupation contingents) in helping to build up public administration in general and in assisting to uphold public order in particular. It was rather artificial of course, even more so because it was agreed to that in any sort of severe crisis, the Brits, and eventually the Americans, would come to the help of the Dutch with all the firepower they would see fit. This was one of the hard-learned lessons of the drama at Srebrenica: Dutch troops should and would never be deployed again without the guaranteed back-up of a senior military partner. Surely, to begin with, in order to be able to defend themselves, the soldiers operated under robust rules of engagement, essentially derived from those applied by the United Kingdom, as the relevant lead nation. One last crucial caveat in the context of these arrangements deserves to be mentioned: under all circumstances the Netherlands would hold on to 'full command' over its troops, to be exercised by the highest military authority, the Chief of Staff, on behalf of the Minister of Defence (Brief Regering 2003: 14).

To reiterate, the mandate of the Dutch battalion was not without an artificial ring to it. Because of that, as we will see later on in this chapter, in the harsh reality of Iraq some friction could not be avoided. It was not that beforehand decision-makers were totally unaware of the possible strains and risks. All in all though, the mission was looked upon as justifiable and feasible. So in the end, during the parliamentary vote, not only the government bloc, but also the biggest opposition party, the social democrats, supported contributing to SFIR. Polls suggested that two-thirds of a Dutch public poll gave the mission its blessing as well (van der Meulen and Soeters 2005: 548). Whatever hard feelings were harboured against the Anglo-American coalition, helping post-Saddam Iraq to become secure and democratic tended to be looked upon as a default option; what in today's world an expeditionary military organization was meant to do in the first place.

In the course of July the soldiers and their equipment were shipped to Iraq, and on 1 August 2003, the Dutch battalion took over command in the assigned area of operation. The initial commitment was set to six months although extending the mission was not ruled out. Eventually it would last until March 2005.

Tokyo: no combat

For Japan the principle of sending soldiers abroad was anything but self-evident and the decision to deploy troops in Iraq was deeply contentious. To understand why, it is helpful briefly to analyse some recent and crucial changes in Japan's security and defence policies. Since the first half of the 1990s, the long political and 'theological' debate on the legitimacy of the JSDF was more or less settled.[1] Its constitutionality had been recognized across the political spectrum, with the inclusion of the Socialist Party. During this period the focus of public debate shifted to the new agenda of the constitutionality of *operations* by the JSDF. Moving away from the 'cheque-book diplomacy' of the first Gulf War, Japan's operational scope gradually broadened. The dispatch to the Persian Gulf of six vessels of the Maritime Self-Defence Forces (MSDF), three months after the Gulf War, marked the first overseas operation in the history of the JSDF.

In August 1992, the International Peace Cooperation Law (PKO Law) was voted. Perceived as 'a pivotal event' or a major 'turning point' in the post-war military history of Japan in the eyes of the Japanese people (Yanai 1996; Heinrich *et al.* 1999), it made possible the dispatch of 600 JSDF peacekeepers to Cambodia. For the first time in its history, a Ground Self-Defence Force (GSDF) unit was deployed beyond the national border to conduct a United Nations peacekeeping mission, albeit only in support of the peacekeeping force (Morrison and Kiras 1996; Kawano 2002). Also in 1992, the International Disaster Relief Law was amended so that the JSDF personnel could join international disaster-relief operations.[2] Taken together the two legislations opened a new page in the JSDF history of international operations, making possible a range of worldwide deployments, aimed at peacekeeping, humanitarian aid and disaster relief.

When the Koizumi administration tried to dispatch JMSDF ships to the Indian Ocean after the September 11 terrorist attacks, the constitutionality issue arose again since this operation seemed much more problematic than the UN peacekeeping missions and the international disaster relief operations. An Anti-Terrorism Special Measures Law (ATSML) was passed within 60 hours of deliberation (Dobson 2003: 129). Based on this new law, the JSDF joined the US-led coalition force in support of the Afghanistan campaign mainly by providing fuel for the allied ships operating in the Indian Ocean. It was the first major overseas operation by JSDF with the US-led coalition force.[3]

However, joining the coalition force invited a public debate. The new front of the constitutionality debate was over the issue of *collective defence*. The official interpretation of the Constitution maintains that Japan has the right of collective defence but does not 'exercise the right' due to the limit set by Article 9.[4] Providing combat support for the coalition force engaged in combat operations in Afghanistan was considered unconstitutional because it would violate the prohibited exercise of the right of collective defence. Thus, the Anti-Terrorism Special Measures Law only allowed the JSDF to provide non-combat support to the US coalition force (Cossa and Glosserman 2005; Defence White Paper 2005).

In 2003 the collective defence issue once again resurfaced when the Koizumi government decided to send JSDF troops to Iraq in support of the US-led coalition force. Prime Minister Koizumi insisted that the area near As Samawah, the capital city of Al-Muthanna, where Japanese Ground Self-Defence Force (JGSDF) troops would be stationed, was not a combat zone, and that the JSDF was going to dispatch troops for a humanitarian reconstruction mission. However, on a particular point a subtle modification was made to the previous interpretation of the Constitution. According to this interpretation, the Air Self-Defence Force (ASDF) was not allowed to transport any weapons or ammunition for other countries. After reinterpretation it was said the ASDF was allowed to transport 'soldiers who are carrying weapons' (Cossa and Glosserman 2005:11). Thus the Iraq operation by the JSDF to some extent pushed further the borders of what, according to the Constitution, was considered legitimate.

In the meantime, the political debate over the proposed bill, the Special Measures Law for Humanitarian and Reconstruction Assistance in Iraq (SMLHRAI), was tumultuous. The opposition parties, such as the Japan Democratic Party, the Communist Party, and the Social Democratic Party strongly opposed the bill because the dispatch of JSDF units to the seemingly 'combat zone' of Iraq would be against the Constitution. Even among members of the ruling Liberal Democratic Party, some were against the bill (Morimoto 2004: 264–267). Nonetheless, the government of Japan maintained that the area of the JSDF operation, near As-Samawah, would not constitute a combat zone, and therefore, that the Iraqi operation was constitutional. Apart from that, the government's view was that a vital national interest was at stake, given the fact that Japan is heavily dependent on imported oil, more than 90 per cent of which comes from the Middle East. Taking into account the needs of the United States and the 'Coalition of the Willing', and using UN resolution 1483 as a rationale for legislation, the final political decision was made against the political opposition and the majority of public opinion as well.

On 3 June 2003, the bill was submitted to the Diet, and the law was passed in late July. The law took effect on 1 August 2003. On 29 November, while preparation was in progress, two Japanese diplomats were killed in Iraq. Nevertheless, the Basic Plan for the JSDF dispatch was approved by the government on 9 December.[5] Following a preparation team, the first GSDF unit was dispatched to As-Samawah in February 2004. The last Japanese troops would leave Iraq in the summer of 2006.

Cooperation light

All in all, during their time in Iraq, Dutch and Japanese soldiers worked side by side for some 13 months. With their respective camps some 5 km apart, on average there was scant contact, give or take the occasional social event or soccer match. As we noted in the introduction to this chapter, more important than the physical separation was the difference in task and mandate and, we might add here, in rules of engagement. These differences precluded any kind of really joint operations. That being said, the 'cooperation light' that crystallized during the period under review brought with it a number of relevant stories and lessons. The main one of which was, in our view, that the impact of differences in organizational practices and cultural patterns, real as they were, was a lot less important than the consequences of certain political caveats.

We can draw only a sketchy picture of Dutch–Japanese cooperation. We do not have at our disposal any kind of systematic case study or survey. So we have to rely on the odd article (by journalists, scientists and officers), which mostly treats our subject as a sideline or in relation to a particular incident. Luckily we did receive more thorough background information from a number of military insiders, on both sides, who were in a position to watch closely the events (and non-events) in the Japanese–Dutch neighbourhood. We were also given access to fieldnote-like information of miscellaneous sorts. In this section in particular, we use our sources, oral as well as written, mostly in a general way, i.e. without specific references to who said or wrote what. From a scientific point of view this is not very satisfying, but of course it will always be possible to correct our description with alternative experiences and perceptions. Basically, however, we consider our sketch to be a plausible and trustworthy one.

Tasks and contacts

Before the Japanese troops had time to set up their own encampment, advance parties had stayed at Camp Smitty, the main base for the Dutch battalion. During this early phase GSDF (Ground Self-Defence Force) units heavily relied on Dutch soldiers for their security. A Japanese journalist who witnessed the way a group of five GSDF members, visiting a local market in downtown As-Samawah, was being protected by a Dutch military police unit, showed himself 'deeply impressed' by this 'perfect example of force-protection' (Kakitani and Kikuchi 2005: 69). However, in the eyes of a GSDF officer who was in As-Samawah from February to August 2005, the Dutch troops seemed much less concerned with force protection than the GSDF.[6] No doubt the latter observation was correct, for reasons we will address in the next paragraph, but at the same time the journalist's quotation probably echoed a feeling not uncommon among Japanese officers as well. Generally speaking, they held the professionalism of the Dutch troops in high regard and considered them as experienced, 'combat-ready' soldiers, devoting a lot of time to practising their skills and drills. In the field of logistics also, the Dutch troops were perceived as better experienced in carefully figuring out the best options available among various loci of operation and means of procurement (Sankei Shimbun News Service 2004: 147).

Once they were settled in their own camp, where they took care of their own force-protection, the JSDF soldiers went about their business. As clearly stated in the law, the major purpose of the JSDF 'dispatch' to Iraq (a preferred term for JSDF overseas operation since 'deployment' has an unconstitutional connotation), was strictly for humanitarian relief and reconstruction assistance. In particular, JSDF units were assigned for providing water supply (one of their major tasks), medical assistance, reconstruction for public facilities such as schools and roads, as well as for providing logistical support and local transportation for humanitarian relief activities.[7] Besides, ASDF aircrafts provided air transportation for the US and other Coalition Forces.

Extensive Civil–Military Cooperation (CIMIC) activities also belonged to the tasks of the GSDF units. Many cultural exchange activities such as visiting local schools, entertaining children with plays and picture-bodes, teaching origami, the traditional Japanese paper-folding art, performing Japanese music by the voluntary military band, constituted an important part of the CIMIC by GSDF (Defence White Paper 2005: 284).

The Dutch troops, which were in fact located in a number of facilities around As-Samawah, were given three main tasks: reconstruction, security sector reform (SSR) and maintaining public order. The first task involved the repair of infrastructure (electricity, telephone, fuel) as well as (other) CIMIC-like projects, all of which were meant to win over the population by showing visible results. The second task was considered to be the most important one: training and educating Iraqi professionals belonging to the police, the military and other security services. The third task brought with it around the clock patrolling in the designated area, on foot as well in armoured vehicles (Klep and van Gils 2005: 471–473). As we shall see in the next section, at times this latter task turned out to be a risky one and a number of fatal incidents could not be avoided.

On an official and daily basis liaison officers (LO) from both sides took care of Japanese–Dutch communication, of formal issues of mutual interest, of task-related arrangements as well as of informal contacts and meetings of a more representative kind. The LOs served as ears, eyes and helping hands, and were by far the most knowledgeable officials at the organizational and operational interface of both contingents. There were other regular contacts as well, like medical personnel meeting weekly in order to exchange information and to plan for a coordinated response to any eventualities. If necessary Japanese troops could always count on Dutch helicopter-transport, just as mutual requests in other practical matters as well usually were dealt with positively.

As far as core tasks were concerned, working together was limited to CIMIC-related activities. This could hardly have been otherwise, given the fact that the scope of the JSDF was strictly humanitarian and that neither security-sector reform nor the maintenance of public order fitted in with its mandate. CIMIC officers from both contingents met weekly and talked over projects and plans underway. However, while the Dutch also attended CIMIC meetings at the divisional level of the Multinational Force (MNF), the Japanese did not. Probably this reflected the fact that formally the JSDF was not part of the MNF command system. This ambivalent position played out in a number of other areas as well. For instance, while the Dutch conducted Information Operations (Info Ops), as an integral part of MNF-promotion, the Japanese ran their own public-relations campaign in the very same area. It took some time before a more coordinated effort in reaching out to the Iraqi population could be worked out.

Differences and frictions

Much of the contact between Dutch and Japanese representatives went well enough, based as it was on mutual respect and shared professionalism. Inevitably though, as with any kind of international cooperation, at times strains manifested themselves as well. Language for one, seems to have been experienced as a source of friction (Knops 2005: 21). Dutch officers have been heard complaining that their Japanese counterparts, although lacking skills in English, still preferred not to communicate with the help of the Dutch–Japanese interpreter.

Of course in a more general sense, organizational and cultural differences did not go unnoticed. According to a GSDF officer who belonged to an operation support unit, the Dutch troops, within the overall framework of their tasks, acted flexibly. His observation was that in comparison British troops, which took over Camp Smitty after the Dutch deployment ended, followed the Japanese style of work. Both countries, Japan and the UK, tend to follow and implement well-detailed plans. 'Uncertainty avoidance' is one of the major concerns among the GSDF members and the Dutch sometimes were struck by the degree to which their Japanese colleagues checked and double-checked before taking action.

It is true that as a rule the Japanese system of decision-making took much longer than the Dutch troops expected. In general, the Japanese bureaucracy tends to be slow in making decisions, due to the time needed for the participating members to reach a consensus. Once the decision is made though, implementation tends to be very effective indeed. In the words of the CEO of Tokyo Electron 'in Japan it takes a long time to make one decision but once it is decided, the action is very quick' (Chappell 2001: 2). These kind of characteristic modi operandi are well-known from workplace studies on Dutch–Japanese cooperation in the field of business and industry. Especially the different ways in which the construction of consensus plays a crucial role in both cultures, has been researched thoroughly. Normally these differences – not only with regard to consensus and decision-making, but also to hierarchical relationships and work ethos – do not preclude successful cooperation (Hofstede and Soeters 2002; Noorderhaven et al. 2007).

However, what added gravely to the cultural pattern of decision-making in these circumstances was the politically delicate nature of the Iraqi operation for the GSDF. Because of that, any unexpected change of plan or any contingency that should occur could not be decided upon by the local commander himself. He had to consult with GSDF HQ in Tokyo and often it took a long time before political approval reached him. Even though they might not like it, this was something the GSDF commanders and their staff had to live with. Their Dutch counterparts were fully aware of this problem and even if at times they might have felt a bit irritated by slow decision-making, they realized that it would be unfair to blame their Japanese colleagues. For instance, a Dutch officer who was under the impression that the GSDF, notwithstanding a large budget, was lagging behind in implementing CIMIC projects, immediately knew why: Tokyo had to give permission first (Knops 2005: 21). From their perspective sometimes the Japanese would have the impression that the Dutch were not that interested in really working together. There were no hard feelings though; just small frictions.

Dealing with risks

Even without the turmoil of post-Saddam Iraq, the province of Al-Muthanna would have been a demanding environment. Very early in the mission the Dutch Department of Defence concluded that the extreme desert climate made it necessary to shorten the tours of duty from six to four months. The Japanese soldiers were rotated likewise according to a system which differed from previous UN peacekeeping operations. Instead of six months, the Iraqi operation rotated the major JSDF units after three months, due to the anticipated stressful conditions. Under the circumstances, the Dutch could not quite understand why the Japanese would stick to their usual working hours, instead of having a siesta. In Al-Muthanna, in the summer, temperatures can reach 60°C.

But of course the climate was not the main stress factor. Even though, as we pointed out in the introduction to this chapter, both countries took pains to select a relatively safe region for stationing their troops, there were real risks out there. Al-Muthanna had its own share of political struggle and social tension, of crime and of revolt. Besides, it was hardly immune to what happened in the rest of Iraq. When in consecutive years the overall level of violence increased, there was bound to be a spill-over to the south of the country.

Dealing with these risks constituted a major challenge for both contingents. In a way, it was the ultimate benchmark for the public and political evaluation of the mission. However, it was done in rather different ways, as a consequence of dissimilar mandates, tasks and rules of engagement. The no-combat motto issued from Tokyo did not have the same implications as the no-occupation battle-cry resounding in The Hague. Similarly, while fulfilling their tasks, the troops followed their own courses of action and reaction in confronting and minimizing risks. First we will describe the Japanese approach, with its very strict rules of engagement and its heavy emphasis on force protection. Thereafter we will depict how the Dutch went about maintaining public order and unfortunately could not avoid taking and making casualties.

Force protection

While the operation in Iraq was by far the most dangerous one for the JSDF, the security of the troops was of utmost concern to the politicians who made the decision to send them abroad. However, no matter how dangerous an operation, due to the Peace Constitution, JSDF troops are not allowed to engage in any type of 'armed conflict'. 'The threat or use of force as a means of settling international disputes' is strictly prohibited. As a consequence, the general rules of engagement for the JSDF are quite different from the ones practised by the armed forces of other nations. In fact, it is more like a guideline 'to use weapons' in case of an unexpected emergency situation. JSDF members are allowed to use their weapons for legitimate self-defence and emergency evacuation only.

Since 'collective defence' is unconstitutional, JSDF members cannot counter-attack with any kind of overwhelming force on behalf of another nation's soldiers. Even when they witness a nearby foreign unit under attack, Japanese soldiers are not allowed to come to its help, unless they receive hostile fire themselves. This may sound rather awkward to other countries, but for the JSDF there is no other way, given Japan's Peace Constitution. In fact, before the Anti-Terrorism Special Measures Law of 2001, the rules for using weapons were even more strict. Until then, while on a UN peacekeeping mission a JSDF member, unless fired upon himself, could not fight back even to protect another JSDF member under attack. Only after 2001 the law authorized the use of weapons to protect the lives of 'those under control' of JSDF members. Moreover, since then senior officers have been granted the power to order subordinates to fire.[8]

The troops in Iraq made the best effort to prepare for unexpected emergency situations, like armed attacks and suicide bombings. Far more extensive shooting training allowed GSDF soldiers to fire live ammunition in a close range by the hundreds of thousands of rounds. It is also notable that many elite infantry soldiers such as Rangers and Paratroopers were selected to join the Iraqi operation, though exact numbers are not disclosed.

In order to strengthen force protection, a range of measures were taken, stretching from aerial surveillance for monitoring suspicious movements around Camp Samawah to customizing weapons and equipment. Each vehicle was coloured dark green and marked with clearly recognizable Japanese national-flag paintings, so that any hostile party would not mistake them for other national forces. By the same token, GSDF members distinguished themselves by wearing green battle-dress uniforms with clearly recognizable Japanese national-flag emblems.

These precautions notwithstanding, in the course of its dispatch the GSDF was attacked a number of times. Mortar-fire hit the camp on the outside as well as on the inside. These incidents elicited the construction of heavily protected container shelters, in which all personnel were required to spend the night. On

23 June 2005, a light armoured vehicle was damaged by an improvised explosive device (IED), but no one was injured. Also an incident took place where local protesters surrounded some vehicles and began throwing stones. Following standard operating procedures, the soldiers involved succeeded in calming down the situation.

During its stay in Iraq, the JSDF suffered no casualties. However, three Japanese civilians were killed, and three other civilians were taken hostage by local terrorists, but they were released unharmed. It goes without saying that these incidents stirred emotions at the home front. Reportedly six GSDF members and one ASDF member who were dispatched to Iraq committed suicide after returning home.[9] Whether these tragic deaths were mission-related cannot be established with total certainty. It has been speculated that there were a number of cases in which GSDF veterans suffered from mental disorders after returning from Iraq. Exact percentages of those who suffered from post-traumatic stress disorder (PTSD) are not disclosed by the GSDF. It is, however, a reminder that no matter how stringent and successful is force protection, there always will be a risk of psychological wounding manifesting itself afterwards.

Public order

Within the confines of their encampment, Japanese troops took care of their own force protection. For their security in a wider sense, however, they relied heavily on the presence and the operational capabilities of the nation which, within the command of the multinational force, had been given responsibility for maintaining public order in this particular, shared area. The GSDF troops were well aware that their rules of engagement were qualitatively different from those of other contingents. For their part, soldiers from other nations had no difficulty in telling the difference either.

On the one hand, the Dutch could not help being struck by the extremes of Japanese force protection. On the other hand, they realized that yet again this was something 'political', and that their GSDF colleagues had no choice but to stick to their rules of engagement. However, now and again friction popped up. The sharing of information in particular, proved to be a sensitive issue. Sometimes the Japanese felt left out of the loop about critical situations or specific operations. The Dutch were of the opinion that in certain circumstances they were entitled to practise a need-to-know-only policy. For example, given the GSDF would not participate in any kind of patrolling, it made no sense to share the details of operational plans beforehand. Briefings afterwards seemed reasonable enough – but the Japanese thought otherwise.

Without overstating the issue – most of the available intelligence and information was shared as a matter of routine – it should come as no surprise that problems arose, typically with regard to security. Because, even while their rules of engagement offered rather more room for robust action, the Dutch were not at all oblivious of risks for themselves. At the same time, as we have already explored, there was this delicate notion of not wanting to be seen as an occupation force. Effectively safeguarding public order while minding risk and reputation, at times proved to be a difficult task indeed.

In Al-Muthanna a number of circumstances and developments added turmoil to what, by Iraqi standards, still was a quiet region. Shortage of fuel(!) was one of the major sources of unrest, leading quite often to angry protests. In the rain season especially, when many trucks would get stuck, looters targeted the convoys of the multinational force. And then there was the political unrest, getting ever more manifest in 2004, when in many parts of Iraq Shiite factions struggled for power, Muqtada Al-Sadr and his constituency prominently among them. All of this was watched closely from The Hague, where extra reinforcements – like additional special forces and Apache helicopters – were decided upon at regular intervals, in order to enhance operational capacities and force protection (Klep and van Gils 2005: 471–478).

Measures like these though could never take away the inherent risks of maintaining public order by patrolling among the population, whether on foot or in armour. Attacks became more common and during two such confrontations, the first in May 2004, the second that August, two Dutch sergeants were killed. There was public grief about both casualties, to which political anger was added, especially in the second case. Intelligence suggested that within the Iraqi security establishment, information had been available about the impending ambush but had not been shared with Dutch counterparts. Obviously, this was a ground for bitterness, if not a blow to the assumption of cordially and constructively working together with the local authorities. After all, this wasn't meant to be an ordinary occupation, was it?

Earlier, in the same vein, another incident had already problematized the legal and moral status of the military's presence. It involved the killing of an Iraqi looter by a Dutch sergeant-major, in December 2003. Doubts about whether the rules of engagements had been followed correctly led to his arrest and prosecution – as well as to a lot of indignation, among politicians and in the media alike. The sentiment prevailed that it was unheard of to criminalize soldiers for firing at local 'scum', in a situation where they felt threatened. Certainly the bitterness among fellow marines was tangible, part of which was projected on the military police (*Onderzoek Ondervragingen in Irak* 2007: 19). In the spring of 2005 the sergeant-major was finally acquitted by the Supreme Court. All the time though, the affair lingered on as a focal point for much broader questions about the rationale of this mission, the rules of engagement and dealing with risks.

Final remarks

Almost two years after the deployment to Iraq ended, debate flared up in the Netherlands once again. In the autumn of 2006 a newspaper came forward with evidence that during their stay Dutch troops not only had detained Iraqi prisoners illegally, but had also mistreated them, up to the point of using torture. Formally, the troops had been entitled to arrest anyone who would try to endanger their safety. However, they were not empowered to detain or interrogate them. Criminals should be transferred to the Iraqi authorities, while rebellious elements should be handed over to the British, being the lead nation in Al-Muthana. In fact, this was one of the central arrangements guaranteeing the Dutch the status of a non-occupational force.

Precisely this latter status, an official committee concluded, must be looked upon as the main source for what went wrong. The mandate proved to be a rather artificial political construction, which fell flat in the complexities of Iraq. For the soldiers in the field, some of its basic assumptions were unworkable. To wit, according to the committee, the treatment of detainees, while not faultless, definitely fell short of torture (*Onderzoek Ondervragingen in Irak* 2007).

Yet again these ex-post-facto revelations and reflections illustrate the degree to which the Netherlands tended to be preoccupied with its own mission, its own debates, and its own sensitivities. Surely the same can be said about the JSDF dispatch to Iraq. In a way this even may be looked upon as the ultimate point in case. Because of the depths of its constitutional pacifism and the overriding priority of its force protection, Japan still is the odd man out when it comes to the application of military force.

The two countries having been accidental neighbours in Al-Muthanna, it made sense to analyse and compare the political and operational characteristics typifying the Dutch and Japanese contributions to SFIR. No doubt the whereabouts of other countries participating in this mission could be scrutinized likewise. In fact, it would be worthwhile to make such a comparative study, at the political–military interface, for all contingents which were (or still are) present in Iraq.

Of course the same perspective is relevant for other missions as well. The current deployment of the International Security Assistance Force (ISAF) in Afghanistan might offer an even more striking array of national approaches in the context of one and the same mission. To be sure, this does not have to be looked upon only in a negative way. To some degree the diversity of countries, especially with regard to political commitments, may strengthen the international legitimacy of the mission. However, when as a result of national agendas, operational caveats create an uneven distribution of danger, this may hamper cooperation. Therefore, political mandates and rules of engagement not only have to reflect the realities in the field, but in order to facilitate further (cultural) interoperability, they also and especially have to accommodate cross-national discrepancies in dealing with these realities.

Notes

We wish to thank major Ronald van der Heijden for providing us with rich, invaluable data about Dutch–Japanese cooperation. Without his insights the sections 'Cooperation lite' and 'Dealing with risks' could not have been written.

1 However, in February 2006, the Social Democratic Party, successor of the Socialist Party, reversed its political stance on JSDF claiming that, given the current overseas military operations, JSDF is in unconstitutional situation. 'Social Democratic Party Declaration': www5.sdp.or.jp/central/02sengen.html (accessed on 3 April 2006).

2 The Law Concerning the Dispatch of International Relief Teams, originally enacted in 1987, was amended in 1992 so that JSDF could participate in international disaster relief operations. The JSDF activities include: 1) medical services 2) transport of goods, patients, and disaster relief teams and 3) ensuring water supplies using water-purifying devices (Defence White Paper 2005: 312).

3 This naval operation was extended a number of times. In September 2007 another debate on the possibility of extension led to the resignation of the Japanese prime minister, Shinzo Abe.

4 The Article 9 of the 1947 Constitution of Japan states as follows:

CHAPTER II: RENUNCIATION OF WAR

Article 9: 1) Aspiring sincerely to an international peace based on justice and order, the Japanese people forever renounce war as a sovereign right of the nation and the threat or use of force as means of settling international disputes.

Japan, as a sovereign state, has the right of collective defence, but exercising the right of collective defence goes beyond the limit of self-defence authorized under Article 9 of the Constitution (Defence White Paper 2005: 103–105).

5 The Basic Plan was changed later: 1) the original one-year term was extended for two years; 2) necessary measures can be taken, should any situational change arise; 3) a mandate to build facilities for civilian Iraqi reconstruction assistance personnel was deleted (Defence White Paper 2005: 221).

6 Interview conducted on 22 March 2006.

7 According to the law, GSDF can send up to 600 personnel and 200 vehicles, ASDF up to eight aircrafts, and MSDF up to two ships including a transport ship and up to two escort ships.

8 According to the SMLHRAI, 1) the use of weapons are allowed to the extent judged reasonably necessary for the defence of life (lives) and body (bodies) of one's own or other personnel, the staff for the Iraqi relief and reconstruction mission, or those placed under one's control in implementing the duty; 2) when there is one's own superior officer on the site, weapons shall be used by his/her order; 3) except for cases of justifiable defence and emergency evacuation, it is not allowed to injure others (Defence White Paper 2005: 273).

9 According to *Shimbun Akahata*, 10 March 2006. See www.jcp.or.jp/akahata/aik07/2007–01–14/2007011401_01_0.html.

Chapter 13

The formation of the global soldier

Managing identities in multinational military units

Anne-Marie Søderberg and Merete Wedell-Wedellsborg

Introduction

The stereotypical ideal of military units has been that of indistinguishable individuals marching to the same tune. In few organizations is the concept of "identity" as literal as in military organizations: looking alike, thinking alike and acting in perfect coordination are key disciplines. The idea that a strong collective identity yields strong performance has been one of the core assumptions of military management practice.

In the long period of operating under the framework of *nationally organized*, *territorially based* military units, collective identity was forged using classical "us" versus "them" narratives, often based on national stereotyping, patriotic rhetoric and shared national imagery and symbols. The idea of defending the nation has been central to both corporate identity and the identity of individual military managers. These mechanisms of identity formation are well described by military sociologists, anthropologists and management researchers – as well as military practitioners (Gareis *et al.* 2003; Lang 1965; Nørgaard 2004; Sabrosky *et al.* 1982; Soeters *et al.* 2003). Recent theoretical developments (Gioia 1998; Parker 2000) have challenged both the assumption that a central, distinct and enduring identity is sustainable and the proposed direct link between identity and performance.

Whereas the drive towards a *uniform corporate identity* has been the cornerstone of nation-based military organizations, new developments in the missions (e.g. international peacekeeping operations), context (e.g. new multinational command structures) and configuration of military organizations (e.g. truly multinational units) have radically changed conditions for identity formation – both at the organizational level and at the individual level.

This chapter deals with how the formation of corporate identity is conceived and managed in a new temporary, mission-specific, multinational military organization in which a multiplicity of cultures and identifications emerge. In our view identity formation and management is tied to the construction of an ideal figure, which we call "the global soldier". This global soldier is different from his national antecedent in many ways – he is fighting against a diffuse enemy in a much more heterogeneous context governed by military, political, legal, religious and humanitarian logics.

Our overall research interest is to explore how a global military mission and a multinational context change the way military managers think about the formation of corporate identity and how they cope with their own identities as well as with the multinational unit's multiple identities.

We concentrate on studying military managers because they still have an advantage in defining and giving sense (Gioia and Chittipeddi 1991) to the social reality of an organization. By articulating certain values and prescribing certain codes of behaviour, these managers are in a privileged position to define what the organization and its corporate identity is or should be and thus give sense to actions and events. We are well aware that a corporate identity cannot be imposed and communicated top-down and unilaterally. But we are, nevertheless, interested in studying how corporate identity constructions are conceived by managers before they are negotiated with other organizational actors.

In this chapter, we do not address all aspects of the overarching research question; rather we take a step towards establishing both a theoretical and empirical foundation for understanding collective identity work in a multinational setting. First, we discuss the changing framework conditions for organizing and managing what we call "global soldiers". Second, we present, briefly, our theoretical approach and research design, before entering a case study of a multinational military headquarters in Poland. Finally, we present some empirical observations concerning the formation of collective identity and discuss some theoretical and practical implications of our empirical findings. While we try to avoid a priori judgement on what aspects of identity are most important, we take particular interest in the tensions existing between corporate identification and various constructions of individual managerial identity.

We suggest that formation of collective identity must be regarded through two orders of discourse. The first order identity discourse concerns the substance of the collective identity – who we are, why we are here, what we stand for – i.e. questions and answers that help individual members make sense of the collective. The second order discourse deals with the conceptualization of identity – what does it mean to have a collective identity, how may it be created, and what are the functions of identity in the organization. This is a much more subtle and reflective dimension, which we usually consider the domain of academics, but our case study shows that it is also central to managers' daily identity work and that it has a huge impact on both the process and its outcome.

We also suggest that both orders of discourse influence how managers conceive and construct their own identity as an integral part of the collective identity construction. The chapter therefore concludes by encouraging military managers to reflect more on how they deal with identities in a multinational setting in order to make their identity management less an instinctive practice and more a mindful deployment of a broader repertoire of practices.

The main contribution of this chapter lies in the way it supplements the *first order* research focus on the "content" and process of collective and individual identity work with a *second order* interest in what might be called the "identity ideology", i.e. how identity is conceived by military managers. We do that by combining different strands of identity theory to shed new light on the managers' "mental models" of identity and challenge certain managerial practices through which the military tend to deal with multiple cultures and identities. We have devoted most space and thought to analysing and reflecting on this second order identity discourse.

The changing framework conditions for identity formation

Life in uniform is probably the first association most people get when thinking of the armed forces, and indeed the uniformed organization – looking alike – is a trademark of the military. Traditional military cultures are fairly rigid and "stubborn" with an emphasis on dress code, rules, hierarchy and disciplinary control (Winslow *et al.* 2003: 307).

However, various developments point at the emergence of a more contemporary civilian culture within the modern military. Many modern wars and militarized disputes have involved coordination between national armies. During the last decade, internationalization has intensified – primarily as a result of the emergent threat scenario where terrorism and weapons of mass destruction are seen as defining security challenges. Indeed, the core historical task of "defending national territory" has ceded importance and given way to "out of area" operations, such as humanitarian interventions and peacekeeping missions.

Building armies and the capability to engage in warfare might be seen as a symbolic, even defining feature of what it means to be a nation. Thus, the internationalization trend presents not only a set of practical challenges concerning managing diversity, but also a symbolic challenge to the very concept of the nation. Whereas earlier, "internationalization" of the military was a question of coordination between separate national armies, many military units are now "born" as true multinationals parented by command structures that transcend international "coordination forums".

Also, many other elements of diversity come into play in modern military units, thus challenging the ambition to build a cohesive and homogeneous unit. For instance organizations turn more diverse due to differences between the religious and sexual orientations of their members, but the inclusion of women and other ethnic groups in the armed forces also needs to be taken into consideration (Nuciari 2003; Segal 1995; Soeters and van der Meulen 2007).

As we see it, some of the differences between traditional and new conditions for organizing and managing armed forces may be summarized as follows.

The making of the global soldier may be seen as an increased humanization of the soldier. While this may be seen as good in a moral sense, it also adds new

Table 13.1 National vs global soldiers

	Conditions for organizing and managing national units	Conditions for organizing and managing multinational units
Purpose in establishing organization	Create and work in stable, tightly coupled units for the long term.	Create mission-specific, temporary communities/task forces.
Fundamental *raison d'être* and motivation	Territorial patriotism: willingness to give your life for your country.	Non-territorial internationalism: willingness to give your life for "the international community".
Time horizon	Stable organizations with an expected long lifespan.	Temporary organizations with uncertain lifespan.
Task characteristics	Well-defined task/mission.	Changing tasks/missions.
Organizational context	Parent organizational structure is stable and well-known. Clear procedures and chains of command.	Parent organizational structure is fundamentally changing. Chains of command are multinational.
Governing logic	Military logic predominates.	Military, political, legal, religious as well as humanitarian logics. A need for negotiation between them.
Language	Common language (the mother tongue), common concepts and codes.	English as a shared working language (lingua franca). Aligned concepts and codes.
Symbols/artefacts	Identical uniforms and visible symbols (e.g. regimental badges).	Different uniforms, different symbols.
Identity	Different cultural and individual identities, but common national identity and often common ethnic identity.	Different national, ethnic and religious identities as well as gender identities.

burdens to being a soldier: the global soldier has to individually cope with potential conflicts between humanistic and militaristic values and is thus to a wider extent individually responsible for deliberating and resolving dilemmas that were previously resolved at a higher managerial level.

We will attempt to make the outlined differences more concrete through empirical illustrations from a case study of the NATO Joint Forces Training Centre in Poland (JFTC). The case will be introduced below, but first we will present the theoretical approach we use to understand the implications of this shift to individual and collective identity work.

Theoretical positioning: identities as social constructs

The literature on identity is as vast and diverse as may be expected given that it deals with the factors that shape who and what we conceive ourselves to be. A full review is not in order here; rather we provide a glance at social constructivist identity research as it forms the theoretical framework within which we analyse and discuss identity formation and management.

The perspective implicit in social constructivist identity theory seems particularly relevant for dealing with the changing conditions for identity formation in the armed forces. In our view, the proliferation of the social constructivist perspective in academia somehow reflects underlying changes in the ways many contemporary organizations work. It mirrors the shift from capital-intensive, mass-production organizations primarily concerned with optimizing efficiency in the production of a clearly specified output – which would require relatively stable identities – to knowledge-based, technology-intensive organizations that frequently revise not only their targets but their entire purpose – which would require relatively flexible identities.

While these changes are well described in civil society contexts (Bauman, 2004; Bell 1997; Hylland-Eriksen 2001; Sennett 1998), their validity for military organizations has not been discussed as thoroughly, perhaps because the military has been seen to occupy a special position, relatively autonomous in relation to these societal forces.

A social constructivist view emphasizes an understanding of the processes through which identity distinctions emerge and become salient to individuals and groups in organizations (Alvesson 2002a and 2002b; Alvesson and Sköldberg 2000; Hatch and Schultz 2004; Martin 2002; Parker 2000; Sackmann 1997; Søderberg and Vaara 2003). First, it problematizes the existence of a "core", describing identity as not stable, nor fixed, but socially and historically constructed and subject to contradictions, revisions, and change (Hall 1992). Thus, identity is not a given or a constant, and the multiple identities at play in an organization "take colour" from the social context in which they are enacted.

Second, social constructivists focus their attention on the discursive processes that constitute identities. The construction of a person's identity is not only enabled, but also constituted by the use of language (Ainsworth and Hardy 2004). Identity construction is about sense-making (Weick 1995), and sense-making is both a process of cognitive modelling and a linguistic act. Members of an organization have understandings and identities that are specific to their locale, but which are also influenced by understandings that circulate more widely within society. The construction of these identities is an "ongoing argument" that never ends (Coupland and Brown 2004).

Thus the constructivist perspective also problematizes the distinction between collective identity and individual identity. The "story" of the organization – Who are we? Where are we going? – is intrinsically linked to the story of the individual manager or employee – Who am I in relation to the collective? How do I fit in? Thus, constructivism also implies an attempt to bridge the classic academic division of labour with individual identity formation as belonging to the domain of psychology, and collective/organizational identity as belonging to the domain of organization theory (Schultz 2005).

The term "collective identity" is in itself ambiguous. It covers three overlapping aspects of identity: organizational identity, which regards identity from the perspective of members of the organization and is closely linked to the organization's culture; corporate identity, which we reserve for management's strategic articulation of the organizational self; and finally, public identity or image which denotes the identity as seen from the perspective of its external stakeholders (Schultz 2005). In this chapter, based on our interest in managerial identity we focus on the interplay between individual military managers' identifications with various communities and management's efforts to construct a corporate identity.

Heeding Alvesson and Sköldberg's (2000) call for awareness of the constitutive effect of employing any analytical concept, we must point out a caveat regarding our use of the concept of corporate identity: this concept implies that an organization is a unit – a "corpus" (Christensen *et al.* 2007) – and that it is the management's task to express and organize the organization's identity on the basis of its *raison d'être*, its mission, and its desired image. However, we must be very cautious about assuming that there are shared values, habits, meaning systems in a new, temporary, multinational organization; multiple identities may exist within a single organization as well as multiple perceptions of the organization's mission and values, and members of the organization may be able to communicate and collaborate without sharing many basic ideas and beliefs. Behind a façade of some common artefacts and corporate statements that serve integrative purposes, we may thus find strong evidence of differentiating and fragmenting forces articulated in many different – and sometimes even conflicting – identities at play (Martin 2002). With this caveat in mind, we find a social constructivist approach fruitful as framework for understanding how military managers think of and deal with identity issues, i.e. for tapping into their sense-making and sense-giving processes (Gioia and Chittapeddi 1991; Weick *et al.* 2005).

A framework for understanding identity formation in organizations

How does the new multinational context change the way military managers think about and work with the formation of corporate identity – and what is the relationship between corporate identity work and their individual work on managerial identity?

In all organizational contexts there are many layers of culture and many potential identifications – or cultural memberships – at stake at the same time (see for example Sackmann 1997 and 2004). Members of an organization are unlikely to be restricted in their membership to one single organizational culture or subculture, because people may also identify with their gender, ethnic background, parent and spouse roles, sports club, city, profession, work organization etc. Thus, our basic analytical approach is to parse out the multiple identities that are at play in the organization at the same time.

This also ties into one basic premise of Social Identity Theory, namely that people use social categories to make sense of what they are doing and what kind of organization they are part of (Tajfel 1982; Jenkins 1996). The description of the organization as well as the positioning of the managers' private and professional selves revolve around social categories, some of which are universal (gender, nationality, ethnicity), and some of which are unique to the organizational context (e.g. military rank and tenure).

What is often missing in social constructivist mapping of identities at play in an organization, is the attention to what might be called *existential moments* where a person is forced to choose between different identities. It is indeed possible that multiple identities can coexist without one dominating the other for long periods of time – this may even be the normal state (cf. Parker 2000). But as pointed out by Hoffmann (1993), people are occasionally forced into situations where they have to choose between different identities; situations where they have to decide whether being Danish, a soldier, a Christian, a father or a democrat is most important to them. In such situations, identities and cultures are never parallel and equally important, but instead momentarily fixed in a hierarchy. They may choose a specific course of action simply because one identity or cultural affiliation is more important than another to them.

In our view, the requirement to resolve such identity dilemmas is often overlooked in constructivist research. The observation that multiple identities coexist most of the time has perhaps led to an assumption that identities are generally malleable, ambiguous and open to reconstruction/rearticulation. This may be correct as a general observation; identity hierarchies may not be consistent across time and place. But in specific situations, where identity issues frame actions and interactions, the dilemma must be at least temporarily resolved – and structured in a hierarchy. Our focus on "existential moments" in military managers' individual and collective identity work seeks to balance the current constructivist interest in ambiguity and ambivalence.

Research design

The nature of the subject lends itself to a qualitative and open methodological orientation aimed at gaining depth and density of information. In the overall project, we conducted a number of case studies, but in this chapter we illustrate our argument with findings from one case only. We employed a three-way approach to gathering data. Our primary method for collecting empirical material was semi-structured single-person interviews. Twenty interviews with military managers were conducted in situ on two field trips to the Joint Forces Training Centre (JFTC) in Poland in 2005 and 2006. Our ambition was to create a form of interview that left the interviewees space to articulate their perceptions and retrospective interpretations, while at the same time covering the subjects of the interview guide. Second, we conducted a number of expert interviews with Danish military managers who knew the military environment in Poland very well. During our field studies we gathered more data via informal conversations, participating in meetings and observing the interactions of the personnel under their normal work conditions, as well as observing the physical setting and the environment. Third, we collected and studied official documents, surveys and data from NATO and the JFTC as well as press releases. The purpose of the study was to investigate managerial identity work and highlight some consequences of different ways of managing multiple identities.

Analytically, we chose a two-step approach. First, we determined what identities were at play in the organization. Second, we analysed selected conflict situations connected with the work of forming a corporate identity, in order to understand the dynamics of identity work.

Hence, the first research issue was to identify the multiple identities at play in the organization. Identities are often latent or unarticulated and therefore hard to detect if they have no linguistic representations. The question "Who am I?" is intimate and often perceived as difficult to answer in depth. Sometimes people are reluctant to speak about their identity. Sometimes they may not be fully aware of – or capable of expressing – the identities they represent.

Following this argument, identity may be hard to articulate directly, and may not be part of a person's self-conscious reflection. As emphasized by Stryker and Serpe (1994), researchers must therefore distinguish between members' *self-ascribed* identity hierarchies (which they name "psychological centrality") and the identifications that govern their behaviour (what they call "identity salience"). This is why we found it fruitful to study *conflicts* as scenarios for individual and organizational identity work.

Conflicts are situations in which people make explicit claims of their identities, or at least situations in which identities are enacted. Conflicts may function as windows for the researchers into the internalized identity hierarchies of an individual and an organization, especially because identities are often activated by their counterparts – and made salient and contrasted to what people think they are not. Conflicts in organizations, whether between units, nationalities or professions, contain clues as to the multiple identities at play. Conflicts can be seen as microcosms that express who or what the organization is, thus contributing to the search for identities at play.

The risk of this approach is, of course, that conflicts may bring people to enact identities in psychologically distorted ways (Wetherell 1996; Zimbardo 1972). Keeping this risk in mind, we nevertheless see conflicts as a potentially fruitful entry point into the study of identity formation.

The case: the NATO Joint Forces Training Centre

As case study, we chose a multinational military NATO unit in Poland: the NATO Joint Force Training Centre (JFTC) located in Bydgoszcz.[1] The JFTC is a young organization: its creation was agreed upon in May 2003, but it was only when a Polish Implementation Planning Team began working in January 2004 that the concept of the JFTC was taken forward. According to official documents, the JFTC's mission is to enhance allied combined and joint training at the tactical level, and to prepare, manage and execute NATO's combined and joint training events. The JFTC is a NATO training body aimed at joint, combined training of tactical-level command posts and staff.

The training centre provides collective battle staff training for component level headquarters and below as well as staff training for partner and new member nations. The JFTC facilitates joint experimentation and the development and implementation of joint doctrine and NATO standards. The facility uses computer modelling and simulation capabilities to further interoperability and transformation within NATO.

The JFTC is authorized with a peacetime establishment of 120 personnel and contractors. The Directorship is a permanent Danish position. The position as Deputy Director is held by a Pole. The Chief of Staff position is shared between Bulgaria and Greece on a rotational basis. The staff includes personnel from 15 nations.

Identities at play at the JFTC

Even at the very first glance through the lenses of our analytical framework, it becomes apparent that many different identities are indeed at play. During the days of observing and interviewing, we saw and heard accounts of a number of conflicts containing clues to the identification and formation of identity groups. The following table summarizes the identifications that were expressed in interview statements about different conflicts at the JFTC.

The overview of identifications, fault lines, identity expressions and conflict issues highlights the complexity of identity issues in this multinational military organization. But the interesting part of the analysis is not the descriptive registration of the different identities that are expressed in the organization and in respondents' accounts. Rather it is the way in which these identities are enacted

Table 13.2 Identifications at the JFTC

Identification	Fault lines	Identity expressions	Conflict issues
National	Danes vs Germans vs Poles, etc.	Different uniforms/languages, sense of affiliation. Few overt expressions, hidden issue, noted in private, informal conversations and with lowered voice. Use of "Eastern/Western European" labels.	Work habits, social skills, norms about professional conduct and standards. Latent sense of inferiority/superiority. Utterances interpreted in the context of being ahead of the curve vs being behind the curve.
Regional	Former East Bloc (i.e. Warsaw Pact) members vs. former West Bloc (i.e. original NATO) members.		
Sector level	Military system vs. civil society, the political system and/or the business community.	Uniformed vs casual clothes.	Competing logics in relations to policy decisions.
Local	Local hosts vs. foreign guests.	Self-identification as guest/host countries.	"Home-base advantages" Foreigners' expectations of hospitality vs locals' expectations of gratitude and respect for hosting the NATO Training Centre.
Organizational/ collective	"Insiders/members" vs "outsiders/ external parties".	External communication maintains image of a unified "we". Internal contest about the degree and substance of "the we". Clear distinctions between outsiders/ insiders.	Maintenance of a coherent public (external) image vs internal disassociation.
Functional domain	Specialists vs managers.	Functional groupings, technical jargon.	Management skills/judgement vs professional skills and judgement. Formal vs informal authority. Peer group formation.
Hierarchy/rank	Executives/Officers/Non-commissioned Officers/Privates	Decision-making competencies. Expressions of authority/deference. Articulation of collective interests based on rank.	
Length of stay	The "newcomers" vs the "settlers".	References to "we/they were here first".	Divergence over the right to lay out the ground rules and assert informal authority.
Ethnicity	Northern European vs Slavic.	Ethnic markers: physical appearance, language, religious affiliation, ethnic history.	Stereotyping, attribution about competency levels and social skills with reference to ethnicity.
Age/experience	Senior officers vs junior officers.	Distinctions between generations. Attitudes associated with generation	Experience as basis for authority/power vs dynamism as basis for authority/power.
Gender	Female vs male officers.	Physical attributes. Separate quarters.	Attributions about physical and emotional strength and "tone of voice".

("activated") in conflicts, integrated into the managers' self-ascribed identity, and used in managerial sense-giving as explanations for decisions and pre-scribed behaviour.

For example, in conflicts about what it means to be a professional military manager, the officers referred to their national norms. Polish and American managers told us that they were used to shouting and yelling when educating junior staff, because they saw this as a defining expression of what it means to be in charge. As an American officer says: "In my army, especially as lieutenant-colonel or full colonel, you just have to raise your voice and everything happens. In NATO that's not how you do business". Scandinavian managers frowned at this practice because they felt it conflicted with the non-authoritarian ethos that constituted part of their Scandinavian identity.

First-order identity discourse: the battles about "who we are"

The first-order identity discourse concerns the negotiation of the content of corporate identity and its relation to other identities at play. We have analysed a number of conflict situations in order to understand the identities at play in JFTC. A detailed description of all cases of conflict that we have studied is beyond the scope of this chapter, but we will highlight one of these conflicts to illustrate the dynamics of collective/individual identity work at the JFTC and dig deeper into the rich empirical material.

Introducing a Memorandum of Agreement (MOA), which serves as a standard working policy between NATO and the host nation, turned out to be a very difficult negotiation. The Polish civil servants in the town of Bydgoszcz wanted NATO officers to conform to Polish standards on a number of areas that seen from a NATO perspective were non-negotiable. As a senior-ranking American officer describes it:

> The single best indicator for multinational integration at the JFTC is the infamous MOA. It is almost as if the Polish representatives are trying to intimidate us. For example they want us to hand in our driving licenses, get our passports stamped, our non-EU cars rebuilt, etc.

The Polish JFTC employees were also very frustrated and sometimes embarrassed with this situation. The employees were divided in two camps on this issue. One group of civilian employees had a lot of patience with "the system" and often gave the other nations ideas and thoughts on how to handle the situation. A group of Polish officers were more aggressive and angry with the local authorities whom they felt sometimes envied their job situation[2] and therefore tried to obstruct work at the JFTC.

Many organizations facilitate social validation by institutionalizing temporal markers of progress, known as *rite de passage*. Entry into a group or an organization is often marked by rituals of varying formality and complexity. The MOA negotiations can be viewed, from a NATO point of view, as a *rite de passage* towards adapting a multinational organizational identity and leaving behind a strong identification with the host nation and national (Polish) interests.

An American officer makes sense of his observations about the MOA when he mentions the so-called "Warsaw Pact Syndrome" – to grow up in a society where things more or less stay the same for a long period – as a reason for this struggle between the NATO multinational identity and the host-nation identity. According to several Western officers, some of the Polish officials believed that it was their "duty" to make life hard on the Western European NATO members through sabotage, resistance and aggressive behaviour during the negotiations of the Memorandum of Agreement.

However, as a Bulgarian officer described it, due to deficient English-language skills it was not always an easy task for Eastern Europeans to participate in the multinational working groups. Some of the young Polish officers who did not face these language problems themselves even referred to their older superior colleagues as the "Jurassic Park" and explained that they had so many problems understanding the English language that they sometimes deliberately delayed and obstructed work processes. However, a Polish civilian academic at the JFTC theorized that the observed reluctance towards working in multinational groups could also have something to do with some Eastern Europeans' lack of self-confidence:

> The Western Europeans are more self-confident, they feel more comfortable or at least they show it. [...] The Eastern European people are less self-confident, they are talking less. [...] From Eastern Europeans I hear: I'm only a major so I can't do anything. I haven't heard that from any Western European.

Although we observed a struggle between different national and regional identities, the JFTC management believed that if they kept focusing on the support and training of the young Polish officers and reinforced a strong multinational and corporate identity among them, the forms of resistance expressed by the senior Polish officers (the "Jurassic Park") would decrease.

It is, however, important to stress that neither the corporate identity nor national identities are clearly and consistently articulated or enacted at the JFTC. All identities are to some extent still open to negotiation and re-articulation. In this perspective, there seems to be a need for members of the top management group to present the outcome of their discussions and negotiations concerning identity issues both to themselves and to their subordinate officers in order to protect the non-negotiable issues. These issues are, according to an interviewee, that "At the JFTC we work in multinational groups, we deal only with legitimate business, we will not accept any corruption."

The analysis of this conflict suggests that the discursive negotiation of the corporate identity often takes the form of a competition between various identifications. While management has a privileged position to impose norms and rules and regulate identities, they often weigh and balance their own social identities against the corporate interest.

Second-order identity discourse: the conceptualization of corporate identity

The case study does not only capture the conflicts about the content and status of the collective identity vis-à-vis other identities; it also exposes – somewhat more subtly – the second-order identity discourse. That is, it contains a discourse on the nature, meaning and status of the concept of identity – as a management objective, a tool, and a cultural phenomenon. The reflection on the concept of identity is at times explicit, but mostly it is tacitly implied in the managers' accounts and reflections in the interview sessions as well as in their actions and strategic communication in the organization.

Consider for example one officer's reflection on the settler/newcomer issue: "If I were ever to give advice on how to start a military multinational organization I would say: never have one national unit there first – start up as a multinational unit. Otherwise it hinders integration among the different nations."

This, together with numerous other statements, demonstrates that the construction of an integrated corporate identity is a priority (and a standing source of frustration) for top management in the case of the JFTC. The espoused ideal is that members of the organization must give primacy to the corporate identity. For example they are expected to subdue their national affiliations and let their actions be guided by collective values. And the corporate identity is articulated and backed up by managerial authority, e.g. when top management presents who will be working together in the multinational groups. But it may be wrong to equate an espoused corporate identity with an organizational identity, given that it is not enacted by all or a majority of the organizational members. Perhaps it may be more correct to speak of the corporate interest and managerial effort to launch a corporate identity. In almost all instances, the corporate interest at the JFTC was protected by a "guardian of the corporate code"– doing things the "JFTC way". For example, national identity was always salient at JFTC, but rarely allowed to dominate. As exemplified by a Danish officer stating:

> In a national setting you can issue orders – and sometimes tell people in a harsh way to get something done. In a multinational setting you have to be very careful not to push any nationality too strongly. On the other hand, you cannot be too nice either. We have had officers asking me why the Danish Director is so kind. They are simply not used to being treated with respect and calmness by a general. Some of the officers are used to being yelled at and therefore they consider that a normal situation.

It was very important to the Director of the JFTC to maintain this calm and respectful tone within the unit. As several interviewees pointed out, it was often emphasized by the director at the weekly staff meeting that part of the JFTC vision is to treat people with respect, and that everyone at the JFTC was responsible for all victories and failures. Doing things the JFTC way was a team effort: "It is never a single person who gets the credit."

The preferred strategy for building a corporate identity at the JFTC seemed to be a "command-and-control" strategy, outlawing the pursuit of national interest and enforcing the corporate interest. Whenever national identity threatened to take over within the identity hierarchy, the corporate identity was enforced by top management. For example it was frowned upon if two officers during a meeting began whispering to each other in their own national language. Building a corporate identity was a key managerial objective at the JFTC. When conflicts started to emerge, corporate interests were forced upon the multinational organization. The "command-and-control" strategy was highly visible in conflict situations and sometimes served as an overall method for solving problems in the building of the organization.

This recognized drive towards a unifying idea is even more pronounced when it comes to JFTC's external relations. As a Danish officer remarked:

> When it comes to being a NATO unit we have to be very specific about our corporate selves. We are very explicit about the JFTC way when presenting projects to 'outsiders'. However, I think that we are more open to debate and different opinions when we are working here and no special guests and meetings are scheduled.

The Danish officer explained that "doing things the NATO way" meant that top management had to be very precise in establishing "the right corporate code". This ambition was very pronounced, and several interviewees mentioned the introduction interview they had with the Director where he described the JFTC mission and the way to cooperate as a team at the JFTC. This *esprit de corps* was very apparent when a NATO general visited the JFTC or when the Director and his staff went to the NATO headquarters in the US to present the mission. In these situations an officer described how every word was discussed and balanced to make sure that neither a political agenda nor a national community were offended.

While the JFTC put much effort into conforming to the external expectation that it should appear as an integrated unit, normal day-to-day routines were more differentiated. According to several interviewees, the Director's orders were often debated and the tone during staff meetings was informal and pleasant. As an interviewed senior-ranking officer explained it, the JFTC corps identity expressions were more fluid and constantly balanced to meet the different demands of the outside world, NATO and the employees. The deliberate efforts to create and launch a corporate identity at JFTC may, however, be counterproductive inasmuch as identities, according to our theoretical perspective, are products of mutual negotiation, not something fixed and established.

Even though many strategic initiatives were taken to build a corporate identity, management often explained performance problems at the JFTC as a result of the absence of a common identity. When other identities were competing with the corporate identity, the managers' strategy was to suppress them in order for the corporate identity to prevail. The military managers' ideal is a monolithic/tightly aligned culture where a strong corporate code exists. The principal fear expressed by JFTC managers is to be dominated by autonomous subcultures. Below we will depict the mental model of the JFTC managers:

This JFTC conceptualization of identity conforms quite well to the identity ideology that historically has characterized national military units: an emphasis on sameness, integration, and priority to the corporate code. At JFTC, management expected of themselves and others that they would subdue the impulse to enact a social identity that would work to the detriment of the corporate/collective identity. JFTC management clearly viewed it as its job to manage identity and resolve identity dilemmas. But this is not a given truth; in fact, in some other NATO headquarters it is much more unclear whether management considers it part of its job to manage identity (Wedell-Wedellsborg 2007).

The orders of identity discourse and individual identity construction

The conceptualization of corporate identity is interesting in itself, but it is also important because it is central to the construction of individual managerial iden-

Table 13.3 Conceptualization of corporate identity

Conceptualization of corporate identity	JFTC manager's mental model
Ideal	Monolithic/tightly aligned identity strong corporate code.
Strategy for managing corporate identity	Command and control. Alignment around specific values and norms.
Importance assigned to identity as a driver of performance	High – identity issues (especially lack of common identity) often seen as explanation for problems and performance.
Perspective on other identities at play	Other identities compete with corporate identities and must be kept down in order for corporate identity to prevail.
Principal fear/Antitheses	Organization dominated by autonomous subcultures.
Typical statements	"We need to build a strong common culture". "Our greatest challenge is to become a unit".

tities. Military managers at the JFTC are expected – and impose on themselves – to be guardians of the corporate code, to disregard national differences, and to abstain from engaging in subcultural work, because it conflicts with the ideal of being "One Unit".

Of course, individual managers may or may not conform to these expectations, but they certainly form the sounding board against which the managers make sense of their role and their tasks. Thus, it is not only the substance of "who we are" that matters to individual identity formation, but also the conceptualization of what it means to develop and maintain a corporate identity.

The case study suggests that managers' construction of their individual identities cannot be separated from their notion of the collective. As managers depict and conceptualize an organization's corporate identity, they construct the roles, expectations and subject positions to which they must relate and inscribe their own professional selves. This is particularly salient for managers, because an implicit part of any manager's job is to create and maintain a clear and compelling idea of why the collective makes sense. Thus, the distinction between collective identity (whether organizational or corporate) and individual identity may be analytically helpful, but it also obscures the intricate relationship between the two. As shown above, individual identity formation is linked to the construction and use of social categories. Military managers make sense of their roles and actions in relation to how they make sense of their organization.

Concluding arguments

We began the case study with an ambition to answer the research question: *how do the new military missions and the multinational context change the way military managers think about and work with the formation of corporate identity.* The theoretical discussion and empirical analyses presented in this chapter contribute to answering that question.

We have analysed some observations and discussed some implications of the new conditions for organizing and managing multinational teams in the military. These new conditions for military collaboration probably require more than just modifications to existing management practice in a national context. Rather, they set a new stage for a conscious and reflexive management of identity issues. Working from the notion that our way of thinking about identity – both in theory and in practice – should be contingent on the context for identification, we suggest that the time has come for military leaders to rethink both how identity should be conceived, and how it should be managed in a multinational context.

The JFTC case is interesting in that there are complex international agendas to identify *with*, but no visible threat and no clearly defined common enemy to unite *against* – and hence nothing that may help management define and demarcate the specific corporate identity of JFTC. In this regard, we claim that there is a difference between ad-hoc multinational peacetime units and multinational units operating in war zones, even though we are well aware of the fact (and recent studies based on terror management theory go in the same direction) that a common enemy not necessarily creates any unity or cohesion (Dechesne *et al.* 2007). However, our case study of JFTC still gives rise to the question: if a corporate identity cannot be constructed against a visible threat or an image of the enemy, what might then serve as the logic behind shared identifications among soldiers? And which concepts and tools can military managers use in their strategic communication and identity management?

In the JFTC case, we found that the idea that it is imperative to forge a strong corporate identity based on integration and uniformity was still prevalent among military managers as a sort of reminiscence of a traditional mindset for identity formation and management. But at JFTC there was only a modest use of common artefacts and social gatherings that could have served the function of socializing the various national groups and building a corporate identity. Therefore, management in JFTC was struggling with the many challenges to a fragile corporate identity and frustrated by its actual state. Perceived national differences in attitudes, work habits and social skills were pointed out as the greatest barriers to building a shared multinational identity as well as to the emergence of relatively autonomous subcultures. The analysis of the empirical material suggests that there were numerous other identities at play; some of them were perceived by the members of the organizations as being just as important as the multinational identity.

Polemically, one might say that the dominant identity management concept, which we found present among JFTC managers, preaches undivided loyalty to the unit and the adoption of a singular identity, while at the same time presenting the organization's members with the ideal of "the global soldier" who is capable of negotiating and reflecting on his loyalties and identities.

The empirical analysis of culture and identity formations in the case study of JFTC raises a key question: how can managers of multinational peacetime military organizations cope reflexively with identity formation and identity management?

From our point of view, the central challenge for military managers in a peacetime multinational organization seems to be to create a certain amount of cohesion and commitment without pressing for an unattainable, uniform corporate identity. We suggest that both the managers' mindset and the tools available to them must be tuned to build an identity that allows for coexistence of multinational, national and other identities. In our opinion the way to develop a stable organizational identity is not by forcing a corporate identity on the organization, but by involving its members and negotiating with them what could be building blocks and how various identifications could be balanced.

In the multinational ad-hoc military organization, the usual quest for uniformity, shared values and common identity is only one option within a broader repertoire of identity concepts and practices. Another identity concept, the diversity concept, would not only pay respect to diversity within the military organization, but also emphasize diversity as an asset and thus require of the military leader that he is able to contain a multiplicity of identities and facilitate a constructive interplay among them.

We do not give priority to any particular identity concept and identity management practice; we rather encourage military leaders to be aware that there is a broader repertoire and thus make mindful choices of concepts and tools that correspond to a specific mission and fit well into a specific context.

Notes

1 Two other cases, Multinational Corps North East, Poland, and NATO Defence College, Rome, are analysed in detail in the PhD thesis (Wedell-Wedellsborg 2007).
2 At the time of the research project in 2005–2006, almost 35 per cent of the inhabitants in Bydgoszcz were unemployed. According to a Polish officer, working at the NATO Joint Force Training Centre was considered a steady job with a good salary.

Chapter 14

Smooth and strained international military cooperation

Three cases in Kabul[1]

Joseph Soeters, Delphine Resteigne, Rene Moelker and Philippe Manigart

Introduction

At the beginning of the twentieth century, rebellious groups, called the Boxers, attacked the foreign community as well as thousands of converted Christian Chinese people in the city of Beijing (Preston 2002). The foreign community consisted of a variety of nationalities, including Americans, British, Australians, Russians, Germans, French, Italians, Austrians and Japanese. They were diplomats, tradesmen, military men, journalists and their families. The fights were severe: there were thousands of casualties, especially among the missionaries and the Chinese converts. Inside the besieged area in China's capital city and during the military campaign set up to relieve the foreigners under attack, troops of the various nationalities assembled and fought side by side. This may have been one of the first well-documented examples of international military cooperation. This campaign was fairly successful: the besieged were rescued and the number of casualties among the military was not very high.

Nonetheless, it was clear from the beginning that mutual stereotypes and rivalries between the various national troops would not fade away during the siege and the following military campaign. Quite systematically, the American and British troops were considered to be the best and bravest, the least dirty and those least taking part in the looting and punitive actions after the hostilities had ceased. At any rate, the Americans and British citizens were inclined to think this way (Preston 2002: 66, 93, 195). On the other hand, continental European military men – in particular the Germans and the French – deemed the British behaviour as too bold, reckless and presumptuous. They criticized the fact that the British would not accept a foreigner to command their troops and that they had claimed the victory that was actually won by the brave actions of others (Preston 2002: 92, 117, 175, 194). Even the way injured soldiers behaved displayed remarkable differences along national lines: the French and the Italians were said to "make the most of their wounds", whereas the British and the Americans were found to be eager to return to the battle (Preston 2002: 186). Clear rivalries between the national troops developed after the campaign, sometimes even causing fights between soldiers of the various nations. These hostilities did not come as a surprise. As a general of one nation had prophesied, there would be fighting coming up, but "not with the Chinese" (Preston 2002: 321–322).

Clearly, in today's international military cooperation, there is no fighting going on between the contributing troops (e.g. Elron *et al.* 1999). This is important because – within the framework of international institutions such as NATO, the UN or the EU – national forces tend increasingly to work with forces of other nations. Due to budget cuts many national forces – especially in Europe – lack sufficient resources to engage in large-scale operations. Moreover, military collaboration with other nations enhances a mission's legitimacy. Both arguments apply to all national military organizations, even to the sizable US forces as the operations in Iraq demonstrate. Consequently, the importance of the success and effectiveness of such cross-national military collaboration can hardly be overestimated (Duffey 2000; Soeters *et al.* 2006).

Yet, it would be naïve to assume that all of today's international military missions proceed smoothly, nor can one expect that they are effective all of the time. International collaboration in business, such as international mergers, alliances, joint ventures and partnerships have not always been very successful, to put it mildly. Cultural, institutional and (changing) power differences between the partnering organizations often account for less than optimal performance of the newly founded organizational entities (e.g. Olie 1994; Inkpen and Beamish 1997). In fact, in multi-organizational arrangements coherence and unity of purpose are often lacking (Clegg *et al.* 2002). Similarly, international military cooperation is unlikely to yield exclusively results that are up to or even above standard expectations.

In this chapter we aim to describe and analyse three examples of international military cooperation. All of these operations were part of NATO's ISAF mission (International Security Assistance Force) in Kabul that started early 2002. Two of our case studies regard bi-national cooperation within the framework of the multinational ISAF mission; the scope of the third one is truly multinational, in that it analyses how the everyday collaboration between more than 20 countries takes place at Kabul International Airport (KAIA). We deem two of these cases to be examples of strained cooperation, whereas we consider the third one to be running fairly smoothly, although even this case is not without problems in regards of cooperation. We consider a cooperation to be strained when there is little trust between the partnering forces (Das and Teng 1998), when there is only a limited degree of commitment to make the cooperation become a success (Doz 1996), when there is no collective identity (Hardy *et al.* 2005), and when the cooperation is ended prematurely and unplanned (Inkpen and Beamish 1997). Using existing literature on cross-cultural cooperation, we try to compare the three cases and point at possible factors explaining the differing outcomes.

Although the military traditionally has played a central role in organization studies (Lang 1965; Smith *et al.* 1995: 7–8), international military cooperation is an under-researched field of study. It is an example of "managing exceptional organizations working in exceptional circumstances" (Mintzberg 2001: 759). The cases' exceptional circumstances derive from three elements. International military cooperation brings together organizations that derive their core – and perhaps even their sole – identity from national sovereignty (e.g. Elron *et al.* 1999; Chapter 13, this volume). They are state institutions par excellence, in principle designed to defend the own nation *against* the armed forces of other nations. In addition, the organizations featured in this chapter operate under threatening circumstances where human lives are at stake. As Terror Management Theory (Schimel *et al.* 1999) demonstrates, awareness and acceptance of death play a role in the willingness to work with people from other groups, i.e. groups with different identities. Clearly, this is not a factor organization scholars are inclined to include in their analysis of international, inter-organizational arrangements. Thirdly, military personnel in these three cases perform their activities in *camps* or *gated communities* (Diken and Laustsen 2005). There is reason to believe that the dynamics inside those camps are reflected in the way people, i.e. the soldiers, behave outside the camps while on mission. And their activities outside the camps in the city of Kabul are the only reason that they are in this area anyway. We will reflect on the connection between the dynamics inside and outside the camps at the end of this chapter. In this way, we hope our work will be conducive to the further development of organization theory in exceptional circumstances.

Existing literature on cooperation within (international) organizations

Cooperation between units within an organization is at least as important as cooperation between individuals or cooperation between organizations. Cooperation is imperative if tasks are too extensive, complex, risky and hazardous to be performed by one single individual, unit or organization. In addition, cooperation may provide people within and between organizations with learning opportunities, work satisfaction and stress reduction (Argyle 1991; Smith Ring and Van de Ven 1994). Yet, cooperation does not always have such positive results, certainly not if the cooperation consists of people and organizations from different nationalities (e.g. Olie 1994). Examining the literature on collaboration, we have identified seven relevant factors that may help explain why international collaboration between organizations in general, and military organizations in particular, sometimes fails and sometimes flourishes. We have focused on structural and contextual factors because previous studies have led us to believe that these have a more pervasive impact than process-related characteristics of the cooperation. Nonetheless, process-related elements will not be excluded from the analysis and discussion.

Composition of the multinational cooperation

Nowadays, it is generally accepted that the composition of teams and organizations in terms of nationality – its national demography, so to speak – plays a role in the success of international collaboration (Adler 2002). Current understanding based on the work of the late sociologist George Simmel makes it clear that proportions between demographic minorities and majorities account for numerous social and behavioural patterns in groups, organizations and societies. Kanter (1977), for example, has demonstrated that the quantitative distribution of men and women in organizations plays a major role in explaining social dynamics in gender-mixed work situations. In a similar vein, recent studies have revealed a U-shape relationship between national composition and performance. Highly heterogeneous teams – with many nationalities of equal size (ten times 10 per cent for example) – and highly homogeneous teams – with few nationalities and one nationality clearly outnumbering the others (in a 90/5/5-per-cent-ratio or so) – outperform teams and organizations that are moderately heterogeneous (Earley and Mosakowski 2000; Adler 2002). In other words, high and low heterogeneous teams show the least amount of conflict, the most effective communication patterns and the highest level of satisfaction, planning and cooperation. The highly heterogeneous teams for their part emphasize rules and practices that are inclusive rather than exclusive; this means that heterogeneous teams tend to be more open to participants' ideas and inputs. Hence, these teams develop the highest levels of team identity. Moderately heterogeneous teams – for instance, teams composed of two or three more or less equally sized nationalities – on the contrary, tend to display dysfunctional interactions. The members of such teams are likely to accuse one another of not fully understanding or even being the source of a problem. Additionally, such teams show many difficulties in communicating as well as low levels of team identity (Early and Mosakowski 2000: 36, 45). Recent research shows that the level of disintegration in such mixed teams is larger when the demographic fault lines are clear from the outset, pre-existing and salient to all people involved, i.e. when team members have been instructed to represent their own group or at least when they feel that way (Li and Hambrick 2005; see also Barinaga 2007). This is more likely to be the case in moderately heterogeneous groups than in high and low heterogeneous groups. An illustration of this "mechanism" in the field of international military cooperation can be found in a working paper by Søderberg and Wedell-Wedellsborg (2005). In that paper they compare a multinational corps, consisting of personnel from three countries, i.e. Germany, Denmark and Poland, with a multinational military training centre consisting of personnel from 15 countries. As they write, in the latter organization, "national identities play a minor role, whereas at the former organization national identification seems to be almost an organising principle – the basis for coalitions, a source of conflict and the standard explanation for problems".

Cultural diversity

International cooperation is intercultural cooperation, bringing together people with different demeanours, languages, cognitive schemas and values (Hambrick *et al.* 1998; Adler 2002). Cultural differences also exist between military organizations, even within the ones belonging to NATO (Soeters *et al.* 2006). First, it does not seem too speculative to assume that within the Western world an Anglo-Saxon cultural "cluster" exists, consisting of the so-called ABCA countries (America, Britain, Canada and Australia), which indeed have a common history and attitudinal coherence (Lammers and Hickson 1979; Ronen and Shenkar 1985) as well as elaborate forms of joint defence policies and practices. The affinity between the British and the American military organizations during the campaign against the Boxers in Beijing in 1900 (Preston 2002) seems to have continued to exist until today (e.g. Ballard 2002). This is not to say that these four countries always operate in a completely identical style; in general, the Americans (and the Australians) have been reported to make a much more tough and distant impression with regard to their contact with the local population than the British (and the Canadians) (Duffey 2000; Caniglia 2001; Fitz-Gerald 2003). However, in matters of discipline and hierarchy these four countries act quite similarly, which is distinct from the working style in many continental European armed forces who seem to be more easy-going and perhaps less ambitious when it comes to operational-military affairs (Soeters *et al.* 2006). Given these differences, it should come as no surprise that ABCA-armed forces know lesser degrees of civilianization than armed forces from the West European continent. For instance, in the ABCA-armed forces military unions are not allowed, or in the case of Australia and the UK they have been admitted only very recently. In countries such as the Netherlands, Belgium and Germany military unions have existed for a considerable period of time (Bartle and Heinecken 2006). Another cultural gap that seems to exist within NATO concerns the interactions with armed forces perceived to be of "lower (professional) status". Previous research on Dutch–Turkish military cooperation in Kosovo and Afghanistan revealed that the cultural distance between the two military organizations is fairly large, and that – on top of that – derogatory stereotypes of the "Turkish migrant worker" seem to be prevalent among West European soldiers (Soeters *et al.* 2004). A similar rift seems to exist between soldiers from "old" and "new" NATO member states – such as between Danes and Germans on the one hand and Poles on the other (Søderberg and Wedell-Wedellsborg 2005). Hence, even among NATO countries clear cultural differences between nationalities have existed and continue to do so (Soeters *et al.* 2006). More often than not, these differences are detrimental to the development of mutual trust, because the partnering organizations lack informal sets of congruent expectations and assumptions about each other's prerogatives and obligations (Smith Ring and Van de Ven 1994: 100). One can only guess what this means for missions in which NATO and non-NATO armed forces work together. Not surprisingly, this type of international military cooperation does not occur frequently.

Internal cohesion and status of units

Military organizations are characterized by a high degree of functional and structural differentiation, based on the existence of different services (land, air and sea), functional groupings (engineers, signals), and teeth-versus-tail positions (i.e. military core versus support and staff units). One special distinction refers to so-called "elite units". "Elite units" – e.g. air manoeuvre and airborne troops – are designed and trained to operate under dangerous conditions, and to use and sustain violence. "Elite units" generally are considered to be high-status groups – or at least this is what they think they are. They tend to emphasize group bonding, disregarding and actually looking down upon others (Winslow 1999). In correspondence with their (self-)attributed high status and their inner-directed elite culture, these units are not likely to accept orders, instructions and inspections from people who do not belong to their own units. In general, soldiers in such units are critical of outsiders and protective of the ones inside. This deliberately created attitude of internal solidarity and bonding has proven to be useful in battle and clear friend-and-foe situations. Not surprisingly, the "leave-no-man-behind" ideology is particularly strong among "elite" troops. Yet, it is noteworthy that this ideology specifically pertains to casualties from the own unit and not from casualties of other units, even if they belong to the own national forces (Wong 2005). In today's fuzzy, multinational peace support operations, however, displaying an open mind and developing ties to others in the mission is at least as important. If such a "bridging" attitude is lacking, units tend to become isolated and oblivious of negative feedback from other parts of the organization, while tending to stick to internal (within unit) communication and territorial behaviour (Browne et al. 2005). All this lowers their general performance and creativity in situations that are new, ambiguous and unclear (Granovetter 1983; Ancona and Caldwell 1992; Kratzer et al. 2004).

Technology

Although the national cultural factor clearly plays a role in aviation (Helmreich and Merritt 1998; Soeters and Boer 2000), the cultural impact on air force operations seems to be far less pervasive than among land forces. Air forces, especially the ones operating in NATO, are subject to isomorphing, technology-driven impulses (e.g. DiMaggio and Powell 1991). In the air forces uniformity in technologies (F-16s, Blackhawks, or helicopters in general) as well as common operating procedures and training reduce variation in human behaviour; hence, the impact of the cultural factor decreases. In air force operations tasks are mostly based on relatively objective standards for assessing the correctness or superiority of a particular solution. Performing such tasks is generally expected to be unrelated to cultural diversity (Hambrick *et al.* 1998: 194–196; Jackson 1992). Comparable findings have been demonstrated at the – also very technology-driven – European Air Space Agency; here, however, one might claim that the creativity needed for the design of air space technology profits from cultural diversity (Jackson 1992; Zabusky 1995). Land operations – especially peace operations – however, allow for much more variation in procedures and behaviours. These operations are far less technology-driven, but they do require an "elaborate and well-orchestrated interaction among groups members" (Hambrick *et al.* 1998: 194). Hence, these operations are subject to endless discussions on how things should be done (Soeters *et al.* 2006), simply because there are no sets of congruent expectations and assumptions (Smith Ring and Van de Ven 1994) or compatible frames of reference (Doz 1996: 72) among the partnering forces. Brocades Zaalberg (2005), for instance, has described the many different ways national armed forces interpret and operationalize the concept of Civil–Military Cooperation (CIMIC). Previous studies have repeatedly shown that even a seemingly simple activity such as patrolling the streets can be done – and actually is done – in many ways: weapons on the back or not, wearing sunglasses or not, having interpreters in the squad or not, driving in armoured vehicles or not, driving slowly or not, etc. The role of technology also comes to the fore in Søderberg and Wedell-Wedellsborg's (2005) comparative case study. They found that the multinational military organization that was relying on training facilities using technology-driven computer modelling and simulation experienced lesser difficulties in cooperation than the other organization in their analysis. This was a headquarter tasked with executing strategies and policies – clearly a type of work entailing endless debates and discussions as well as limited mutual adjustment among group members (Hambrick *et al.* 1998).

The organization of tasks

The way tasks in multinational operations are organized and allocated seems to play a role as well in the possible success or failure of international military collaboration. The work that needs to be done in a collaborative effort of many can be divided in at least two different ways (Argyle 1991): *parallel tasking* in which (national) units are assigned their own geographical area of responsibility where they can act fairly independently versus *reciprocal tasking* in which each (national) unit, on the one hand, is providing a discrete, complementary contribution to the whole while, on the other hand, being supported by the whole and, hence, impregnated by the other units (Thompson 1967: 54–55). Combining these structural arrangements with possible cultural outcomes when culturally distinct organizations come together, the following picture emerges (Nahavandi and Malekzadeh 1988; Berry 2004). *Parallel tasking*, i.e. the allocation of specific geographical areas of responsibility to different national units, implies a *separation* strategy which will produce positive outcomes, if the work of one unit has no impact on the work of another. However, if the different units remain connected in one way or another (for instance, through joint living facilities or due to the impact of other units' actions), problems may occur. In a *reciprocal organizational set-up*, either *assimilation* (one group submits to the dominating group), or *integration* (the formation of a "third culture") may follow. As we noticed earlier, assimilation – leading to uniformity – can be observed in technology-driven operations, or when one nation clearly outperforms the other nations and indeed is deemed to be superior by these nations. If the other nation's (claimed) superiority is not accepted, however, cooperation is likely to be strained. The integration outcome is more likely to occur if the commander successfully sets superordinate and supranational goals, maintaining a balance between "assertive and cooperative talk" (Hardy *et al.* 2005), emphasizing goal interdependence and goal sharing, as well as a strong common code, culture and coinciding values (Gray 1985; Chen *et al.* 1998; Søderberg and Wedell-Wedellsborg 2005). On the contrary, if the commander is not capable of preventing ambiguity and information asymmetry to occur between the partnering forces (Doz 1996: 72), the operation tends to become flawed. In sum, the structural and cultural elements of an organizational set-up should match for a mission to be successful.

Shift in bargaining power

Inkpen and Beamish (1997) have convincingly argued that shifts in the balance of bargaining power between partners may render inter-organizational arrangements unstable to the extent that these arrangements can be unexpectedly or prematurely ended. Such shifts in the balance of power may occur when one partner acquires sufficient (local) knowledge, skills and resources to eliminate dependency on a partner and make the inter-organizational arrangement in fact obsolete. This may be the result of one partner deliberately striving for less dependency, but this may also be the consequence of changing contextual factors rendering the contribution of the other organization(s) less important. In international business there are numerous cases of unplanned terminations of international, inter-organizational arrangements – for instance between Japanese and American firms – simply because the other partner's knowledge and resources were no longer needed. Such change in power and dependency relations may evolve during the inter-organizational arrangement, but also in a sequence of collaborative arrangements between the same partnering organizations. It is important to underline that unequal power relations are not the issue per se; it is the change in those power relations that renders the cooperation less than successful.

Danger and threat

When people and organizations experience adversity, forms of mental and organizational rigidity are likely to occur. Sociological and psychological research has shown that under conditions of threat information processing is restricted and control is constricted, leading to lesser degrees of individual and organizational flexibility and even inducing "primitive forms of reaction" (Staw et al. 1981: 505). Soldiers, however, are likely to experience more than general forms of adversity only. In their perception a threat may endanger their lives, which impacts on what they think and how they behave. Recent social-psychological studies have demonstrated that people realizing the fragility of their lives tend to increase stereotypical thinking. This implies that people under such conditions focus their frustration on out-groups, cling to values that are essential to their own common identity and worldview and tend to reject people who are different (Schimel et al. 1999; Pyszczynski et al. 2003). While these studies mostly rely on laboratory experiments, more realistic evidence is also available. A quasi-experiment measuring cultural values among US students before and after September 11 2001 revealed that students had become less cosmopolitan and more power-oriented after the attack had occurred (Olivas-Lujan et al. 2004). This implies that they were less inclined to value foreign people and cultural manifestations, such as music and food from abroad. The implication of these findings for our purpose is that international military co-operation is quite likely to develop less smoothly, if there are signals indicating that life-threatening situations may occur in the area of operations. A study conducted among Dutch troops in Kabul and Europe has confirmed these behavioural tendencies to a large degree (Dechesne et al. 2007).

In summary, we expect international military cooperation to be more strained, if this multiorganizational arrangement:

a   is moderately heterogeneous in composition;
b   concerns interactions between soldiers from the European continent and from ABCA countries, and/or from supposedly "higher (professional) status" versus "lower (professional) status" armed forces;
c   concerns interactions between so-called "elite" and "non-elite" units;
d   is less technology-driven;
e   is based on organizational set-ups in which structural and cultural elements do not fit very well;
f   has experienced a shift in bargaining power between the partnering organizations; and
g   is executed under conditions that are experienced to be life-threatening.

Although the listing of these factors creates the impression that they all work independently, this is probably not true; in reality, there will be many interactions and mutual dependencies. But for the sake of clarity we have chosen to present them as independent elements of multinational military cooperation.

Research methodology

Given the under-researched and exceptional character of our subject, we have chosen to use a qualitative methodology based on comparative case-study analysis. The methodology in the case studies relies on semi-structured interviews and participatory observation, and comes close to what has become known as organizational anthropology (e.g. Gellner and Hirsch 2001). The research approach has been more than merely exploratory, because we could make use of the existing knowledge presented above, even though this knowledge had not been tested in exceptional circumstances. During the interviews, the authors focused first on the way everyday intercultural interactions were taking place or had taken place (i.e. the description of the cooperation including its smooth and/or strained character), pursuing with questions leading to the explanations of the descriptive data. In addition to the possible factors the authors mentioned in the interview (cultural diversity, composition, organization of tasks, etc.), the interviewees had ample space to come up with factors they deemed to be important. In this way we made sure that we did not miss any important issues. Hence, our research methodology has been deductive and inductive at the same time.

Study 1 on German–Dutch cooperation in Kabul is based on retrospective data collected in Germany and the Netherlands, hence outside the area of operation. In May 2003 the first and third author had in-depth interviews with 13 Dutch and 10 German NCOs and officers with binational working experience in the German–Netherlands Corps HQ in Münster, Germany. The interviewees not only talked about the situation at HQ, but also provided information on the collaboration taking place in Kabul, given that, at the time of data collection, more than 25 per cent of the HQ's staff was in Afghanistan commanding the ISAF operation. Our interviewees in the Corps' HQ were – through telephone calls and emailing – in close contact with their colleagues in Kabul, so they knew about the situation there. During one of the interviews, a colleague in Kabul called and commented on what was being said during the interview. Prior to this round of interviews, the first author had already interviewed 16 Dutch soldiers and NCOs who had just returned from Kabul. They had been deployed to Afghanistan as operational ("air-manoeuvre") units working closely together with German operational troops. The interviews were conducted in Dutch and English (the HQ's working language).

Study 2 on the multinational cooperation at Kabul International Airport (KAIA) is based on data that were collected at the airport in Afghanistan between 27 January and 3 February 2005. Hence, this approach can be seen as a form of "Blitz fieldwork" (Gellner and Hirsch 2001). During this period the first and second author stayed at the airport on a 24/7 basis. They conducted formal, in-depth interviews (lasting one to two hours each) with ten Belgian NCOs and officers, four Dutch servicemen, three French soldiers, one Turkish officer and two local interpreters. In addition, they continuously had informal conversations with other people, mostly Belgian and Dutch service (wo)men, who were deployed at the airport. The interviews were performed in French, Dutch/Flemish and English.

Study 3 on the binational Belgian–Canadian cooperation in Kabul partly relies on the same data as study 2. A visit to Camp Julien (the "Canadian" camp in Kabul) enabled the researchers to do five more interviews with Belgian officers and NCOs, who were working with Canadians deployed at the camp. These interviews were conducted in French or Dutch/Flemish. In all cases the researchers stopped with the formal interviews when they decided the study had reached a degree of saturation.

In all three studies the authors have used various sorts of additional evidence, in particular data from a survey conducted among Belgian service(wo)men in Kabul (both at KAIA and Camp Julien), evaluation reports, newspaper articles, "talks at the bar" and organizational artefacts such as pictures and banners expressing vision statements (Yin 2003; see also Clegg *et al.* 2002). The interviews were analysed on the basis of extensive interview notes, following the structure of the interview scheme and taken by the researchers independently of one another. The Turkish officer requested us not to take any notes, which necessitated us to draft a summary of the interview afterwards, based on our memories of what he had said. In all three studies the first author drafted (in English) preliminary reports on the findings. These preliminary reports were then checked independently by the other researchers who relied on their own field and interview notes. With respect to study 2 and 3 the second researcher drafted her own report in French, independently and not knowing the content of the first author's report. On the basis of both reports the authors cross-checked their accounts. The confrontation of the insights of the different researchers led to a number of changes and additions in the final reports. The results of study 1 have been formally presented a number of times to audiences consisting of people who had been in Kabul. These presentations elicited various "member-check" comments varying from "this is a fair description and analysis" to "it was far worse than that". We have, however, preferred to remain on the safe side, avoiding the risk of exaggeration. We have also received a number of "member-check" comments (from people who had been there but had not been interviewed) with respect to study 2 and 3. All these comments underlined that our description and analysis concur with the servicemen's own experiences.

Three cases of international military cooperation

German–Dutch cooperation in Kabul

In 1995 the first German–Netherlands Corps (1GNC) was founded. The start of the binational cooperation was slow, but gradually the integration deepened. Mutual appreciation increased step by step, as was shown in surveys among both German and Dutch servicemen in 1995, 1997 and 2000 (Moelker *et al.*

2007). In the years after its inception the HQ has been awarded the status of NATO High Readiness Headquarters, which has been regarded as a major achievement that could be attributed to the joint efforts of both the Germans and the Dutch. The first combined deployment in Kosovo in 1999 was rated favourably by external examiners and the German and the Dutch military themselves. The 2000 survey showed that despite some differences in style and work orientation the Germans and Dutch really liked working together, especially at the Corps' HQ; this impression was confirmed in the interviews we did in May 2003.

However, everything changes and nothing ever remains the same. In 2002 the Corps was tasked to contribute operational (infantry) troops to the ISAF operation. In 2003 the Corps HQ was ordered to take over the command of the mission in Kabul for a period of six months. Both deployments turned out to be less successful than might have been expected given the previous positive developments. From the onset of the deployments in 2002, especially the Dutch felt uncomfortable with the German dominance in personnel, material resources and command. At HQ there had always been a careful equilibrium in numbers and responsibilities, but in Kabul this precarious balance was absent due to political decisions made by both national governments.

The relations soured considerably and that became public via newspaper articles quoting Dutch soldiers saying that "the Afghans are not the problem, the Germans are". This referred to the situation in the operational camp ("Warehouse"). In this camp some 2,300 troops, consisting of 1,400 Germans, more than 300 Dutch servicemen, and 600 troops of 18 other countries were working and living together. This was a case of binational cooperation against the background of a multinational mission, but the contribution of the two countries was clearly not balanced. The whole camp was densely populated, housing the Dutch service(wo)men in tents that were located closely to one another at one side of the camp. Hence, a tendency to isolate themselves developed.

In an isolated position internal gossip and complaints are likely to develop, which indeed happened among the Dutch. They continuously complained about the supply of goods (including weapons and ammunition), about logistics in general, the safety policies implemented by the Germans, the insufficient availability of telephones, the quality of the food, as well as the alcohol policies which varied between the Germans and the Dutch. In general the Dutch criticized the way the Germans conducted the mission and the assignments the Germans ordered them to do. All these complaints were vented with an air of superiority: the Dutch air-manoeuvre soldiers considered themselves to be far more experienced in peacekeeping. In addition, the Dutch did not understand why the Germans had better housing facilities and financial allowances. The resentment among these Dutch soldiers was so pronounced that they met with criticism from their compatriots at HQ: these Dutch staff officers commented that their fellow Dutchmen at the camp should stop whining and should "leave their corner every once in a while and join the others".

Table 14.1 Summary of findings of the three case studies

	Nature of activities	Organizational set-up	Mutual appreciation	End of situation
German–Dutch cooperation (in a multinational context)	Operational duties (patrolling, manning check points, de-mining, civil–military cooperation, etc.) since 2002. Command of mission in 2003	ISAF-HQ was equally manned by Germans and Dutch (in 2003). In the operational camp the Germans dominated in overwhelming numbers and command. Operational tasks in distinct geographical areas in Kabul were allocated to each nation.	Dutch operational troops harshly criticized German ways of working, commanding and behaving. Dutch staff officers had far fewer problems, and even disapproved of their compatriots' attitudes; nonetheless, they experienced souring relations with the German staff officers in Kabul as well.	Command of mission (ISAF HQ) ended according to plan in 2003. Operational binational cooperation (in Camp Warehouse) ended fairly suddenly (in 2003) because of other obligations of the Dutch elsewhere.
Multinational cooperation at KAIA	Running military and civilian airport, air and land patrolling.	Multinational staff and command unit. All national operational units are roughly equally large, and all have been assigned one specific, independent operational task.	Mutual stereotyping especially vis-à-vis the (growing numbers and increasingly more powerful) Turkish military. All units are relatively satisfied with living and working conditions at the base.	Continues to present.
Canadian–Belgian cooperation (in a multinational context)	Operational duties only (patrolling, manning check points, de-mining, civil–military cooperation, etc.).	Canadians in charge of camp Julien. Operational duties in distinct geographical areas in Kabul separately assigned to national units.	Belgians felt dominated by condescendingly acting Canadians. Old memories revived.	Ended in 2005 according to plan.

This situation did not improve, not even when the first rotation of soldiers were replaced by other Dutch units. The problems at Camp Warehouse resonated in Münster (the Corps' HQ) and at ISAF HQ in Kabul, where the binational staff of the Corps HQ had taken over command of the mission in 2003. This was remarkable because – as already mentioned– the relations between the Germans and Dutch staff officers in Münster had proven to be rather good. After the planned return of the HQ personnel to Münster, the Corps' Dutch and German commanders felt the need to pay considerable attention to improving the relations between their staff officers that had soured in Kabul. The operational German–Dutch cooperation in Camp Warehouse ended fairly suddenly in the fall of 2003, because of new obligations for the Dutch military in Iraq. Even though the formal cooperation between the Dutch and the Germans in the Army Corps and the recently founded EU battle group still exists, there has never been a joint deployment since then (however, the numbers of deployed troops of both national armed forces has increased continuously). Given all these processes and outcomes, we consider this case to be an example of strained international military cooperation.

Multinational cooperation at Kabul International Airport (KAIA)

At the start of the ISAF mission at the end of 2001, the most important priority was restoring air traffic at Kabul airport that had been impossible during the hostilities in the period before. The airport serves both civilian and military purposes. Because almost all of ISAF's resources have to be supplied by air transport, the airport has been one of the most strategic elements in the mission. Therefore, a command and staff unit, consisting of officers and NCOs from nearly all NATO air forces, was tasked by NATO with keeping the airport running. The command is rotated every six months over representatives of various nations. The operational tasks at the airport have been assigned to "normal" units from separate nations: for instance force protection to a Belgian unit, de-mining to a Czech detachment, air transport with Black Hawks to a Turkish unit, air reconnaissance with Apaches to a Dutch air-force unit, land patrolling among others to a French company, medical services to a Spanish contingent, etc. Hence, every national operational unit performs its duties fairly independently and, therefore, coordination costs are kept to a minimum. Every national unit is housed per section on the premises, but eating facilities are centrally provided. In total some 25 nations contribute troops, and no single country dominates in numbers.

The operations at the airport are running fairly smoothly and successfully, even enabling an increasing number of civilian airliners to operate their flights. The interviewees at the airport stressed that this KAIA operation is "business as usual". People are encouraged to report "challenges instead of problems" (a slogan made visible on banners and posters), quite similar to the way they used to do at their own NATO bases. The personnel's attitude is said to be service-oriented: "they want to help maintain Afghanistan's door open to the world". Clearly, the international composition makes the base a bit more "messy" than one would see in the USA or at a base entirely run by the US Air Force, as some respondents said. Not surprisingly, since 2001 there have been a number of language-related problems. The most prominent one referred to the medics who did not master the English language sufficiently, inducing people in case of emergency to seek medical help outside the base at the German medical facilities at ISAF HQ. In addition, different national rules and regulations sometimes caused discipline-related problems. Furthermore, the pace of decision-making was sometimes criticized and attributed to the complex international chain of command.

During our stay at the base the command was transferred from a general from Iceland to a Turkish general. This caused a certain discomfort among a number of Western European service(wo)men. Rumours and gossip flourished indicating that "once the Turkish commander would take over command, alcohol would be banned, female soldiers would no longer be allowed to leave their premises after 1900 hours and the military hierarchy would become far more important." As one of the Western European interviewees indicated, "for the Turks the commander is God, for us he is only a little God". A Turkish officer, confronted with these "expectations", responded astonished and irritated, pointing at the various female jet-fighter pilots in the Turkish air force and the fact that the use of alcohol is permitted on Turkish bases. Other examples of multiple realities could be observed in the "book of complaints" in the dining hall. Turkish military personnel wrote down that "they don't understand that this kebab is made of pork instead of lamb", and that "they don't want Chinese food". Some others, clearly not Turkish personnel, wrote that "they don't understand that recently olives are being served at breakfast". However, all this calmed down very soon after the Turkish general had taken over command. Things became quickly "business as usual" again.

This leads us to conclude that, despite some problems, people at KAIA in general were satisfied with the mission and considered their work in Afghanistan as "just another job". In addition, the continuously increasing number of civilian airline connections to and from Kabul demonstrates the success of the KAIA operation. We, therefore, deem this case as an example of fairly smooth international military cooperation.

Canadian–Belgian cooperation in Kabul

The same cannot be said about our last case study. This example of international cooperation revolves around a trinational battle group, consisting of some 230 Belgian Airborne troops, a Norwegian reconnaissance squadron and a Hungarian light infantry company. This trinational battle group was located at a large Canadian base, called Camp Julien, where Canadian soldiers (of unilingual

Canadian units) dominated in numbers. In general, the commanders of the trinational battle group were fairly satisfied with the work of their units; the battle group had been very effective in a number of critical incidents. But they were less satisfied with the life at the Canadian Camp. Especially, the Belgians reported to feel uncomfortable working and living with the Canadians. A small survey among the Belgian servicemen showed that slightly more than half of them indicated that their contacts with the Canadian military were "(very) bad".

In addressing these findings, some of our Belgian interviewees pointed out that this particular Belgian unit had operated under the command of the Canadian General Romeo Dallaire in Rwanda in 1994, during the genocide in that country. In a book describing his experiences at that time, Dallaire (2004) had not only heavily criticized the Belgian political decision to pull out its troops after they had suffered ten casualties at the beginning of the upheaval in April 1994, but also the behaviour of the Belgian paratroops regiment (its alleged lack of discipline, etc.). According to some interviewees, this caused a certain deep-seated resentment among some of the members of the Regiment. Furthermore, in Kabul they felt the Canadians treated them in a condescending manner, which can only be understood by closely examining the interaction of the two working styles.

The Canadian soldiers displayed a professional attitude characterized by a high degree of discipline and strict rule orientation. Besides, the Canadians often punish collectively even if a single person or a very small number of persons in a unit have committed the offences. Even informally, reactions to breaches of the rules (for instance, when servicemen forget to take off their hat when entering the mess[2]) are loud and aggressive. Since Belgians do not tend to have such habits, they were rather frequently addressed in this rude way. In addition, the Belgians were not used to the presence of rank-segregated messes that, in the words of our respondents, seemed to be separated by "walls".

In contrast to these specific Canadian practices, Belgians seemed to be somewhat more relaxed, laid-back and easy-going, and superiors reacted to misconduct in a far less sharp, let alone aggressive way. While fines going from several hundred euros to a full monthly allowance are not unknown in the Canadian military, Belgian service(wo)men were completely unfamiliar with such penalties. After working hours, privates, NCOs and officers in the Belgian army were used to socializing in the "all ranks bar", drinking a beer and discussing problems that may have occurred during the day. Belgian service(wo)men indicated that they were shocked when they were confronted with (collective) penalties like being banned from the bar. Furthermore, they felt uncomfortable for they had the impression that the Canadians looked down upon them, in particular with respect to an insufficient degree of professionalism and discipline. Of course, the Belgian rank-and-file refuted such claims and saw things differently. In contrast to the interactions with the Canadians, the contacts with the Norwegians and the Hungarians did not create many problems. The problematic Canadian–Belgian interaction, however, lasted until Belgians returned home. All in all, we deem this case of international military cooperation to be rather strained, although less so than the German–Dutch cooperation in study 1.

Analysis

The three case studies provide three different pictures of international military cooperation. None of these cases provides a picture of perfect cooperation. Even the second case (Kabul International Airport) shows national isolation and stereotype-related friction occurring among the service personnel of the various nations. However, this case of international military cooperation has been (and still is) fairly successful with respect to both its effectiveness and mutual relations. The two other cases have turned out to be much more problematic in terms of mutual trust and commitment to make the inter-organizational arrangement successful. The German–Dutch cooperation is clearly the most problematic as indicated by the fact that it was terminated fairly suddenly and to date has not been followed up by other missions where the two nationalities would work together again. The question is how these differing outcomes can be explained. As Doz (1996: 77) noted with respect to failing inter-organizational (civilian) cooperation, it appears that small – seemingly insignificant and innocent – events in the beginning can have big consequences at the end. Using the seven insights we have discussed before, we now want to analyse the processes and outcomes of international military cooperation in the three different cases. Each of the seven "mechanisms" has its own influence, but if they coincide within one single case, their impact becomes more powerful.

Table 14.2 Summary of the analysis (+ = high impact; +/– = moderate impact; – = low impact)

Strained international military cooperation due to:	German–Dutch cooperation at Camp Warehouse	Multinational cooperation at KAIA	Belgian–Canadian cooperation at Camp Julien
1 moderate heterogeneity	+	–	+
2 cultural distances: interaction between continental and ABCA militaries and/or between "higher"- and "lower"-status militaries	–	+/–	+
3 cooperation involving "elite" units	+	–	+
4 lesser degree of technology orientation	+	–	+
5 no fit between structural and cultural elements of organizational set-up	+/–	–	+/–
6 shift in balance in bargaining power	+	–	–
7 danger and treat	+	+/–	+

Relative size clearly plays a role in our three case studies. The KAIA case is an example of high heterogeneity involving more than 20 national contingents of about equal size, a condition we now know to be most conducive to optimizing processes and outputs. The other two cases were examples of moderate heterogeneity having two sizable participating partners, who easily form two "blocks" continuously frustrating one another. As interviewees in the German–Dutch case study stressed, it is not a matter of Germans and Dutch, it is a matter of being only two. At Camp Julien too, most frictions developed between two sides: the large minority of Belgians versus the Canadians clearly outnumbering all other nationalities.

With respect to cultural distances we witnessed Western European military at KAIA expressing discontent with Turkish staff being in command, which was often attributed to Turks being culturally distinct. This comes close to what other studies involving Turkish military personnel have shown and to what has been reported with respect to the way Danish and German soldiers perceive their Polish colleagues when cooperating with them (Chapter 13, this volume). More tellingly with respect to cultural distances seems to be the Belgian–Canadian interaction, because this case illustrates the aforementioned cultural "cluster" of the ABCA countries within NATO. While interviewing the Belgians in Kabul, we were struck by the resemblance of their stories with accounts from a case study into British–Dutch cooperation in Cyprus (Soeters and Bos-Bakx 2003). The similarities of the data in both studies with respect to hierarchies, discipline and punishments were astonishing. Clearly, the Dutch and the Belgian armed forces have more in common than with the English and Canadian forces, let alone the American troops (Soeters *et al.* 2006). At KAIA (study 2) there were hardly any representatives of the ABCA countries, let alone in a dominating position.

It was striking that in the two cases in which cooperation was less successful, problems and accusations against the other party were almost exclusively aired by members of so-called "elite" units. In the Dutch–German case the problems were the greatest when Dutch air-manoeuvre units had to cooperate with German paratroopers. The problems decreased when German "Bergtruppe" (mountain units) relieved the German "Fallschirmjäger" (paratroopers) in the course of 2003. It appeared, the "Bergtruppe" do not have such an explicit elitist (self-)image as the paratroopers do. As mentioned before, Dutch servicemen from other, non-elite units blamed their compatriots from the air-manoeuvre companies for complaining too much and not being sufficiently constructive. Similarly, in the Belgian case the frictions particularly arose among the paratroopers. In KAIA, there were no "elite" units; so this phenomenon was not present.

The rather successful results of the operations at KAIA can undoubtedly also be attributed to technology-driven normative and professional isomorphism (e.g. DiMaggio and Powell 1991). Air force operations are completely routinized because of the danger that is inherent to flying. The risks are well-known and the ways to cope with those risks are incorporated in procedures that are enforced upon the servicemen with a large degree of discipline. These procedures are identical for all servicemen at KAIA. In the army operations of the other two case studies, however, every aspect of the work can, and indeed is, debated. These discussions most of the times follow national lines.

In all three cases, different operational tasks were divided among the participating national units. Each national unit in case studies 1 and 3 had their own geographical area of responsibility, where they were tasked to control the situation, safeguard the area against hostilities and develop projects in cooperation with civilians. However, the various national contingents were not really independent: as far as living conditions were concerned all nationalities were put together in a camp hosted by one nation, and also in the operations the national contingents were supervised by one nation (study 1: Germany; study 3: Canada). At the airport (case study 2) every national unit was assigned a specific functional task, such as de-mining, force protection or air patrolling. Such a structure is based on reciprocal interdependence (Thompson 1967: 54–55), implying that every unit makes a discrete, complementary contribution to the whole, in such a way that the outputs of each becomes the input for the others. The way these processes are administered, however, differs among the three cases. Administration implies reciprocal interdependence and mutual adjustment. Only in KAIA's case does this mutual adjusting at staff level take place in a truly international atmosphere, necessitating everyone to interrelate heedfully all the time, thereby creating what can be called a collective mind (Weick 2001: 266–268). In each of the other two operational camps (Warehouse, Julien), however, only one country pulled the strings, enabling staff to easily overlook the concerns of personnel of other nationalities under their command, hence hampering conditions that facilitate inter-organizational collaboration (Gray 1985).

The German–Dutch cooperation in Kabul was the offspring of a broader structural alliance between the Dutch army and parts of the much larger German army. In this structural alliance – the German–Dutch Corps – the size of both national contributions is equal with all strategic and command positions meticulously distributed between the two nations. In the Kabul deployment, however, Dutch politicians had opted to make the Dutch contribution – in terms of resources and troops – much smaller than the 50 per cent the Dutch are used to in the Corps. Hence, a considerable shift in bargaining power resulted when the troops were transported from the Netherlands and Germany to Afghanistan. Suddenly, the Dutch saw themselves confronted with Germans dominating all decision-making positions, not only at the level of the strategic apex but also at the more mundane level of logistics, where decisions are made that are of immediate concern to ordinary soldiers (availability of telephones, appropriate food, safety devices and the like). This shift was so pervasive – in fact the 1,400 German troops did not really "need" the 300 Dutch servicemen – and so sudden, that mutual relations soured almost immediately after the arrival in Kabul, leading to seriously conflicting frames of reference between the two forces (Doz

1996: 72). This is a clear example of shifts in bargaining power between partnering organizations leading to the instability – often to the premature end – of inter-organizational arrangements (Inkpen and Beamish 1997). In the two other cases there were no such developments.

Even though, since ISAF arrival, Kabul is not officially seen as a war zone, the situation in the area has, at times, been really dangerous. Especially during ISAF's first year (2002–2003) there were several missile attacks as well as assaults with grenades and other small explosives on Camp Warehouse and ISAF's HQ (Dechesne *et al.* 2007). This applies particularly to the first case study in this article. As for the other two more recent case studies, while the actual danger had, at the time of our field observations, substantially decreased (although not fully disappeared), some of the friction can be attributed to the danger and death awareness that still existed among the military personnel. The air-force operations have for a long time incorporated the well-known risk of their operations in everyday routines and procedures, as we mentioned before. Furthermore these operations attract virtually no concrete hostile attention, because they hardly interact with the local population, unlike land forces which are continuously in interaction with locals during patrols, transports, house searches and the manning of road blocks and check points. The danger – unpredictable and hidden as it is – particularly lurks in these close contacts. If the aforementioned laboratory studies are right (Schimel *et al.*, 1999), these differences in threat perception are – in cases 1 and 3 relatively more than in the second case and in case 1 more than in case 3 – likely to account, at least partially, for the differences in process and outcome of the three cases.

Conclusions and reflections

In this chapter we have identified seven factors that are propitious for reaching satisfying results in international military cooperation: (1) a heterogeneous (or the opposite: a nearly homogeneous) composition of the mission in terms of nationality; (2) as much as possible, agreement about operational matters enabling the bridging of cultural distances; (3) insistence on an open mindset toward others in the mission, especially among so-called "elite units"; (4) uniformity of technologies and working procedures; (5) an organizational structure in which all nationalities contribute in a recognizable and respected way to the grand output of the mission; (6) the absence of a shift in bargaining power between the partnering organizations; and (7) a thorough preparation of the soldiers with respect to coping with risk-inducing situations, if these are expected to occur. If all these conditions are met, cross-cultural military cooperation is more likely to be smooth, as in the case of KAIA.

However, even the operation at KAIA was not without flaws. The general collaboration, mutual appreciation and professional atmosphere at the base for instance were threatened when the Turks, who were perceived as culturally distant, took over command. This did not persist, however. Nonetheless, commanders of international military missions should continuously try to foster collaboration by paying attention to the different cultural baggage national troops bring along with them (Chen et al. 1998). For commanders to be able to do so, they need to be made aware of this and trained accordingly. In general, in multinational military cooperation one should try to seek ways to create "a collaborative commitment and transparency into the moral fibre of the project", a "governmentality" among all participants so to speak (Clegg et al. 2002: 325) as well as a sufficient degree of cultural intelligence (Triandis 2006). This can be done by emphasizing a strong mission culture (with clear goals and performance indicators), a respecting attitude towards all, but perhaps also by creating conditions in which power is not put in the hands of one stakeholder only (Gray 1985: 927). A certain "circularity of power" (Romme 1999) – as could be most clearly seen at KAIA – is likely to strengthen collaborative commitment among all participants of the mission.

This way of organizing at KAIA can even be enhanced through possible changes in the organizational structure at the airport. Now the various functional operational tasks at KAIA are separately assigned to the different national units. This division of labour will produce satisfactory results as long as every national contingent performs adequately. But, as the problem with the medical unit not mastering the English language sufficiently illustrates, a functional structure is inherently vulnerable if one contributing part fails. Not only are the operations threatened, but the whole idea of international cooperation runs the risk of becoming a fiasco in an organizational arrangement where the different functions are allocated to the various national contingents.

Therefore, it would be wise to experiment with cross-cutting national/ functional group structures (see also Brewer 1996), creating complementary and overlapping skill bases among the partnering forces (Doz 1996: 72). This could for example imply that the Belgian contingent performing the force protection and safety tasks at the airport would be mixed with service(wo)men from other nations (e.g. with soldiers of the French company whose task it is to patrol outside of the airport). Or that the Turkish unit responsible for logistics at the base would be mixed with military (wo)men of other nations. Of course, this would require a certain degree of preparation and gradual implementation. This idea, though, is far from being unrealistic given the fact that the command and staff unit at the airport is both fully internationally composed and operating smoothly. At the airport's international command and staff unit, people take care of each other, interrelate heedfully and form a sort of collective mind. This example demonstrates that cross-cutting the functional/national structure could prevent the mutual stereotyping and blaming we witnessed at the base. So, even though KAIA on the whole can be deemed to be fairly successful, the existing social dynamics at the base render the cooperation less than optimal. In addition, the operations at KAIA were relatively routine at the time of our study. We have no idea how this international, inter-organizational arrangement at KAIA would perform should the situation become more violent, flammable and unstable, for instance in case of a concerted attack on the airport. Would the servicemen of the participating countries in such conditions still perform as professionally as they are used to do in circumstances that – taken altogether – are not that different from peacetime conditions? Or will the latent frictions that clearly exist come to the surface, jeopardizing the whole operation at the airport?

This brings us to our final point. As mentioned, the three case studies are all examples of international military cooperation in *camps* or *gated communities*. Diken and Laustsen (2005: 79–100) have argued that camps often function as islands in a larger context, signifying a clear distinction between life inside and outside the camp. Most people in those military gated communities hardly ever come outside the camps. Those who have to work outside the camps, however, may experience the same frictions in the outside world as they do inside the camp. For instance, those who have derogatory feelings towards military personnel from countries perceived to be of lower status, will also be likely to have the same kind of attitude toward the local people. If so, this will be detrimental to the quality of their work which mainly consists of communicating, in fact cooperating, with the local population. As has been argued in the field of international business in emerging markets (London and Hart 2004), being successful in non-Western contexts requires the military to develop socially embedded strategies leveraging the strengths of the existing environment. It may be assumed that militaries experiencing problems while collaborating with military colleagues from other countries will face even more difficulties in developing such interactions with local people. If so, the study of cross-cultural military cooperation becomes even more important, because it may uncover indications of both internal and external effectiveness of military operations. Of course, this idea needs further corroboration and it requires more studies to follow.

Notes

1 This is an expanded and updated version of a chapter published in Hagen *et al.* 2006. The research is supported by a long-term research contract of the Belgian Defence Ministry (contract ERM HF-04). We are grateful for the constructive comments we received from C.J. Lammers and Lt-Col. H. Koolstra, as well as for the editing work by A. Hendricks and H. Kirkels.
2 The "fascination" in the Canadian military with (removing) headgear goes a long way. Canadian Hindustani soldiers are allowed to wear a turban, but only with a metal symbol attached to it that they can take off as a sign of respect at the same time that their fellow soldiers take off their hats. This information was communicated to us by Dr Alan Okros from the Canadian Military Academy (Amsterdam, 3 July 2007).

Part III

Afterthoughts

Chapter 15

Epilogue

Joseph Soeters and Philippe Manigart

Multinational military cooperation is here to stay. Like firms in international business, national armed forces are increasingly compelled to work together because of the frequency, nature and scale of the missions they are tasked to do. In addition, politicians and wider audiences – the general public, the recipients – want these missions to be legitimized, which can best be achieved by having more partnering countries involved. The United Nations and NATO prefer their operations to be conducted by international forces because of this quest for legitimacy.

The logic of multinational military collaboration applies to all nations and national armed forces, including the most sizable ones such as the US forces. This logic pertains, however, even more to the smaller nations all over the world, whose military ambitions and resources are simply too small to conduct today's military operations independently. In putting their resources, capabilities, experience and know-how together, national armed forces engage in so called "win–win" combinations. As inter-organizational theory predicts, cooperation between organizations pays (Alter and Hage 1993), even if, or perhaps especially if, this happens in a multinational setting.

In this volume we have seen a number of cases demonstrating that multinational military cooperation indeed works the way it was intended to do. Even though national armed forces in multinational missions need to give up their autonomy, sometimes have to deal with less professional armed forces, face constraints and difficulties that seem inherent to working with others, the overall result of those missions seems satisfying. The UN missions in East Timor analysed by Ballard have proven to be rather successful. Equally fruitful, although not always completely unproblematic are the UN missions in the Middle East described by Elron, the example of German–Italian cooperation in Kosovo in Tomforde's chapter, the cooperation in the trinational brigade depicted by Jelušič and Pograjč, as well as the international military force running Kabul International Airport and the NATO Training Centre analysed by Söderberg and Wedell-Wedellsborg. Politically, the Japanese–Dutch and the Turkish–Gambian military cooperation, described in the chapters authored by respectively van der Meulen and Kawano, and Varoglu and associates, have fulfilled the goals of the strategic "masterminds" who initiated these unexpected acts of collaboration. And even though the Swedish–Irish cooperation in Liberia presented in the chapter by Hedlund and his fellow researchers was not much of a success, UNMIL as a whole has, however, considerably improved the security and political situation in this war-ridden African country. There are more examples of strained cooperation in this volume (such as in the ISAF operation in Afghanistan), but never does this seem to have gone at the expense of the overall effectiveness of the mission or the multinational unit.

This is perhaps not too surprising. In international business, failing cross-bordering or cross-cultural endeavours can lead to bankruptcy or dissolution. In the public sector, to which the military belongs, organizations are not bankrupted even if they do not reach the goals that were originally set for them (Downs 1967). Nonetheless, today's public sector organizations will do their best to prevent becoming "permanently failing" (Meyer and Zucker 1989), because they see the risk of future budget cuts and the danger of becoming small and irrelevant. They want to achieve and maintain a degree of effectiveness that is acceptable in the eyes of their masters, i.e. the leading politicians and the general public. This is even more so for military organizations if they want to remain relevant in the field of international military cooperation. There are three strategies to achieve such an acceptable level of effectiveness in the context of multinational, cross-cultural military cooperation. These are based on a framework developed by cross-cultural psychologist John Berry (2004), and applied to the military by, among others, Moelker and colleagues (2007).

The first strategy is *assimilation* implying that one nation tends to become similar to the (culture of the) other nation. This strategy is likely to emerge in lead-nation missions, where one country – for instance the UK (Chapter 6, this volume) – or a cluster of countries such as the ABCA countries (Chapter 7, this volume) direct the execution of the mission. This lead nation, or set of nations, formulates the mission's tactics, the doctrine as well as the organizational set-up. Assimilation is likely to occur if the leading (cluster of) nation(s) is much more sizable than the partnering forces. Those smaller partnering forces are naturally inclined to adapt themselves to the leading forces as they deem those leading forces to be more powerful, experienced, and even protective in case operational conditions turn rough. Also in technology-dominated branches, such as in air operations, the superior partner is in the position to dictate standard operational procedures, daily practices and training programmes, much more than in land operations. As has been observed elsewhere, a technology-driven professional culture drives out cultural differences between nations; technology is a uniformizing force (e.g. Zabusky, 1995).

Often, however, assimilation does not always come as natural or easy as some would deem necessary to reach a high degree of effectiveness. Among land forces technological uniformity is much less present and, hence, it is much less influential in daily operations. Moreover, the contribution of partnering nations in terms of personnel and resources is often quite substantial, making a pattern of adaptation or assimilation less likely. In such cases, in fact in most cases of today's multinational military operations (Iraq, Afghanistan, Lebanon), a *separation* strategy is therefore chosen (see Chapter 12, this volume). In such a strategy every national military force is assigned an "own" geographical area of responsibility. This enables them to develop their own way of working in this specific area, to maintain contact with their home countries and to have their servicemen living in their own compounds, i.e. in an atmosphere that feels like home. If there is any sort of cooperation between national armed forces, it is only "cooperation light", in the words of van der Meulen and Kawano. Interestingly, this strategy produces varying experiences based on the different operational styles that national armed forces display, each in their own area of responsibility. For instance, in the Northern part of Afghanistan various national armed forces (Germany, UK, the USA, and the Netherlands) have deployed so called Provincial Reconstruction Teams (PRTs). Each of these PRTs tends to work out new types of Civil–Military Cooperation in a different way. Carefully comparing such varying experiences may help to understand what works best in the fuzzy, ambiguous and dangerous operations the world's military organizations are facing nowadays. In such an operational set-up, i.e. giving room to the national armed forces' diversity, the opportunities for learning are most straightforward.

Yet, not all elements of today's operations can be organized in an isolated way. To coordinate the operations, headquarters are needed, and most of the times HQs are run by a multinationally composed workforce. Also, if the geographical space is limited (such as in the Kabul area), working and living facilities cannot easily be divided and, hence, these must be shared by the troops of more than one country. And if in such conditions the various functional tasks (e.g. force protection, logistics, medical assistance) are allocated to the units of different countries, multinational cooperation is really put to the test. In such a complex yet vulnerable operational configuration the *integration* approach is most needed. In this approach there is no superior or dominating country or operational style. On the contrary, every contributing national force is deemed equally important, and – in the ideal situation – the strengths of each contributing nation's working style are identified, brought together and combined into a new, better supranational working style. In these conditions the importance of adequate leadership (Chapter 4, this volume) can hardly be overestimated and the integrative mechanisms described by Elron in Chapter 3 are enormously important. Furthermore, it is in these conditions that language skills on both sides (especially native and foreign English speakers) need most attention, because neglecting the dynamics of this factor has been demonstrated to result in less effective policy-making and implementation, and even to frustration among the officers involved (Chapter 5, this volume).

Multinational military cooperation, especially in its integrative form, comes with problems and frictions related to national politics, and – at the more operational level – to differences in formal regulations, operational styles, leadership modes, sanctioning approaches, perceptions of professional status, and even to different pay systems and other labour conditions. This observation, however, may seem a bit gloomy. The good news is that military commanders and military personnel in general tend to get used to and tolerant of these differences. In general, military personnel are increasingly experienced and trained in *cultural awareness*, and are encouraged to develop a certain degree of *cultural intelligence*. If they have not yet learned to do so, commanders of multinational military missions need to understand how to create a certain degree of cohesion without striving for an unattainable, uniform corporate identity. This means that they have to learn to think in organizational paradoxes and dialectics, which is working with contradictions as well as the interplay of – and tensions between – functions and dysfunctions of different national operating working styles (e.g. Vlaar *et al.* 2007).

Against the background of globalization, the development towards integration coincides with worldwide tendencies of increasing transnationalism and multiculturalism among national populations (Lutz 2007). Especially younger people – and most military personnel are young – tend to display an increasing international outlook enabling them to switch between various identities: they feel themselves for instance German, Danish or Dutch and European at the same time. Even though there are now and then nationalist set-backs in some countries, national "myopia" seems to become less and less prevalent among younger generations. In the military anyway, it has been observed (Chapter 9, this volume; Ben-Ari and Elron 2001) that soldiers are increasingly capable of displaying double loyalties, i.e. to their own national troops as well as to the international military mission they belong to.

The future of multinational military cooperation may even be more promising. Based on insights from organizational sociology, we know that organizations working in a similar environment tend to become more alike over time. This process has been labelled *isomorphism* (DiMaggio and Powell 1991). Such isomorphism may be *coercive* (evolving under the pressure of governmental mandates and regulations), *normative* (due to the influence of professional affiliations) or *mimetic* (imitation as a consequence of taking over best practices and benchmarking). It can easily be argued that similar learning processes may evolve in multinational peace operations. To begin with, supranational organizations such as the UN, NATO and the EU (with their newly founded international battle groups) are increasingly inclined to standardize policies, doctrines, resources and training programmes. Given the fact that more and more countries belong to these supranational institutions, the impact of these standardization processes will improve the degree of interoperability and bring the varying cultural mindsets of military personnel closer together. Winslow (Chapter 2) has clearly demonstrated how the UN is improving its policies in order to reach such increased interoperability. Of course more needs to be done in this respect, both in a general way but particularly in the preparation of specific missions.

In a similar vein, military personnel with a learning attitude will try to ascertain how their colleagues in another area of responsibility conduct their operations (for instance how they interpret the Rules of Engagement), and how successful or failing these different approaches appear to be. Through *lessons-learned* and *after-action-reviews* this learning attitude may lead them to imitate those practices that seem to be most propitious in achieving the goals of the mission. They will learn from each other how to communicate with local people, how to use violence when appropriate, how to deal with hostile people and terror, and how to develop productive nation-building activities, all this in the context of potentially life-threatening circumstances. After all, these are all new activities for the military. Learning by variation, in fact by doing *something else*, seems most profitable to innovate (Schilling *et al.* 2003), and innovating in peace operations is what the military are asked to do. The result of this may be that mutual organizational learning (e.g. Huber 1991) will lead to a new sort of isomorphism in the military, one that is based on hard – dead-or-alive – experiences: *experiential isomorphism*.

All in all, we are fairly optimistic about multinational military cooperation in the time to come. Even though there are substantial differences between national armed forces in terms of national interests, ambitions, military resources, the way the military conducts operations, the use of violence, personnel policies and cultural frameworks, and even though these differences sometimes lead to frictitious forms of cooperation, the general tendency seems positive. We hope this volume has provided enough support for such optimism. Perhaps the very fact that today's military operations are almost always conducted in some sort of multinational military framework, helps to improve military organizations to optimize their efforts in today's fuzzy, but dangerous, peace operations. After all, in organizational learning, diversity of experiences is better than uniform experiences, as outlined earlier.

A last caveat: using military force is the last resort, only to be used if all other instruments have proven to be powerless. We therefore should refrain from using it too frequently, since, as history has shown, we often expect too much from it. But perhaps we also expect too much from epilogues (Stewart 2007: 405).

References

Abbott, A. (1988) *The System of Professions*, Chicago: University of Chicago Press.

Adler, N. (2002) *International Dimensions of Organizational Behaviour*, Cincinnati, OH: South-Western.

Adnani, J. (2005) 'The brotherhood expansion and the Turco-African relations from 17th to 19th Century', paper presented at the 1st International Turkish–African Congress, 'Rising Africa and Turkey', Istanbul, October 2005.

Ainsworth, S. and Hardy, C. (2004) 'Discourse and identities', in Grant, D., Hardy, C., Oswick, C. and Putnam, L.L. (eds), *The Sage Handbook of Organizational Discourse*, Thousand Oaks, CA: Sage.

Allport, G.W. (1954) *The Nature of Prejudice*, Cambridge: Addison-Wesley.

Almén, A. and Sörensen, K. (2007) *Erfarenheter från Sveriges deltagande i UNMIL*, Stockholm: FOI-rapport.

Alter, C. and Hage, J. (1993) *Organizations Working Together*, Newbury Park, CA: Sage.

Alvesson, M. (2002a) *Understanding Organizational Culture*, London: Sage.

—— (2002b) *Postmodernism and Social Research*, Buckingham: Open University Press.

Alvesson, M. and Sköldberg, K. (2000) *Reflexive Methodology. New Vistas for Qualitative Research*, London: Sage Publications.

Anand, V., Clark, M. and Zellmer-Bruhn, M. (2003) 'Team knowledge structures: matching task to information environment', *Journal of Managerial Issues* 15: 15–31.

Ancona, D.G. and Caldwell, D.F. (1992) 'Bridging the boundary: external activity and performance in organizational teams', *Administrative Science Quarterly* 37: 634–665.

Andersson, L. (2001) *Militärt ledarskap – när det gäller. Svenskt militärt ledarskap med fredsfrämjande insatser i fokus*, Stockholm: HLS förlag.

Annan, K. (2004) *Report of the Secretary-General: Implementation of the Recommendations of the Special Committee on Peacekeeping Operations*, New York: United Nations, Doc. A/59/608.

—— (2005a) *Report of the Secretary-General: In Larger Freedom: Towards Security, Development and Human Rights for All*, New York: United Nations, Doc. A/59/2005.

—— (2005b) *Secretary-General's Keynote Speech at Conference on Reforming the United Nations, Columbia University*. Online. Available on: www.un.org/apps/sg/sgstats.asp?nid=1742 (accessed 1 July 2006).

Appadurai, A. (1991) 'Global ethnoscapes: notes and queries for a transnational anthropology', in R. Fox (ed.), *Recapturing Anthropology*, Santa Fe, NM: School of American Research Press.

Argyle, M. (1991) *Cooperation. The Basis of Sociability*, London: Routledge.

Arias, M.E. and Guillen, M. (1998) 'The transfer of organizational techniques across borders: combining neo-institutional and comparative perspectives', in J.L. Alvares (ed.), *The Diffusion and Consumption of Business Knowledge*. London: Macmillan.

Arnstberg, K.-O. (1989) *Svenskhet: den kulturförnekande kulturen*, Stockholm: Karlssons.

Ba Banutu-Gomez, M. (2003) 'Leadership in the government of Gambia: traditional African leadership practice, shared vision, accountability and willingness and openness to change', *Journal of American Academy of Business* 2: 349–359.

Baker, K.M. and Edmonds, R.L. (2004) 'Transfer of Taiwanese ideas and technology to the Gambia, West Africa: a viable approach to rural development', *The Geographical Journal* 170: 189–211.

Bakhtin, M. (1984) *Rabelais and His World* trans. Hélène Iswolsky, Bloomington, IN: Indiana University Press.

Ballard, J.R. (2002) 'Mastering coalition command in modern peace operations: Operation "Stabilise" in East Timor', *Small Wars and Insurgencies* 13 (1): 83–101.

Banerjee, D. (1995) 'An Indian Approach to UN Peace-Keeping Operations', *Strategic Analysis* 18: 5–21.

Bani, U. (2007) *SHIRBRIG: In Service for the United Nations*. Online. Available on: www.un.org/Pubs/chronicle/2007/webArticles/022807_shirbrig.htm# (accessed 11 September 2007).

Barabé, J.G.J.C. (1999) *Coalitions and the Peace Support Operations Continuum: 'Reading the Peace-field' – an Unbalancing Experience*, Toronto: Canadian Forces College.

Barinaga, E. (2007) ' "Cultural diversity" at work: "national culture" as a discourse organizing an international project group', *Human Relations* 60: 315–340.

Barth, F. (1969) 'Introduction', in F. Barth (ed.), *Ethnic Groups and Boundaries*, Oslo: Universitetsforlaget.

—— (2002) 'Toward a Richer Description and Analysis of Cultural Phenomena', in R. Fox, Richard and King, B. (eds), *Anthropology beyond Culture*, Oxford, New York: Berg.

Bartle, R. and Heinecken, L. (eds) (2006) *Military Unionism in the Post-Cold War Era: A Future Reality?*, London: Routledge.

Bartlett, C.A. and Ghoshal, S. (1989) *Managing Across Borders: The Transnational Solution*, Boston, MA: Harvard Business School Press.

Basch, L., Glick Schiller, N. and Szanton Blanc, C. (1994) *Nations Unbound: Transnational Projects, Postcolonial Predicaments, and Deterritorialized Nation-States*, Langhorne, PA: Gordon and Breach.

Bass, B.M. (1998) *Transformational Leadership*, Mahwah, NJ: Lawrence Erlbaum Associates.

Bauman, Z. (2004) *Identity*, Cambridge: Polity Press.

Bell, D. (1997) *Cultural Contradictions of Capitalism*, London: Basic Books.

Bellamy, A.J., Williams, P. and Griffin, S. (2004) *Understanding Peacekeeping*, Cambridge: Polity.

Bellamy, C. (1996) *Knights in White Armour: The New Art of War and Peace*, London: Hutchinson.

Ben-Ari, E. and Elron, E. (2001) 'Blue helmets and white armor: multi-nationalism and multi-culturalism among UN peacekeeping forces', *City & Society* 13: 275–306.

Ben-Ari, E. and Sion, L. (2005) ' "Hungry, weary and horny": joking and jesting among Israel's combat reserves', *Israel Affairs* 11: 655–671.

Benner, T., Binder, A. and Rotmann, P. (2007) 'Learning to build peace? United Nations peace building and organizational learning: developing a research framework', Global Public Policy Institute, Research paper series No. 7.

Ben-Shalom, U., Lehrer, Z. and Ben-Ari E. (2005) 'Cohesion during military operations: A field study on combat units in the Al-Aqsa intifada', *Armed Forces and Society* 32: 63–79.

Berggren, A.W. (ed.) (2005) *Människan i NBF. Med särskilt fokus på internationella insatser*, Stockholm: Försvarshögskolan.

Berkes, N. (1978) *Türkiye'de Çağdaşlaşma* [Modernization in Turkey], Istanbul, Doğu Batı Yayınlari.

Berry, J.B. (2005) 'Living successfully in two cultures', *International Journal of Intercultural Relations* 29: 697–712.

Berry, J.W. (2004) 'Fundamental psychological processes in intercultural relations', in D. Landis, J.M. Bennett and M.J. Bennett (eds), *Handbook of Intercultural Training*, 3rd edn, Thousand Oaks, CA: Sage.

Bhabha, H.K. (1994) *The Location of Culture*, London: Routledge.

Billig, M. and Tajfel, H. (1973) 'Social categorization and similarity in intergroup behavior', *European Journal of Social Psychology* 3: 27–52.

Biscop, S. (2007) 'For a "more active" EU in the Middle East: transatlantic relations and the strategic implications of Europe's engagements in Iran, Lebanon and Israel-Palestine', in: R. Nathanson and S. Stetter (eds), *The Middle East under Fire? EU–Israel Relations in a Region Between War and Conflict Resolution*, Berlin: Friedrich Ebert Stiftung.

Bisho, A. (2004) *Multinational Operations*, Toronto: Canadian Forces College.

Black, J.S. and Mendenhall, M. (1990) 'Cross-cultural training effectiveness: a review and a theoretical framework for future research', *Academy of Management Review* 15: 113–136.

Blomgren, E. (2007) *Caglavica 17 mars 2004: sex militära chefer berättar om ett upplopp i Kosovo*, Stockholm: Försvarshögskolan, Institutionen för ledarskap och management.

Blomgren, E. and Johansson, E. (2005) *Hemma övas man – Borta prövas man. Att vara bataljonschef i en internationell kontext*, Stockholm: Försvarshögskolan, Institutionen för ledarskap och management.

Boene, B. (2001) 'Relations with officers from other nations in military operations other than war and the impact of comparisons on professional self-perceptions', in G. Caforio (ed.), *The Flexible Officer*, Rome: Centro Militare di Studi Stragegici.

Born, H., op den Buijs, T. and Vogelaar, A. (2000) 'Dutch experiences with international military operations in Bosnia', paper presented at a conference of the European Research Group on Military and Society, Prague.

Bos, G. and Soeters, J. (2006) 'Interpreters at work: experiences from Dutch and Belgian peace operations', *International Peacekeeping* 13 (2): 261–268.

Bourdieu, P. (1977) *Outline of a Theory of Practice*, Cambridge: Cambridge University Press.

—— (1984) *Distinction. A Social Critique of the Judgement of Taste*, London: Routledge and Kegan Paul.

Bowman, E.K. and Pierce, L.G. (2003) *Cultural Barriers to Teamwork in a Multinational Coalition Environment*, Proceedings of the 23rd Army Science Conference.

Bowman, S. (1997) 'Historical and cultural influences on coalition operations', in T.J. Marshall, P. Kaiser and J. Kessmeier (eds), *Problems and Solutions in Future Coalition Operations*, Carlisle: USAWC Strategic Studies Institute.

Brewer, M. (1996) 'When contact is not enough: social identity and intergroup cooperation', *International Journal of Intercultural Relations* 20: 291–303.

Brocades Zaalberg, T. (2005) 'Soldiers and civil power. Supporting and substituting civil authorities in peace operations during the 1990s', unpublished thesis, University of Amsterdam.

Browne, G., Lawrence, T.R. and Robinson, S.L. (2005) 'Territoriality in organizations', *Academy of Management Review* 30: 577–594.

Cady, S.H. and Valentine, J. (1999) 'Team innovation and perceptions of consideration: what difference does diversity make?', *Small Group Research* 30: 730–750.

Callaghan, J. and Schönborn, M. (eds) (2004) *Warriors in Peacekeeping. Points of Tension in Complex Cultural Encounters. A Comparative Study Based on Experiences in Bosnia*, Münster: LIT Verlag.

Caniglia, R.R. (2001) 'U.S. and British approaches to force protection', *Military Review* 79: 73–81.

Cartwright, S. and Cooper, C.L. (1996) *Managing Mergers, Acquisitions and Strategic Alliances. Integrating People and Cultures*, 2nd edn, Oxford: Butterworth Heinemann.

Champagne, J.A.G. (1999) *Canadian Forces Transformational Leadership Against the 21st Century Environment and its Neutralizers: The Battle of Our Future Operational Commander*, Toronto: Canadian Forces College.

Chappell, J. (2001) 'Crossing the cultural divide: for Japan, penetrating U.S. and global markets means making changes', *Electric News*, 8 January 2001.

Chen, C.C., Chen, X.-P. and Meindl, J. (1998) 'How can cooperation be fostered? The cultural effects of individualism-collectivism', *Academy of Management Review* 23: 285–304.

Christensen, L.T., Morsing, M. and Cheney, G. (2007) *Corporate Communications. Convention, Complexity and Critique*, London: Sage.

Christian, J., Porter, L.W. and Moffitt, G. (2006) 'Workplace diversity and group relations: an overview', *Group Processes and Intergroup Relations* 9: 459–466.

Clark, W. (2001) *Waging Modern War*. New York: Public Affairs.

Clausewitz, C. von (1989) *On War*, Princeton, NJ: Princeton University Press.

Clegg, S., Pitsis, T.S., Rura-Polley, T. and Marosszeky, M. (2002) 'Governmentality matters: designing an alliance culture of inter-organizational collaboration for managing projects', *Organization Studies* 23: 317–337.

Cooper, D., Doucet, L. and Pratt, M. (2007) 'Understanding "appropriateness" in multinational organizations', *Journal of Organizational Behavior* 28: 303–325.

Cosgrove, P. (2006) *My Story*, Pymble, Australia: HarperCollins.

Cossa, R. and Glosserman, B. (2005) 'U.S.–Japan defense cooperation: has Japan become the Great Britain of Asia?', *Issues and Insights*, Vol. 5: 3, Pacific Forum: www.csis.org/pacfor.

Coupland, C. and Brown, A.D. (2004) 'Constructing organizational identities on the web: a case study of Royal Dutch Shell', *Journal of Management Studies* 41: 1325–1347.

Cremin, D., Mills, M., Phipps, D. and Stewart, K. (2005) 'The challenges of command in multinational environments', *The British Army Review* 136: 54–60.

Crossey, M. (2005) 'Improving Linguistic Interoperability', *Nato Review*: www.nato.int/docu/review/2005/issue2/english/art4.

Cunningham, G.B. and Sagas, M. (2004) 'Examining the main and interactive effects of deep- and surface-level diversity on job satisfaction and organizational turnover intentions', *Organizational Analysis* 12: 319–332.

Dallaire, R. (2000) 'Command experiences in Rwanda', in C. McCann and R. Pigeau (eds). *The Human in Command: Exploring the Modern Military Experience*, New York: Kluwer Academic/Plenum Publishers.

—— (2004) *Shake Hands with the Devil. The Failure of Humanity in Rwanda*, London: Arrow Books.

Da Matta, R. (1991) *Carnivals, Rogues, and Heroes: an Interpretation of the Brazilian Dilemma*, London: University of Notre Dame Press.

Da Matta, R. and Green, R. (1983). 'An interpretation of "carnaval"', *SubStance*, Vol. 11, No. 4, Issue 37–38: 162–170.

Danziger, J.N. (2004) *Understanding the Political World: A Comparative Introduction to Political Science*, London: Sage.

Darboe, M. (2004) 'Asr focus: Islamism in West Africa. Gambia', *African Studies Review* 47: 73–82.

Das, T.K. and Teng, B.-Sh. (1998) 'Between trust and control: developing confidence in partner cooperation in alliances', *Academy of Management Review* 23: 491–512.

Daun, Å. (2005) *En stuga på sjätte våningen: svensk mentalitet i en mångkulturell värld*, Symposium, Eslöv.

Davis, C.J.R. (2000) *Command and Control in Coalition Operations*, Kingston, ON: Canadian Forces College.

Davis, R.G. (2000) *Establishing Trust in Peace Support Leadership*, Toronto: Canadian Forces College.

Dechesne, M., van den Berg, C. and Soeters, J. (2007) 'International collaboration under threat: a field study in Kabul', *Conflict Management and Peace Science* 24: 25–36.

Defence White Paper (2005) *Defense of Japan*, Inter Group Corp.

Den Hartog, D.N., House, R.J., Hanges, P.J., Ruiz-Quintanilla, S.A., Dorfman, P.W. *et al.* (1999) 'Culture-specific and cross-culturally generalizeable implicit leadership theories: are attributes of charismatic/transformational leadership universally endorsed?', *Leadership Quarterly* 10: 219–256.

Diehl, P. (2005) 'Once again. Nations agree genocide must be stopped. Can they find the mechanism to do it?', *Washington Post* 15 May 2005.

Dijk, A. van and Soeters, J. (2008) 'Language matters in the military' (under review).

Diken, B. and Laustsen, C.B. (2005) *The Culture of Exception. Sociology Facing the Camp*, London and New York: Routledge.

DiMaggio, P.J. and Powell, W.W. (1991) 'The iron cage revisited: institutional isomorphism and collective rationality in organizational fields', in W.W. Powell and P.J. DiMaggio (eds), *The New Institutionalism in Organizational Analysis*, Chicago: University of Chicago Press.

DiStefano, J.J. and Maznevski, M.L. (2000) 'Creating value with diverse teams in global management', *Organizational Dynamics* 29: 45–63.

Djelic, M.L. (1998) *Exporting the American Model*, New York: Oxford University Press.

Dobson, H. (2003) *Japan and the United Nations Peace Keeping: New Pressures, New Responses*, London: RoutledgeCurzon.

Docking, T. (2001) *Peacekeeping in Africa*, Washington DC: United States Institute for Peace, special report No. 66. Online. Available on: www.usip.org/pubs/specialreports/sr66.html (accessed 4 July 2006).

Downs, A. (1967) *Inside Bureaucracy*, Boston, MA: Little, Brown, and Co.

Doz, Y.L. (1996) 'The evolution of cooperation in strategic alliances: initial conditions or learning processes?', *Strategic Management Journal* 17: 55–83.

Doz, Y., Bartlett, C. and Prahalad, G. (1981) 'Global competitive pressures and host country demands: managing tensions in MNCs', *California Management Review* 23: 63–74.

Drezner, D.W. (2001) 'Globalization and policy convergence', *International Studies Review* 3: 53–78.

Duffey, T. (2000) 'Cultural issues in contemporary peacekeeping', *International Peacekeeping* 7: 142–168.

Dumont, L. (1986) 'Collective identities and universalist ideology: the actual interplay', *Theory, Culture & Society* 3: 25–33.

Dunn, J. (1996) *Timor: A People Betrayed*, Sydney: ABC Books.

Durch, W.J. (2001) *UN Peace Operations and the "Brahimi Report"*. The Stimson Center. Online. Available on: www.stimson.org/fopo/pdf/peaceopsbr1001.pdf (accessed 1 July 2006).

Earley, C.P. and Mosakowski, E. (2000) 'Creating hybrid team cultures: an empirical test of transnational team functioning', *Academy of Management Journal* 43: 26–49.

Edmondson, A.C. (1999) 'Psychological safety and learning behaviour in work teams', *Administrative Science Quarterly* 44, 350–383.

Eide, E.B., Kaspersen, A.T., Kent, R. and von Hippel, K. (2005) *The Report on Integrated Missions: Practical Perspectives and Recommendations*, Oslo and London: Norwegian Institute for International Affairs and Kings College.

Elron, E. (1997) 'Top management teams within multinational corporations: effects of cultural heterogeneity', *Leadership Quarterly*, 8: 393–412.

—— (2007) 'Renewed partnerships between UNIFIL II, Israel, Lebanon, the United Nations and the international community: implications for mission effectiveness and peace processes in the Middle East', in J. Dufourcq and T. Szvircsev Tresch (eds), *Cultural Challenges in Military Operations*, Occasional Paper No. 23, NATO Defence College, Academic Research Branch, Rome.

Elron, E., Halevy, N., Ben-Ari, E. and Shamir, B. (2003) 'Cooperation and coordination across cultures in the peacekeeping forces: individual and organizational integrating mechanisms', in T.W. Britt and A.B. Adler (eds), *The Psychology of the Peacekeeper*, Westport, CT: Praeger.

Elron, E., Shamir, B. and Ben-Ari, E. (1999) 'Why don't they fight each other? Cultural diversity and operational unity in multinational forces', *Armed Forces and Society* 26: 73–97.

Ely, R.J. and Thomas, D.A. (2001) 'Cultural diversity at work: the effects of diversity perspectives on work group processes and outcomes', *Administrative Science Quarterly* 46(2): 229–273.

Evetts, J. (2002) 'Explaining the construction of professionalism in the armed forces: occupational change within and beyond the nation-state', paper presented at the Special Joint Session of RCs 01, 34 and 52, XVth ISA World Conference, Brisbane, Australia, July 2002.

Feely, A.J. and Harzing, A.-W. (2003) 'Language management in multinational companies', *Cross Cultural Management* 10: 37–52.

Festinger, L. (1962) *A Theory of Cognitive Dissonance*, Stanford, CA: Stanford University Press.

Findlay, T. (2002) *The Use of Force in UN Peace Operations*, Oxford: Oxford University Press for SIPRI.

Fitz-Gerald, A. (2003) 'Multinational landforce interoperability: meeting the challenge of different backgrounds in chapter VI peace support operations', *Journal of Conflict Studies* 23: 60–85.

Foldy, E.G. (2004) 'Learning from diversity: a theoretical explanation', *Public Administrative Review* 64: 529–538.

Fowler, S.M. (2006) 'Training across cultures: what intercultural trainers bring to diversity training', *International Journal of Intercultural Relations* 30: 401–411.

Gareis, S., Hagen, U. vom, Bach, P., Andreasen, T., Doulgerof, I., Kolodziejczyk, A. and Wachowicz, M. (2003) *Conditions of Military Multinationality. The Multinational Corps Northeast in Szczecin*, Strausber: SOWI, FORUM International.

Garza, R. and Santos, S. (1991) 'Ingroup/outgroup balance and inter-ethnic behavior', *Journal of Experimental Social Psychology* 27: 124–137.

Gasperini, G. (2004) 'Soziologische Aspekte der Beziehungen zwischen den einzelnen Kontingenten in multinationalen Verbänden am Beispiel der Italienisch–Slowenisch–Ungarischen Brigade', in K.W. Haltiner and P. Klein (eds), *Multinationalität als Herausforderung für die Streitkräfte*, Baden-Baden: Nomos.

Gasperini, G., Arnejčič, B. and Ujj, A. (2001) *Sociological Aspects Concerning the Relations within Contingents of Multinational Units*, Rome: Artistic & Publishing Company.

Gaunt, G. and Löfgren, O. (1984) *Myter om svensken*, Stockholm: Liber Förlag.

Gelfand, M.J. and Realo, A. (1999) 'Individualism–collectivism and accountability in intergroup negotiations', *Journal of Applied Psychology* 84: 721–736.

Gelfand, M.J., Erez, M. and Aycan, Z. (2007) 'Cross-cultural organizational behavior', *Annual Review of Psychology* 58: 479–514.

Gellner, D. and Hirsch, E. (eds) (2001) *Inside Organizations. Anthropologists at Work*, Oxford: Berg.

Gerstner, C.R. and Day, D.V. (1994) 'Cross-cultural comparison of leadership prototypes', *Leadership Quarterly* 5: 121–134.

Ghosh, A. (1994) 'The global reservation: notes toward an ethnography of international peacekeeping', *Cultural Anthropology* 9: 414–22.

Gibson, C.B. and Vermeulen, F. (2003) 'A healthy divide: subgroups as a stimulus for team learning', *Administrative Science Quarterly* 48: 202–239.

Gillespie, G.L. (2003) *Culture: The Key to Coalition Operations*, Kingston, ON: Canadian Forces College.

Gioia, D.A. (1998) 'From individual to organizational identity', in D.A. Whetten and P.C. Godfrey (eds), *Identity in Organizations. Building Theory through Conversations*, Thousand Oaks, CA: Sage.

Gioia, D. and Chittipeddi, K. (1991) 'Sensemaking and sensegiving in strategic change initiation', *Strategic Management Journal* 12: 433–448.

Graen, G.B. and Hui, C. (1999) 'U.S. army leadership in the twenty-first century: challenges and implications for training', in J.G. Hunt, G.E. Dodge and L. Wong (eds), *Out-of-the-Box Leadership: Transforming the Twenty-First Century Army and Other Top-Performing Organizations*, Stamford, CT: JAI Press.

Granovetter, M. (1983) 'The strength of weak ties: a network theory revisited', *Sociological Theory* 1: 201–233.

Gray, B. (1985) 'Conditions facilitating interorganizational collaboration', *Human Relations* 38: 911–936.

Griffeth, B.T. and Bally, R.E. (2006) 'Language and cultural barriers in the assessment of enemy prisoners of war and other foreign nationals', *Psychiatric Services: A Journal of the American Psychiatric Association* 57: 258–259 and 580–581.

Guler, I., Guillen, M.F. and McPherson, I. (2002) 'Global competition, institutions, and the diffusion of organizational practices: the international spread of ISO 9000 quality certificates', *Administrative Science Quarterly* 47(2): 207–232.

Gullestad, M. (2002) 'Invisible fences: egalitarianism, nationalism and racism', *Journal of the Royal Anthropological Institute* 8: 45–63.

Gupta, A. (1992) 'The song of the nonaligned world: transnational identities and the reinscription of space in late capitalism', *Cultural Anthropology* 7: 63–79.

Gurstein, M. (1999) 'Leadership in the peacekeeping army of the future', in J.G. Hunt, G.E. Dodge and L. Wong (eds), *Out-of-the-Box Leadership: Transforming the Twenty-First Century Army and Other Top-Performing Organizations*, Stamford, CT: JAI Press.

Hackman, J.R. (1987) 'The design of work teams', in J. Lorsch (ed.), *Handbook of Organizational Behavior*, Englewood Cliffs, NJ: Prentice Hall.

Hagen, U. vom, Klein, P., Moelker, R. and Soeters, J. (2003) *True Love: A Study in Integrated Multinationality within 1 (German/Netherlands) Corps*, Strausberg: SOWI, Forum International.

Hagen, U. vom, Moelker, R. and Soeters, J. (eds) (2006) *Cultural Interoperability: Ten Years of Research into Co-operation in the First German–Netherlands Corps*, Strausberg: SOWI, FORUM International.

Halevy, N. and Sagiv, L. (2008) 'Teams within and across cultures', in P.B. Smith, M.F. Peterson and D.C. Thomas (eds), *Handbook of Cross-Cultural Management Research*, London: Sage.

Hall, S. (1992) 'The question of cultural identity', in S. Hall, D. Held and T. McGrew (eds), *Modernity and its Futures*, Cambridge: Polity.

Hambrick, D.C., Canney Davidson, S., Snell, S.A. and Snow, C.C. (1998) 'When groups consist of multiple nationalities: towards a new understanding of the implications', *Organization Studies* 19: 181–205.

Handley, H.A.H. and Levis, A.H. (2001) 'Incorporating heterogeneity in command center interactions', paper presented at the Command and Control Research Technology Symposium, Annapolis, Maryland.

Hannerz, U. (1992) 'The global ecumene', in Hannerz, U. (ed.), *Cultural Complexity: Studies in the Social Organization of Meaning*, New York: Columbia University Press.

Hardy, C., Lawrence, T.B. and Grant, D. (2005) 'Discourse and collaboration: the role of conversations and collective identity', *Academy of Management Review* 30: 58–77.

Hatch, M.J. and Schultz, M. (1997) 'Relations between organizational culture, identity and image', *European Journal of Marketing*, 31: 356–365.

—— (2004) *Organizational Identity – A Reader*, Oxford: Oxford University Press.

Hebegger, B. (2007) 'UN peace operations in transition', *CSS Analyses in Security Policy*, Vol. 2, No. 7.

Heinrich, L.W., Shibata, A. and Soeya, Y. (1999) *United Nations Peacekeeping Operations: A Guide to Japanese Policies*, New York: The United Nations University Press.

Helmreich, R.L. and Merritt, A.S. (1998) *Culture at Work in Aviation and Medicine. National, Organizational and Professional Influences*, Aldershot, Hampshire: Ashgate.

Hoffman, E. (1985) 'The effect of race-ratio composition on the frequency of organizational communication', *Social Psychology Quarterly* 48: 17–26.

Hoffmann, S. (1993) *The Nation, Nationalism, and After: The Case of France*, The Tanner Lectures on Human Values, delivered at Princeton University, 3–4 March 1993.

Hofstede, G. (1980) *Culture's Consequences: International Differences in Work Related Values*, Newbury Park, CA: Sage.

—— (1983) 'National cultures revisited', *Behavior Science Research* 18(4): 285–305.

Hofstede, G. and Hofstede, G.J. (2005) *Cultures and Organizations – Software of the Mind*, New York: McGraw-Hill.

Hofstede, G. and Soeters, J. (2002) 'Consensus societies with their own character: national cultures in Japan and the Netherlands', *Comparative Sociology* 1: 1–17.

Holt, V. (2005) *UN Peacekeeping Reform: Seeking Greater Accountability and Integrity.* Testimony to the Subcommittee on Africa, Global Human Rights, and International Operations, House Committee on International Relations, US House of Representatives, 18 May 2005.

House, R.J., Hanges, P.J., Javidan, M., Dorfman, P.W. and Gupta, V. (eds) (2004) *Culture, Leadership, and Organizations. The Globe Study of 62 Societies*, Thousand Oaks, CA: Sage.

Huber, G.P. (1991) 'Organizational learning: the contributing processes and the literatures', *Organization Science* 2: 88–115.

Hürriyet (newspaper) (2005) http://hurarsiv.hurriyet.com.tr/goster/haber.aspx?id=322323 (accessed 30 May 2007).

Hylland-Eriksen, T. (2001) *Øyeblikkets tyranni. Rask og langsom tid i informasjonsalderen*, Oslo: Aschehoug.

Ignatieff, M. (1998) *Warrior's Honour, the Ethnic War and the Modern Conscience*, London: Chatto and Windus.

Ingold, T. (2002) 'Introduction to culture', in T. Ingold (ed.), *Companion Encyclopedia of Anthropology: Humanity, Culture and Social Life*, London: Routledge.

Inkpen, A.C. and Beamish, P.W. (1997) 'Knowledge, bargaining power, and the instability of international joint ventures', *Academy of Management Review* 22: 177–202.

Jackson, S. (2006) *The United Nations Operation (ONUB) – Political and Strategic Lessons Learned*, New York: UN Best Practices, DPKO.

Jackson, S.E. (1992) 'Consequences of group composition for the interpersonal dynamics of strategic issue processing', *Advances in Strategic Management* 8: 345–382.

Jelušič, L. (2003) 'Conversion of the military: resource-reuse perspective after the end of the Cold War', in G. Caforio (ed.), *Handbook of the Sociology of the Military*, New York: Kluwer Academic/Plenum Publishers.

Jelušič, L. and Pograjč, B. (2006) 'Sociological aspects of cooperation among Italian, Hungarian, and Slovenian soldiers in MLF Unit: diversities for better efficiency or not?', paper presented at the ISA World Congress, Durban, July 2006.

Jenkins, R. (1996) *Social Identity*, 2nd edn, London and New York: Routledge.

Jepperson, R.L. and Meyer, J.W. (1991) 'The public order and the construction of formal organization', in W.W. Powell and P.J. DiMaggio (eds), *The New Institutionalism in Organizational Analysis.*, Chicago: University of Chicago Press.

Johansson, E. (2001) *The Unknown Soldier – A Portrait of the Swedish Peace-keeper at the Threshold of the 21st Century*, Karlstad: Karlstad University Press.

Joint Warfare Publication (JWP) 0–01 (2001) *British Defence Doctrine.* Shrivenham, Oxfordshire: Joint Doctrine and Concepts Centre.

—— (JWP) 5.00 (2004a) *Joint Operations Planning.* Shrivenham, Oxfordshire: Joint Doctrine and Concepts Centre.

—— (JWP) 01 (2004b) *Joint Operations*. Shrivenham, Oxfordshire: Joint Doctrine and Concepts Centre.

Jones, L.T. (2005) *A framework for appreciating and managing the cultural adaptation of multinational peace operations forces to local environments: with case studies of Bougainville and Timor-Leste*, unpublished thesis, Oxford University.

Kakitani, T. and Kikuchi, M. (2005) *Jieitai Iraq Haken no Shinjitsu* [Reality of SDF Dispatch in Iraq], Tokyo: Sanshusha.

Kanter, R.M. (1977) *Men and Women of the Corporation*, New York: Basic Books.

Kavas, A. (2005) 'The Ottoman state's role in the non-establishment of colonialism in Africa until the second half of 19th century', paper presented at the 1st International Turkish–African Congress, 'Rising Africa and Turkey', October 2005, Istanbul.

Kawano, H. (2002) 'The positive impact of peacekeeping on the Japan Self-Defense Forces', in L. Parmar (ed.), *Armed Forces and the International Diversities*, Jaipur: Pointer Publishers.

Keegan, J. (1993) *A History of Warfare*, London: Hutchinson.

Keller, J. and Tomforde, M. (2007) 'Findings from fieldwork on German-Italian cooperation at NMB SW (KFOR)', in J. Dufourcq and T. Szvircsev Tresch (eds), *Cultural Challenges in Military Operations*, Occasional Paper No. 23, NATO Defence College, Academic Research Branch, Rome.

King, A. (2005) 'Towards a transnational Europe: the case of the armed forces', *European Journal of Social Theory*, 8: 321–340.

Kipping, M., Usdiken, B. and Puig, N. (2004) 'Imitation, tension, and hybridization: multiple Americanizations of management education in Mediterranean Europe', *Journal of Management Inquiry*, 13 (2): 98–108.

Kirkman, B.L., Tesluk, P.E. and Rosen, B. (2004) 'The impact of demographic heterogeneity and team leader–team member demographic fit on team empowerment and effectiveness', *Group and Organization Management* 29: 334–368.

Klein, H.A. (2005) 'Cultural differences in cognition: barriers in multinational collaborations', in H. Montgomery, R. Lipshitz and B. Brehmer (eds), *How Professionals Make Decisions*, Mahwah, NJ: Lawrence Erlbaum Associates.

Klein, H.A., Pongonis, A. and Klein, G. (2000) 'Cultural barriers to multinational C2 decision making', paper presented to the Command and Control Research Technology Symposium, Naval Postgraduate School, Monterey, CA, 2000.

Klein, P. (2003) 'Multinational armed forces'; in J. Callaghan and F. Kernic (eds), *Armed Forces and International Security: Global Trends and Issues*, Münster: LIT Verlag.

Klein, P. and Haltiner, K.W. (2004) 'Multinationalität als Herausforderung für die Streitkräfte', in K.W. Haltiner and P. Klein (eds), *Multinationalität als Herausforderung für die Streitkräfte*, Baden-Baden: Nomos.

Klein, P. and Kümmel, G. (2000) 'The internationalization of military life: necessity, problems and prospects of multinational armed forces', in G. Kümmel and A. Prüfert (eds), *Military Sociology. The Richness of a Discipline*, Baden-Baden: Nomos.

Klep, C. and Gils, R. van (2005) *Van Korea tot Kabul. De Nederlandse militaire deelname aan vredesoperaties sinds 1945* [From Korea to Kabul. Dutch Military Participation in Peace-Operations after 1945], The Hague: SDU.

Klep, C. and Winslow, D. (2000) 'Learning lessons the hard way – Somalia and Srebrenica compared', *Small Wars and Insurgencies* 10: 93–127.

Kokot, W., Tölölyan, K. and Alfonso, C. (eds) (2004) *Diaspora, Identity and Religion: New Directions in Theory and Research*. London: Routledge.

Knops, R.W. (2005) 'Mission Iraq', *Carré*, 2: 20–25.

Kratzer, J., Leenders, R.T. and van Engelen, J.M.L. (2004) 'Stimulating the potential: creative performance and communication in innovation teams', *Creativity and Innovation Management* 13: 63–71.

Lammers, C.J. and Hickson, D. (eds) (1979) *Organizations Alike and Unlike. International and Inter-Institutional Studies in the Sociology of Organizations*, London: Routledge.

Lane, R. (2006) 'The command, leadership and management challenges of contemporary multinational command', *RUSI Journal* 151(6): 30–34.

Lang, K. (1965) 'Military organizations', in J.G. March (ed.), *Handbook of Organizations*, Chicago: Rand McNally.

Lang, S. (2001a) 'Multinationalität – zwischen Tradition und Integration', *Europäische Sicherheit* 4: 41–44.

—— (2001b) 'Multinationalität im Spannungsfeld zwischen Tradition und Integration im Hinblick auf die zukünftige verteidigungspolitische Entwicklung innerhalb der NATO', *ÖMZ* 6: 755–759.

Lave, J. and Wenger, E. (1991) *Situated Learning*, Cambridge: Cambridge University Press.

Legault, A. (1967) *Research on Peace-Keeping Operations: Current Status and Future Needs*, Paris: International Centre on Peace-Keeping Operations.

Lescoutre, C.S.R. (2003) *Command Structure for Coalition Operations: A Template for Future Force Commanders*, Kingston, ON: Canadian Forces College.

Levy, O., Beechler, S., Taylor, S. and Boyacigiller, N.A. (2007) 'What we talk about when we talk about "global mindset": managerial cognition in multinational corporations', *Journal of Business Studies* 38: 231–258.

Lewis, R.D. (2000) *When Cultures Collide*, 3rd edn, London: Nicholas Brealey Publishing.

Li, J. and Hambrick, D.C. (2005) 'Factional groups: a new vantage on demographic faultlines, conflict, and disintegration in work teams', *Academy of Management Journal* 48: 794–813.

Liddell Hart, Basil (1933) *The Ghost of Napoleon*, London: Faber.

London, T. and Hart, S.L. (2004) 'Reinventing strategies for emerging markets: beyond the transnational model', *Journal of International Business Studies* 35: 350–370.

Longhurst, K. (2000) 'The concept of strategic culture', in G. Kümmel and A. Prüfert (eds), *Military Sociology: The Richness of a Discipline*, Baden-Baden: Nomos.

Loos, E. (2007) 'Language policy in an enacted world', *Language Problems and Language Planning* 31: 37–60.

Luttwak, E. (1995) 'Toward post-heroic warfare', *Foreign Affairs* 74(3): 109–122.

Lutz, W. (2007) 'Bevolkingsontwikkeling vergroot Europese identiteit op termijn: jongere generaties voelen zich thuis in de EU' [Demographic development enhances European identity in the long run: younger generations feel at home in the EU], *Demos* 23: 1–4.

McCann, C. and Pigeau, R. (eds) (2000) *The Human in Command: Exploring the Modern Military experience*, New York: Kluwer Academic/Plenum Publishers.

MacIsaac, J.R. (2000) *Leadership During Peace Support Operations: 'Mission Impossible'*, Kingston, ON: Canadian Forces College.

Maloney, M. and Zellmer-Bruhn, M. (2006) 'Building bridges, windows and cultures: Mediating mechanisms between heterogeneity and performance in global teams', *Management International Review*, Special Issue on Global Teams, 46(6), 697–720.

Mannix, E. and Neale, M.A. (2005) 'What differences make a difference? The promise and reality of diverse teams in organizations', *Psychological Science in the Public Interest* 6: 31–55.

Marschan-Piekkari, R., Welch, D. and Welch, L. (1999) 'In the shadow: the impact of language on structure, power and communication in the multinational', *International Business Review* 8: 421–440.

Marshall, T.J., Kaiser, P. and Kessmeier, J. (eds) (1997) *Problems and Solutions in Future Coalition Operations*, Carlisle: USAWC Strategic Studies Institute.

Martin, J. (2002). *Organizational Culture – Mapping the Terrain*, Thousand Oaks, CA: Sage.

Mauss, M. (1923–1924) 'Essai sur le Don: Forme et Raison de 'échange dans les Sociétés Primitives', *L'Année Sociologique*, Seconde Série.

Méndez García, M.C. and Pérez Cañado, M.L. (2005) 'Language and power: raising awareness of the role of language in multicultural teams', *Language and Intercultural Communication* 5: 86–104.

Merton, R.K. (1968) *Social Theory and Social Structure*, 3rd edn, New York: Free Press.

Meulen, J. van der and Soeters, J. (2005) 'Dutch courage: the politics of acceptable risks', *Armed Forces and Society* 31: 537–558.

Meyer, M.W. and Zucker, L.G. (1989) *Permanently Failing Organizations*, Newbury Park, CA: Sage.

Miller, D.J., Fern, M.J. and Cardinal, L.B. (2007) 'The use of knowledge for technological innovation within diversified firms', *Academy of Management Journal* 50: 308–326.

Mintzberg, H. (2001) 'Managing exceptionally', *Organization Science* 12: 759–771.

Miura, A. and Hida, M. (2004) 'Synergy between diversity and similarity in group-idea generation', *Small Group Research* 35: 540–564.

Moelker, R., Soeters, J. and Hagen, U. vom (2007) 'Sympathy, the cement of interoperability. Findings on ten years of German–Netherlands military cooperation', *Armed Forces and Society* 33: 496–517.

Morimoto, S. (2004) *Iraku Senso to Jieitai Kaken* [Iraq War and SDF Dispatch], Tokyo: Toyo Kiezai Shinbunsha.

Morrison, A. and Kiras, J. (eds) (1996), *UN Peace Operations and the Role of Japan*, Clementsport, Nova Scotia: The Canadian Peacekeeping Operations Press.

Moskos, C. (1976) *Peace Soldiers. The Sociology of a United Nations Military Force*, Chicago: University of Chicago Press.

Moskos, C., Williams, J.A. and Segal, D. (2000) 'Armed forces after the Cold War', in C. Moskos, J.A. Williams and D. Segal (eds), *The Postmodern Military: Armed Forces after the Cold War*, New York: Oxford University Press.

Multi-national Standby High Readiness Brigade for UN Operations Online. Available on: http://shirbrig.dk/html/main.htm (accessed 11 September 2007).

Nahavandi, A. and Malekzadeh, A.R. (1988) 'Acculturation in mergers and acquisitions', *Academy of Management Review* 13: 79–90.

Nelson, N. (2000) 'The 1st Battalion, RNZIR in East Timor', presentation at Massey University, Palmerston North New Zealand, 27 July 2000.

Niumpradit, B. (2002) *410 Days in East Timor, A Peacekeeper's Diary*, Bangkok: Darnsutha Press.

Noorderhaven, N.G. and Tidjani, B. (2001) 'Culture, governance, and economic performance: an explorative study with a special focus on Africa', *International Journal of Cross Cultural Management* 1 (1): 31–52.

Noorderhaven, N.G., Benders, J. and Keizer, A.B. (2007) 'Comprehensiveness versus pragmatism: consensus at the Japanese–Dutch interface', *Journal of Management Studies* 44(8), 1349–1370.

Nørgaard, K. (2004) 'Tillidens teknologi. Den militære ethos og viljen til dannelse', unpublished thesis, Institut for Antropologi, Det Samfundsvidenskabelige Fakultet.

Nuciari, M. (2003) 'Women in the military. Sociological arguments for integration', in G. Caforio (ed.), *Handbook of the Sociology of the Military*, New York: Kluwer Academic/Plenum Publishers.

Olie, R. (1994) 'Shades of culture and institutions in international mergers', *Organization Studies* 15: 381–405.

Olivas-Lujan, M.R., Harzing, A.-W. and McCoy, S. (2004) 'September 11, 2001: two quasi-experiments on the influence of threats on cultural values and cosmopolitanism', *International Journal of Cross Cultural Management* 4: 211–228.

Oliver, A. and Montgomery, K. (2000) 'Creating a hybrid organizational form from parental blueprints: the emergence and evolution of knowledge firms', *Human Relations* 53: 33–56.

Olonisakin, F. (2003) 'African peacekeeping and the impact on African military personnel', in T.W. Britt and A.B. Adler (eds), *The Psychology of the Peacekeeper. Lessons from the Field*, Westport, CT: Praeger.

Onderzoek Ondervragingen in Irak (2007) 'Report of the Research Committee on Interrogation in Iraq', The Hague, 18 June 2007.

Palin, R. (1995) *Multinational Forces: Problems and Prospects*, Oxford: Oxford University Press, Adelphi Papers 294.

Paris, R. (2004) *At War's End: Building Peace after Civil Conflict*, New York: Cambridge University Press.

Park, Hoon, Dai Hwang, Sun and Kline Harrison, J. (1996) 'Sources and consequences of communication problems in foreign subsidiaries: the case of United States firms in South Korea'. *International Business Review* 5: 79–98.

Parker, M. (2000) *Organizational Culture and Identity: Unity and Division at Work*, London: Sage.

Patterson, H. (2000) 'Rioting in East Timor injures four,' *The Associated Press*, 25 January 2000.

Peterson, M.F. and Thomas, D.C. (2007) 'Organizational behaviour in multinational organizations', *Journal of Organizational Behaviour* 28: 261–279.

Plante, E.D.J. (1998) *Leading a Multinational Force Without Leaving Anyone Behind: The Human Dimensions of Marginalisation*, Kingston, ON: Canadian Forces College.

Pograjč, B. (2006) *Vecnačionalne vojaške enote* [Multinational Military Units], Ljubljana: Univerza v Ljubljani, Fakulteta za družbene vede.

Potts, D. (ed.) (2004) 'Beyond interoperability: part 1', in *The Big Issue: Command and Control in the Information Age*, Vol. 45, Washington, DC: Department of Defense Command and Control Research Program.

Preston, D. (2002) *The Boxer Rebellion. China's War on Foreigners, 1900*, London: Robinson.

Prüfert, A. (ed.) (2002) *Im Dienste einer neuen Friedenskultur*, Baden-Baden: Nomos.

Pyszczynski, T., Solomon, S. and Greenberg, J. (2003) *In the Wake of 9/11. The Psychology of Terror*, Washington DC: American Psychological Association.

Ramsbotham, O. (2000) 'Reflections on post-settlement peace-building', *International Peacekeeping* 7: 167–190.

Rapport, N. and Overing, J. (2000) *Social and Cultural Anthropology: The Key Concepts*, London: Routledge.

Resteigne, D. and Soeters, J. (2007) 'Belgian troops in UNIFIL', in J. Dufourcq and T. Szvircsev Tresch (eds), *Cultural Challenges in Military Operations*, Occasional Paper No. 23, Rome: NATO Defence College, Academic Research Branch.

—— (2008) 'Managing militarily', *Armed Forces and Society* 34 (in press).

Rietjens, S. and Bollen, M. (eds) (2008) *Approaching Civil–Military Interfaces: A Shared Platform for Research and Experience*, London: Ashgate.

Riordan, C.M. and Shore, L.M. (1997) 'Demographic diversity and employee attitudes: an empirical examination of relational demography within work units', *Journal of Applied Psychology* 82: 342–358.

Robertson, L. and Kulik, C.T. (2007) 'Stereotype threat at work', *Academy of Management Perspectives* 21: 24–40.

Robertson, R. (1992) *Globalization: Social Theory and Global Culture*, London: Sage.

Romme, A. (1999) 'Domination, self-determination and circular organizing', *Organization Studies* 20: 801–831.

Ronen, S. and Shenkar, O. (1985) 'Clustering countries on attitudinal dimensions: a review and synthesis', *Academy of Management Review* 10: 435–454.

Rubinstein, R. (1998) 'Cultural aspects of peacekeeping: notes on the substance of symbols', in D. Jacquin-Berdal, A. Oros and M. Verweij (eds), *Culture in World Politics*, New York: Macmillan.

Ryan, A. (2000) *Achieving C3I Interoperability for Coalition Operations: Lessons from INTERFET*, Canberra: Land Warfare Studies Centre.

Sabah (newspaper) (2005) www.sabah.com.tr/2005/05/27/siy103.html (accessed 13 May 2007).

Sabrosky, A., Thompson, J. and McPherson, K. (1982) 'Organized anarchies: military bureaucracy in the 1980s', *Journal of Applied and Behavioral Science* 18: 137–153.

Sackmann, S.A. (ed.) (1997) *Cultural Complexity in Organizations: Inherent Contrasts and Contradictions*, Thousand Oaks, CA: Sage.

—— (2004) 'Cultural complexity as a challenge in the management of global companies', in L. Mohn (ed.), *Corporate Cultures in Global Interaction*, Gütersloh: Bertelsmann.

Salas, E., Burke, C.S., Wilson-Donnelly, K.A. and Fowlkes, J.E. (2004) 'Promoting effective leadership within multicultural teams: an event-based approach', in D.V. Day, S.J. Zaccaro and S.M. Halpin (eds), *Leader Development for Transforming Organizations: Growing Leaders for Tomorrow*, Mahwah, NJ: Lawrence Erlbaum Associates.

Säljö, R. (2000) *Lärande i praktiken*, Stockholm: Prisma.

Sankei Shimbun News Service (2004) *Bushido no Kuni kara kita Jieitai* [SDF coming from the Country of Samurai], Tokyo: Fuso-sha.

Sartori, J.A., Waldherr, S. and Adams, B.A. (2006) *Team Modeling: Literature Review*, Toronto: Defence R&D Canada.

Sassen, S. (1991) *The Global City*, Chichester: Princeton University Press.

Schilling, M.A., Vidal, P., Ployhart, R.E. and Marangoni, A. (2003) 'Learning by doing something else: variation, relatedness, and the learning curve', *Management Science* 49: 39–56.

Schimel, J., Simon, L., Greenberg, J., Pyszczynski, T., Solomon, S., Waxmonsky, J. and Arndt, J.(1999) 'Stereotypes and terror management. Evidence that mortality salience enhances stereotypic thinking and preferences', *Journal of Personality and Social Psychology* 77: 905–926.

Schlenker, B.R. and Weingold, M.F. (1989) 'Self-identification and accountability', in R.A. Giacalone and P. Rosenfeld (eds), *Impression Management in the Organization*, Mahwah, NJ: Lawrence Erlbaum Associates.

Schmitt, B. (2004): 'European capabilities: how many divisions?', in N. Gnesotto (ed.), *EU Security and Defence Policy: The First Five Years (1999–2004)*, Paris: Institute for Security Studies.

Schultz, M. (2005) 'A cross-disciplinary perspective on corporate branding', in M. Schultz, Y.M. Antorini and F.F. Csaba (eds), *Corporate Branding. Purpose, People & Process*, Copenhagen: Copenhagen Business School Press.

Schwartz, S.H. (1994) 'Are there universal aspects in the content and structure of values?', *Journal of Social Issues* 50: 19–45.

Segal, D.R. (1995) 'Five phases of United Nations peacekeeping: an evolutionary typology', *Journal of Political and Military Sociology* 25: 65–79.

Sennett, R. (1998) *Corrosion of Character: The Personal Consequences of Work in the New Capitalism*, New York: Norton.

Shamir, B. and Ben-Ari, E. (2000) 'Challenges of military leadership in changing armies', *Journal of Political and Military Sociology* 28: 43–59.

Sherif, M., Harvey, O.J., White, B.J., Hood, W.R. and Sherif, C.W. (1961) *Intergroup Cooperation and Conflict: The Robbers Cave Experiment*, Norman, OK: University Book Exchange.

Sjöblom, I. (2005) *Interoperabilitet i multinationella operationer. Fallstudie Liberia (LA 01) och tankar inför framtide*, Stockholm: Försvarshögskolan.

Smith, K.G., Carroll, S.J. and Ashford, S.J. (1995) 'Intra- and interorganizational cooperation: toward a research agenda', *Academy of Management Journal* 38: 7–23.

Smith, P.B., Peterson, M.F. and Thomas, D.C. (2008) *Handbook of Cross-Cultural Management Research*, Thousand Oaks, CA: Sage.

Smith Ring, P. and Van de Ven, A.H. (1994) 'Developmental processes of cooperative interorganizational relationships', *Academy of Management Review* 19: 90–118.

Søderberg, A.-M. and Vaara, E. (eds) (2003) *Merging across Borders: People, Culture and Politics*, Copenhagen: Copenhagen Business School Press.

Søderberg, A.M. and Wedell-Wedellsborg, M. (2005) *Challenges to Uniformity: Managing the Changing Identities of Multinational Units*, working paper, Copenhagen Business School and Royal Danish Defence Academy.

Soeters, J. (1997) 'Value orientations in military academies: a thirteen country study' *Armed Forces and Society* 24 (1) Fall: 7–32.

Soeters, J. and Boer, P. (2000) 'Culture and flight safety in military aviation', *International Journal of Aviation Psychology* 10(2): 111–133.

Soeters, J. and Bos-Bakx, M. (2003) 'Cross-cultural issues in peacekeeping operations', in T.W. Britt and A.B. Adler (eds), *The Psychology of the Peacekeeper. Lessons from the Field*, Westport, CT: Praeger.

Soeters, J.L. and Recht, R. (1998) 'Culture and discipline in military academies: an international comparison', *Journal of Political and Military Sociology* 26, 169–189.

Soeters, J.L. and Recht, R. (2001) 'Convergence or divergence in the multinational classroom? Experiences from the military', *International Journal of Intercultural Relations* 25: 423–440.

Soeters, J. and van der Meulen, J. (eds) (2007) *Cultural Diversity in the Armed Forces: An International Comparison*, Abingdon, Oxfordshire: Routledge.

Soeters, J., Poponete, C. and Page, J. Jr. (2006) 'Culture's consequences in the military', in T.W. Britt, A.B. Adler and C.A. Castro (eds), *Military Life. The Psychology of Serving in Peace and Combat*, Vol. 4 (Military Culture), Westport, CT: Praeger.

Soeters, J., Winslow, D. and Weibull, A. (2003) 'Military culture', in G. Caforio (ed.), *Handbook of the Sociology of the Military*, New York: Kluwer Academic/Plenum Publishers.

Soeters, J., Resteigne, D., Moelker, R. and Manigart, P. (2006) 'Smooth and strained international military co-operation', in U. vom Hagen, R. Moelker and J. Soeters (eds), *Cultural Interoperability: Ten Years of Research into Co-operation in the First German–Netherlands Corps*, Strausberg: SOWI.

Soeters, J., Tanercan, E., Varoglu, K. and Sigri, U. (2004) 'Turkish–Dutch encounters in peace operations', *International Peace Keeping*', 11(2): 354–368.

Soeters, J., van den Berg, C.E., Varoglu, A. and Sıgrı, U. (2007) 'Accepting death in the military: a Turkish–Dutch comparison', *International Journal of Intercultural Relations* 31: 299–315.

Stahl, G., Maznevski, M., Voigt, A. and Jonsen, K. (2006) 'Unravelling the diversity–performance link in multicultural teams: meta-analysis of studies on the impact of cultural diversity in teams', paper presented at the Academy of Management Annual Meeting, Atlanta.

Staples, D.S. and Zhao, L. (2006) 'The effects of cultural diversity in virtual teams versus face-to-face teams', *Group Decision and Negotiation* 15: 389–406.

Staw, B.M., Sandelands, L.E. and Dutton, J.E. (1981) 'Threat-rigidity effects in organizational behaviour: a multilevel analysis', *Administrative Science Quarterly* 26: 501–524.

Stewart, K., Cremin, D., Mills, M. and Phipps, D. (2004) '*Non-technical interoperability: the challenge of command leadership in multinational operations*', paper presented at the 10th International Command and Control Research and Technology Symposium.

Stewart, K.G., Macklin, C.M., Proud, A.C., Verrall, N.G. and Widdowson, M. (2004) *Organizational and Sociological Factors of Multinational Forces: Baseline Studies Final Report*, Farnborough, Hampshire: QinetiQ.

Stewart, R. (2007) *The Prince of the Marshes. And other Occupational Hazards of a Year in Iraq*, Orlando, FL: Harcourt Inc.

Storr, J. (2002a) 'A command philosophy for the Information Age – the continuing relevance of mission command' in D. Potts (ed.), *The Big Issue: Command and Combat in the Information Age*, Washington, DC: Strategic and Combat Studies Institute Occasional Papers, 45: 41–48.

—— (2002b) 'The Commander as Expert' in D. Potts (ed.), *The Big Issue: Command and Combat in the Information Age*, Washington, DC: Strategic and Combat Studies Institute Occasional Papers, 45: 49–58.

Stryker, S. and Serpe, R.T. (1994) 'Identity salience and psychological centrality: Equivalent, overlapping, or complementary concepts?', *Social Psychology Quarterly* 57: 16–35.

Swaan, A. de (2001) *Words of the World: The Global Language System*, Cambridge: Polity Press.

Szvircsev, T.T. (2007) 'Cultural challenges in military operations: an overview', in J. Dufourcq and T. Szvircsev Tresch (eds), *Cultural Challenges in Military Operations*, Occasional Paper No. 23, Rome: NATO Defence College, Academic Research Branch.

Szvircsev, T.T. and Picciano, N. (2007) 'Effectiveness within Nato's multicultural military operations', paper presented at the conference 'Cultural Challenges in Military Operations', Rome, NATO Defence College, March 2007.

Tajfel, H. (1982) *Social Identity and Intergroup Relations*, Cambridge: Cambridge University Press.

Tajfel, H. and Turner, J.C. (1986) 'The social identity theory of intergroup behavior', in S. Worchel and W.G. Austin (eds), *The Psychology of Intergroup Relations*, Chicago: Nelson-Hall.

Tatar, S. (2005) 'Why keep silent? The classroom participation of non-native-English speaking students', *Language and Intercultural Communication* 5: 284–293.

Teo, T.M.S. (2005) *Cross-cultural Leadership: A Military Perspective*, Toronto: Canadian Forces College.

Tetsuro, I. (2005) 'Cooperation, coordination and complementarity in international peacemaking: the Tajikistan experience', *International Peacekeeping*, 12: 189–204.

Thomas, D.C and Fitzsimmons, S.R. (2008) 'Cross-cultural skills and abilities: from communication competence to cultural intelligence', in P.B. Smith, M.F. Peterson and D.C. Thomas (eds), *The Handbook of Cross-Cultural Management Research*, London: Sage.

Thompson, J.D. (1967) *Organizations in Action*, New York: McGraw-Hill.

Toh, S.M. and Denisi, A.O. (2007) 'Host country nationals as socializing agents: a social identity approach', *Journal of Organizational Behavior* 28: 281–301.

Tomforde, M. (2006a) 'The emotional cycle of deployment', paper presented at the ISA World Congress, Durban, July 2006.

—— (2006b) 'Einmal muss man schon dabei gewesen sein... – Auslandseinsätze als Initiation in die neue Bundeswehr', in Hagen, U. vom (ed.), *Armee in der Demokratie: Zum Verhältnis von zivilen und militärischen Prinzipien*, Wiesbaden: VS Verlag für Sozialwissenschaften.

—— (2007) 'How about pasta and beer? Intercultural challenges of German–Italian cooperation in Kosovo', in J. Dufourcq and T. Szvircsev Tresch (eds), *Cultural Challenges in Military Operations*, Occasional Paper No. 23, Rome: NATO Defence College, Academic Research Branch.

Triandis, H.C. (2002) 'The study of cross-cultural management and organization: the future', *International Journal of Cross-Cultural Management*, 1:17–20.

—— (2006) 'Cultural intelligence in organizations', *Group & Organization Management* 31: 20–26.

Trondall, J. and Veggeland, F. (2003): 'Access, voice and loyalty: the representation of domestic civil servants in EU committees', *Journal of European Public Policy* 10: 59–77.

United Kingdom Doctrine for Joint and Multinational Operations (1999) Joint Warfare Publication 0–10.

United Nations (2000) *The Report of the Panel on United Nations Peace Operations.* Online. Available on: www.un.org/peace/reports/peace_operations (accessed 4 July 2006).

United Nations Challenges Project (2006) *Meeting the Challenges of Peace Operations: Cooperation and Coordination. Challenges Project Phase II Concluding Report 2003–2006.* Stockholm: Elanders Gotab. Online. Available on: www.challengesproject.net/roach/HOME.do?pageId=13 (accessed 14 November 2006).

United Nations Peacebuilding Commission (2006) Online. Available on: www.un.org/peace/peacebuilding (accessed 4 July 2006).

United Nations Peacekeeping Best Practices Service (2005) *'Re-Hatting' ECOWAS Forces as UN Peacekeepers: Lessons Learned*, New York: United Nations.

Usdiken, B. (1997) 'Importing theories of management and organization: the case of Turkish academia', *International Studies of Management and Organization* 26 (3): 33–46.

——— (2004) 'Exporting managerial knowledge to the outpost: penetration of human relations into Turkish academia, 1950–1965', *Management Learning* 35 (3): 255–270.

Vaara, E., Tienari, J., Piekkari, R. and Santti, R. (2005) 'Language and the circuits of power in a merging multinational corporation', *Journal of Management Studies* 42: 595–623.

Van Knippengerg, D. and Schippers, M.C. (2007) 'Work group diversity', *Annual Review of Psychology* 58, 515–541.

Varoglu, A.K., Bicaksiz, A. and Akyurek, S. (2006) 'A study on cultural divergence and convergence at evaluative and expressive dimensions: does military culture transcend national cultures?', paper presented at 14th national Management and Organization Congress, Erzurum, Turkey, May 2006.

Vinken, H., Soeters, J. and Ester, P. (eds) (2004) *Comparing Cultures. Dimensions of Culture in a Comparative Perspective*, Leiden: Brill.

Vlaar, P.W.L., van den Bosch, F.A.J. and Volberda, H.W. (2007) 'Towards a dialectic perspective on formalization in interorganizational relationships: how alliance managers capitalize on the duality inherent in contracts, rules and procedures', *Organization Studies* 28: 437–466.

Vogelaar, A. and Kramer, E.-H. (2004) 'Mission Command in Dutch Peace Support Missions' *Armed Forces and Society* 30 (3) Spring: 409–431.

Vora, D. and Kostova, T. (2007) 'A model of dual organizational identification in the context of the multinational enterprise', *Journal of Organizational Behavior* 28: 327–350.

Waldherr, S., Sartori, J.A. and Adams, B.A. (2006) *Cultural Modeling: Literature Review*, Toronto: Defence R&D Canada.

Wallerstein, I. (1974) *The Modern World System I: Capitalist Agriculture and the Origins of the European World-Economy in the Sixteenth Century*, New York: Academic Press.

Ward, O. (2006) 'United Nations "army" proposed. International rapid reaction force could be deployed within 48 hours of a UN green light', *Toronto Star* 15 June 2006.

Wasti, S.A. (1998) 'Cultural barriers in the transferability of Japanese and American human resources practices to developing countries: the Turkish case', *The International Journal of Human Resource Management* 9 (4): 608–631.

Watson, W.E., Kumar, K. and Michaelsen, L.K. (1993) 'Cultural diversity's impact on interaction process and performance: comparing homogenous and diverse task groups', *Academy of Management Journal* 36: 590–602.

Wedell-Wedellsborg, M. (2007) 'Den globale soldat. Identitetsdannelse og identitetsledelse i multinationale militære organisationer', unpublished thesis, Copenhagen Business School.

Weibull, L. and Johansson, E. (2006) 'Erfarenheter från tre svenska utlandsmissioner under 2005', unpublished manuscript, Försvarshögskolan.

Weick, K.E. (1995) *Sensemaking in Organizations*, Thousand Oaks, CA: Sage.

——— (2001) *Making Sense of the Organization*, Malden, MA: Blackwell.

Weick, K.E., Sutcliffe, K.M. and Obstfeld, D. (2005) 'Organizing and the process of sensemaking', *Organization Science* 16: 409–421.

Wetherell, M. (1996) *Identities, Groups and Social Issues*, Thousand Oaks, CA: Sage.

Winslow, D. (1999) 'Rites of passage and group bonding in the Canadian Airborne', *Armed Forces and Society* 25: 429–457.

—— (2002) 'Strange bedfellows: NGOs and the military in humanitarian crises', *International Journal of Peace Studies* 7: 35–56.

Winslow, D. and Everts, P. (2001) 'It's not just a question of muscle: cultural interoperability for NATO'; in G. Schmidt (ed.), *A History of NATO: the First Fifty Years*, Basingstoke: Palgrave/Macmillan.

Winslow, D.J., Heinecken, L. and Soeters, J. (2003) 'Diversity in the armed forces', in G. Caforio (ed.), *Handbook of the Sociology of the Military*, New York: Kluwer Academic/Plenum Publishers.

Winslow, D., Kammhuber, S. and Soeters, J. (2003) 'Diversity management and training in non-American forces', in D. Landis (ed.), *Handbook of Intercultural Training*, 3rd edn, Thousand Oaks, CA: Sage.

Wong, L. (2005) 'Leave no man behind: recovering America's fallen warriors', *Armed Forces and Society* 31: 599–622.

Yanai, S. (1996), 'UN peace operations and the role of Japan: a Japanese view', in A. Morrison and J. Kiras (eds), *UN Peace Operations and the Role of Japan*, Clementsport, Nova Scotia: The Canadian Peacekeeping Operations Press.

Yin, R.K. (2003) *Case Study Research. Design and Methods*, 3rd edn, Thousand Oaks, CA: Sage.

Yukl, G.A. (1998) *Leadership in Organizations*, 4th edn, Englewood Cliffs, NJ: Prentice-Hall.

Zabusky, S.E. (1995) *Launching Europe: An Ethnography of European Cooperation in Space Science*, Princeton, NJ: Princeton University Press.

Zaccaro, S.J. (1999) 'Social complexity and the competencies required for effective military leadership', in J.G. Hunt, G.E. Dodge and L. Wong (eds), *Out-of-the-box Leadership: Transforming the 21st Century Army and Other Top-Performing Organizations*, Stamford, CT: JAI Press.

—— (2002) 'Organizational leadership and social intelligence', in R.E. Riggio, S.E. Murphy and Pirozzolo, F.J. (eds), *Multiple Intelligences and Leadership*, LEA's Organization and Management Series, Mahwah, NJ: Lawrence Erlbaum Associates.

Zellmer-Bruhn, M. and Gibson, C. (2006) 'Multinational organizations context: implications for team learning and performance', *Academy of Management Journal* 49, 301–318.

Zimbardo, P.G. (1972) 'Pathology of imprisonment', *Society*, 6: 4–8.

Index